A

PHILOSOPHICAL TREATISE

ON THE

PASSIONS:

SECOND EDITION, CORRECTED.

BY T. COGAN, M. D.

*Format enim Natura prius nos intus ad omnem
Fortunarum habitum.* ———

HORATII DE ARTE POETICA.

PRINTED AND SOLD BY S. HAZARD:
IN CHEAP-STREET.
Sold also by Cadell and Davies, Strand, London: and all other Booksellers.
1802.

PREFACE.

AMIDST the numerous Branches of Knowledge which claim the attention of the human mind, no one can be more important than that which constitutes the subject of the following Treatise. Whatever most intimately concerns ourselves must be of the first moment: the principle of self-love which is inherent in our natures, immediately suggests that no other species of knowledge can stand in competition with it. Every thing is justly deemed interesting that has an immediate relation to ourselves; and the degrees of its importance are measured by the degrees of its influence upon our *wellbeing*. An attention therefore to the workings of our own minds; tracing the power which external objects have over us; discovering the nature of our emotions and affections; and comprehending the reason of our being affected in a particular manner, must have a direct influence upon our pursuits, our characters, and our happiness.

It may with justice be advanced, that the history of ourselves in this department, is of much greater utility than abstruser speculations concerning the metaphysical nature of the human soul, or even the most accurate knowledge of its intellectual powers. For it is according as the passions and affections are excited and directed towards the objects investigated by our intellectual natures, that we become useful to ourselves or others; that we rise into respectability or sink into contempt, that we diffuse or enjoy happiness, diffuse or suffer misery.

An accurate Analysis of these passions and

and affections, therefore, is to the Moralist, what the science of Anatomy is to the Surgeon. It constitutes the first principles of rational practice. It is in a *moral* view, the anatomy of the *heart*. It discovers *why* it beats, and *how* it beats, indicates appearances in a sound and healthy state, detects diseases with their cause, and it is infinitely more fortunate in the power it communicates of applying suitable remedies.

Yet, notwithstanding the superior importance of this Science, it has not engaged the attention of philosophers to an equal degree with the intellectual powers of man. Those who are conscious of the acuteness of their own intellectual powers, have loved to employ them upon subjects the most difficult and abstruse. Their chief delight has been in the study of natures and essences; and their ambition, to solve difficulties which have repeatedly occupied and embarrassed the strongest minds. Patient attention to facts, appeared to them an employment best adapted to plain and common understandings; it is the province of Genius to soar above the common level, and penetrate the mists which surround the regions of intellect.

When it is asserted that the passions of the mind have not employed the attention of the philosophic world, equally with the other branches which relate to Man, the assertion implies that they have not been totally neglected. Philosophers in their study of human nature have not passed them over in silence. They have treated them occasionally, but generally speaking superficially, chiefly as appendages to their other philosophical pursuits. This circumstance, it is acknowledged, has been productive of a train of thought peculiar to each speculator; and thus has each been able to throw some light upon

upon a subject, which it was not his sole or primary object to investigate.

Among the Authors who have paid the most attention to the subject, Professor *Hutcheson*, Dr. *Watts*, Mr. *Grove*, and the Writer of the Article " on the Passions of Men" in the British Encyclopædia, may justly be placed in the first rank. The observations of Mr. Hutcheson chiefly respect the moral uses of the Passions, which it is not the professed object of the present Treatise to investigate. Objections to some of the principles advanced by Dr. *Watts* and Mr. *Grove*, as well as other Writers of eminence, are stated in the Introductory Chapter, and will occasionally appear in different parts of this Work. It will therefore be sufficient to remark at present, that the very small degree of information obtained respecting many essential points, the imperfection of every arrangement hitherto made,—the almost universal

versal disagreement among philosophers in their ideas concerning the precise nature of a Passion, Emotion, and Affection, or in what respect they specifically differed from each other, &c. were the principal inducements to the Author of the following Treatise, to pay much greater attention to the workings of the human mind, than he would have done had their remarks been more satisfactory. In order to find his way through perplexing labyrinths, he was determined to extend the analytical method much farther than it has hitherto been pursued; from a full conviction that, although it is not in general the most popular and acceptable mode, it is much the securest, and best adapted to procure a strength of evidence, in philosophical and moral subjects, which approaches to the nature of demonstration.

The Treatise now submitted to public candour contains the history and the result

PREFACE.

of this procefs; in which, however flow and tedious the fteps, the Author has been frequently relieved, and fometimes amply rewarded by difcoveries which appeared to him equally new and important. If they fhould appear fo to others, he will feel himfelf completely recompenfed for his labour.

As he is not without apprehenfions that the analytical part will appear much too tedious and prolix, thus he fears that the philofophical obfervations and inquiries will appear much too fuperficial; but he would remind the Reader that his fole object is to give an epitome of general and influential principles, and not to purfue the development of any to the extent of which it is fufceptible. The impoffibility of this muft be felf-apparent.

The natural confequences of this immediate application to the genuine fources of knowledge, without any pre-conceived hypothefis, pothesis, are, that in some instances he has traced a perfect coincidence of opinion between his own and those of preceding Writers on the Passions; in many he has *corrected* his own previous ideas; in others, he thinks that he has not only discovered errors, but also the causes of them. Wherever the subject has appeared peculiarly important, the discrepancy great, and the Authorities opposed, respectable, he has stated the subject, and his reasons in the adjoined Notes; that the concatenation of ideas so necessary in the analytical method might not suffer interruption.

Notwithstanding his utmost care, the Analyzer cannot flatter himself that nothing of importance has escaped his attention. Both the extent and intricacy of the subject will, it is hoped, furnish an apology for many defects. Nor can he expect that of the numerous explanations and definitions proposed, fed, they will all be equally acceptable and convincing. Some of them will probably be erroneous. But it may not be improper to remark, that the extraordinary verfatility of language renders it extremely difficult to feize the precife fignification of terms in every connection; and this will fometimes occafion a diverfity of opinion, in cafes where a criterion cannot always be found to which our judgments will uniformly fubmit. If the Reader fhould not agree with him in the precife fignification of particular terms, the utmoft care has been taken that the fenfe in which the Author has ufed them fhall not be mifunderftood: fo that the principles he advances muft either enforce conviction, or lay themfelves fully open to confutation.

The copioufnefs of the fubject has principally confined the Work before us to a *philofophical* inveftigation of the Paffions. Yet in these abstruser investigations, many thoughts occasionally present themselves properly belonging to the departments of *Ethics,* and requiring a larger amplification than would be consistent with the design of the present Work. The Science of *Ethics* opens a field for contemplation still more extensive. Although it has so frequently engaged the attention of Moralists, it appears to be inexhaustible; nor ought we to despair of perpetual additions being added to our stock of knowledge, concerning the nature and importance of our duty.

The degree of acceptance with which the first edition of this Work has been received by the Philosophic World, has encouraged the Author to prosecute his design, and he accordingly proposes to consider the Passions and Affections in a more practical, and perhaps still more interesting point of view.

The

PREFACE. xiii

The apprehensions which naturally present themselves, left public expectation should not be gratified, by much novelty, on a subject that has been so frequently treated, are in some measure silenced by a conviction that his attempts will be received with an indulgence similar to that already experienced.

Although attention has been paid to several minuter corrections, yet the Author has been reluctant to make such alterations in this second edition, as might depreciate the value of the preceding in the opinion of the Purchasers. The most considerable change consists in the divisions of the two first Chapters: the new Arrangements, and introductory Emotions being placed at the commencement of the second Chapter, instead of terminating the *first*: by which he thinks that a more lucid order is preserved. Several additions might have been made, but as these

these can with equal propriety be inserted in a future Volume, that mode is preferred.

BATH:
January 1, 1802.

CONTENTS.

PART I.

ANALYSIS OF THE PASSIONS.

CHAP. I.

General View of the Subject.

		Page.
Sect. I.	On Passions, Emotions, and Affections; the specific difference between them	1
II.	Plans of Arrangement examined	16
III.	Love and Hatred; their Nature	23
IV.	Desire and Aversion	33
V.	Objects of Love and Hatred	38

CHAP. II.

Classification of the Passions according to their characteristic differences.

Sect. I.

	Page.
Sect. I. Efficient Caufes of the Paffions, &c. examined	43
Sect. II. Introductory Emotions	48
Sect. III. Claffification of the Paffions and Affections, as they refpect the Selfifh or the Social Principle	60

CLASS. I.

Paffions and Affections, which owe their Origin to the Principle of SELF-LOVE 61

Order I. Paffions and Affections, &c. excited by the Idea of Good .... *ibid*
 Joy, Gladnefs, &c. 62
  Contentment 65
  Satisfaction .... *ibid*
  Complacency 66
  Pride, &c. 70
  Defire 73
  Hope 86

Order II. Paffions and Affections excited by the Idea of EVIL 90
 1. SORROW. 91
  Grief, Melancholy, &c. 92
  Patience, Refignation, Humility 95
 2. FEAR. 97
  Confternation, Terror, Dread, Defpair, &c. &c. 99
 3. ANGER. 107
  Wrath, Refentment, Indignation, &c. &c. 111

CLASS. III.

	Page.
Passions and Affections derived from the SOCIAL PRINCIPLE	117

ORDER I. Passions and Affections, in which GOOD is the predominant Idea   125

  I. Benevolent *Desires* and *Dispositions*   ibid
    1. Social Affections   126
    2. Sympathetic Affections   131
  II. Affections derived from *Good Opinion*   142
    Gratitude   144
    Admiration   145
    Esteem, Respect   151
    Veneration, &c.   152
    Fondness, &c.   154

ORDER II. Passions and Affections in which EVIL is the predominant Idea   156

  I. Malevolent *Desires* and *Dispositions*   157
    Malignancy, Envy, Rancour, Cruelty, &c.   158
    Rage, Revenge, &c. Suspicion, Jealousy   166

		Page.
II.	Displacency indicated by *unfavourable opinions*	170
	Horror, Indignation, Contempt, &c.	171

PART II.

Philosophical Observations and Inquiries.

CHAP. I.

Observations respecting the Laws of Excitement		181
Observ. I.	Surprise, the efficient Cause of *Passion*	ibid
II.	*Affections* alone permanent	185
III.	Relation of Passions and Affections to each other	190
IV.	Seat of the Passions	204

CHAP. II.

Causes which create a diversity in our Affections, enumerated		219
§ 1.	Experience	220
§ 2.	Difference of Sex	221
§ 3.	Diversity of Temperament	227

		Page.
§ 4.	Progress from Infancy to Age	229
§ 5.	National Customs	232
§ 6.	Force of Habit	235
§ 7.	Self-Love	237
§ 8.	Education	239
§ 9.	Novelty	242
§ 10.	Fashion	244
§ 11.	Love of Singularity	247
§ 12.	Popular Prejudices	249
§ 13.	Associated Affections	252
§ 14.	Manner in which Information is conveyed	258
§ 15.	Imitative Tones and Representations	261
§ 16.	Rhetoric, Oratory, Eloquence	264
§ 17.	The Drama	268
§ 18.	Pre-disposing Causes	270

CHAP. III.

Influence of the Passions.

Sect. I.	*Medical* Influence	278
II.	Influence on *Thought* and *Language*	298
III.	Influence on *Character*	308
IV.	Influence on *Happiness*	317

PART I.

ANALYSIS OF THE PASSIONS.

CHAP. I.

General View of the Subject.

SECT. I.

On Passions, Emotions, and Affections; the specific difference between them.

BY Passions, emotions, and affections, we understand those stronger or weaker feelings, with their correspondent effects upon the System, which are excited within us by the perception or contemplation of certain qualities, which belong, or are supposed to belong, to the objects of our attention; and which in some respect or other, appear interesting to us. In all cases, when the violence of the emotion is not too powerful for the animal œconomy, the feelings or sensations excited are pleasant or unpleasant, according to the nature of the exciting cause, the ideas entertained of it, or the intenseness with which the mind is struck by it. These feelings differ in degrees of strength, according to the apparent importance of their cause; according to certain peculiarities of temperament; and also according to the manner in which the influential qualities are presented to the mind.

One or other of the three terms, Passion, Emotion, Affection, is always employed to express the sensible effects which objects, or ideas concerning them, have upon the mind; but they are so frequently employed in a vague and indeterminate manner, that some difficulty attends the attempt to restore them to their precise and discriminating significations.

The word *Passion*, is thus rendered subject to several peculiarities in the application of it. Sometimes it is used in a generic sense, as expressive of every impression made upon the mind. When we speak of the passions in general, or of a treatise on the passions, we mean not to express the stronger impressions alone; the mildest affections are also included: and if we denominate any one to be a person of strong passions, we mean that he is subject to violent transports of joy, or grief, or anger, &c. indiscriminately. In one instance the word is emphatically

phatically employed to express *suffering;* as *our Saviour's passion:* in another it indicates *anger* exclusively; thus when it is said of any one that he is *in a passion,* it is universally understood that he is very angry. The term *passion,* and its adverb *passionately,* often express a very strong predilection for any pursuit, or object of taste; a kind of enthusiastic fondness for any thing. Thus we remark of one person that he has a passion for musick, or that he is passionately fond of painting, &c. &c. In a sense similar to this is the word also applied to every propensity which operates strongly and permanently upon the mind; as the *selfish* passions, the *generous* passions. Yet when we mean to particularize any of these, a different law of phraseology is observed. The word *passion* is appropriated by the *evil* propensities which are uniformly operative. Thus we do not say the *affection* of pride, or of avarice, but the *passion.* The term *affection* on the other hand is appropriated by the *virtuous* propensities; as the *social, friendly, parental, filial,* affections, &c. though philosophically considered, the relation they bear to the state and workings of the mind is perfectly analogous.

Nor is this capricious latitude of expression confined to common language, where accuracy is not always to be expected; it is also obvious among philosophers

philosophers themselves, so that scarcely two authors, who have written upon the subject of the passions, are agreed in their ideas of the terms they employ. While some consider the Emotions as highly turbulent, others assert that they are in their own nature quiescent:* Some suppose a Passion to constitute the strength of an Emotion, others confine the idea of a passion to the desire which *follows* an emotion: Others again represent the Passions as the calmest things in nature, deeming them to be the steady uniform principles of action, to which reason itself is always subservient.† Hence it becomes highly necessary to seek after some rules which shall render our ideas more consistent and uniform.

In most of these applications no attention has been paid to the primitive signification of the word Passion; although this appears to be the safest method to recall us from those aberrations to which we are perpetually exposed. Few expressions wander so far from their original import, as to convey a sense which is totally foreign. The primary idea annexed to the word is that of *passiveness*, or being impulsively acted upon. In this sense the term properly signifies the sensible effect, the feeling to which

* Lord Kaims.   † Mr. Hume.

the mind is become subjected, when an object of importance suddenly and imperiously demands its attention. If our imaginations be lively, our temperaments susceptible, the object interesting to us, we cannot avoid being affected, or suffering some powerful change on our dispositions, by its recent appearance, or by the suggestion of a something we deem of importance. In all such cases we are obviously passive; we are acted upon without any previous determination of the will, or without any consent of our own.

As several of our passions are of a disagreeable and painful nature, and as this passive or helpless state is so frequently connected with *suffering*, the transition from one signification to the other is not only natural but almost inevitable; and a passion will often be considered as synonimous with suffering. In medical language a person oppressed with disease is called a patient, an involuntary sufferer, and the calmness with which he submits is termed patience; that is, the mind yields with tranquillity to the pains and indispositions of the body. The word pathology, has also the same derivation: it is the history of the sufferings incident to the human frame. The Greeks expressed passions in general by παθος, which signifies *suffering*; and the Latin word *Passio*, from which we have adopted the term *passion*, *paffion*, has the fame fignification. The Stoics alfo gave the name of παθη to all extraordinary emotions of the foul, becaufe they confidered them as mental difeafes, by which the foul, while under their influence, was reduced to a ftate of fuffering. But this fecondary fenfe, as far as it conveys the idea of an unpleafant or painful fenfation, is alone applicable to the effects produced by paffions of a certain clafs; for others are in their own nature pleafing; as joy and hope; whereas the primitive import of the word, that of *paffivenefs*, equally belongs to them all. The mind is equally paffive in every effect fuddenly and unexpectedly produced upon it, whether its influence be of a pleafant, or unpleafant nature. (See Note *A*.)

The term paffion therefore, may with ftrict propriety, be ufed, and ufed exclufively, to reprefent the *firft feeling*, the *percuffion* as it were, of which the mind is confcious from fome impulfive caufe; by which it is wholly acted upon without any efforts of its own, either to folicit or efcape the impreffion.

Probably it is in allufion to this paffive ftate of the mind, that the terms *paffion* and *paffionately* are employed to exprefs the powerful attachment to particular objects mentioned above. They infinuate that the influence of thefe beloved objects, is irrefiftible;

irresistible; and that the mind is completely under their dominion.

The state of absolute passiveness, in consequence of any sudden percussion of mind, is of short duration. The strong impression or vivid sensation immediately produces a reaction, correspondent to its nature; either to appropriate and enjoy, or to avoid and repel the exciting cause. This reaction is very properly distinguished by the term *emotion*. The sensible effect produced at the first instant, by the cause of the passion, greatly agitates the frame; its influence is immediately communicated to the whole nervous system, and the commotions excited in that, indicate themselves both by attitudes and motions of the body, and particular expressions of countenance. These effects are such universal concomitants that no very important change in the state of the mind can take place, without some visible change of a correspondent nature in the animal œconomy.

Emotions therefore, according to the genuine signification of the word, are principally and primitively applicable to the sensible changes and visible effects which particular passions produce upon the frame, in consequence of this reaction, or particular agitation of mind. It is alone by these visible effects, that the subject is discovered to be under the influence of any passion; and it is alone by the particular changes produced, or kind of emotion, that we are enabled to judge of the nature of the paſſion. Thus, although the paſſion exiſts prior to the emotions, yet as theſe are its external ſigns, they muſt indicate its continued influence as long as they continue to agitate the ſyſtem. In conſequence of this immediate connection, the words *paſſions* and *emotions*, are, in familiar diſcourſe, where no philoſophical preciſion is requiſite, uſed ſynonimouſly; though in reality the latter are uniformly the effects of the former. Here, as in innumerable other inſtances, figurative modes of expreſſion are adopted. The *Synecdoche* is perpetually employed, by which, cauſe and effect are confounded, or ſubſtituted the one for the other. Since emotions are faithful indications of their correſpondent paſſions, and ſtrong paſſions are always productive of emotions, we ſhould deem it a pedantic preciſion to ſelect, at all times, the appropriate word, when we mean ſimply to expreſs the general effect.

However the term Emotion is ſometimes expreſſive of lively ſenſations which do not produce viſible effects in any degree proportionate to their feelings. In emotions the mind is not ſo completely, or neceſſarily paſſive. In general it poſſeſſes ſome power over the external ſigns; and in many caſes where the feelings would be too ſtrong to remain concealed,

concealed, were they totally uncontrouled, some other influential affection either of fear, respect, humanity, &c. may serve to repress or moderate their effects, and confine them to *inward* emotions.

Again the term is frequently employed to mark the first impression which particular objects make upon susceptible minds whether they remain concealed or not. Thus in the fine Arts, the charms of musical compositions which are novel to us;—the first view of a gallery of paintings possessing distinguished merit;—the surprise of a beautiful or elevated sentiment, or poetic description, will generally make a more vivid impression upon us, than that which is felt, in a continued, or renewed contemplation of the same subjects; and yet these impressions may not be so forcible as to produce the transports accompanying emotions from other causes. Yet the difference is simply in *degree*, not in *kind*. This species of enjoyment is peculiar to minds highly cultivated, whose repeated enjoyments of a similar nature have gradually moderated transports, and whose emotions have gradually subsided into gentler undulations, if I may thus express myself, in place of those agitations which the inexperienced would inevitably betray upon similar occasions.

The third term *Affection*, has in itself a different signification

signification from either of the above. It always represents a less violent, and generally a more durable influence, which things have upon the mind. It is applicable to the manner in which we are *affected* by them for a continuance. It supposes a more deliberate predilection and aversion, in consequence of the continued influence of some prevailing quality. This distinguishes it from the transient impulse of *Passion*. Nor is it intimately connected with any external signs; which distinguishes it from *Emotions*. The affections sometimes succeed to passions and emotions, because these may have been excited by something that becomes permanently interesting; or they may be gradually inspired by a deliberate attention to the good or bad qualities of their objects.

In this philosophic sense of the word, Affection is applicable to an *unpleasant* as well as *pleasant* state of the mind, when impressed by any object or quality; it may be produced by whatever torments or corrodes the heart, as well as that which charms and delights it. Usage however chiefly applies the word to the kindly and beneficent affections. When we remark that a person has an affectionate heart, we mean to applaud his being under the influence of the best affections, of a social and relative nature.

With other Writers on the Passions we shall always

ways use the term in the philosophical sense; and apply it equally to whatever produces more permanent feelings in the mind, whether they be pleasing or painful, of a benevolent or malevolent character.

As in Passions and Emotions thus in the *Affections* several gradations of influence are observable. Some affections indicate themselves so strongly, that they approach to emotions; some may require a penetrating eye to discover them;—some may be powerfully indulged with such self command, that they shall elude the most critical observation;—and some have such an equal and uniform influence, as to blend, as it were, with the temper, and almost lose the name of affection; as generosity, fortitude, humility, patience, resignation.

When there is a propensity to indulge one particular affection or class of affections more than another, arising from peculiarity of temperament, education, connections, habits, &c. we consider this propensity as an indication of temper or habitual disposition. Thus we speak of a benevolent, grateful, cheerful, timorous, revengeful *temper*. These characters do not imply that the subject is perpetually under the influence of the particular affection, but they mark his propensity towards it. The affections therefore refer to the actual impression made upon the mind by certain qualities real or supposed;

pofed; and the temper or difpofition is that particular caft of mind which renders the perception of certain qualities capable of making a more prompt, or a more durable impreffion upon one perfon than another. We deem that man to be irafcible who is difpofed to be angry at trifles; and him we praife as humane who is always difpofed to commiferate fufferings.

It is hoped that the above explanations of the terms, Paffions, Emotions, and Affections, will obtain the approbation of my philofophic Readers, fince they were fuggefted to the Author by an attention to the workings of the human mind. If approved, they cannot appear unimportant, as they will ferve to indicate both mutual relations and characteriftic differences in the impreffions which furrounding objects, or ideas concerning them, make upon us; and although an attention to thefe minute diftinctions, may not always be neceffary in common language, and would fometimes be abfurd, yet the want of this precifion has been feverely felt in philofophical inveftigations, and is a principal caufe of the obfcurities in which they are too frequently involved. It will be allowed by every attentive obferver, that the procefs which we have characterized by the above terms, *does* take place in the human mind, when expofed to the fudden and

powerful

powerful influence of particularly interesting objects. Such objects are irresistibly forced upon his attention, independent of a will or determination of his own: they often produce great agitations both of mind and body: and when these agitations have subsided, the mind retains some degree of predilection or aversion for them. As these distinctions are clearly and satisfactorily expressed by the particular terms we have given to each, this is a full indication that they are the most appropriate. (See Note *B*.)

The above observations are not confined to a simple process, which takes place from more simple causes. After we have supposed a passion, indicated by an emotion, to be succeeded by some correspondent affection, we may still consider this affection as the parent of new passions, emotions, and affections, according to the variety of circumstances connected with it. It may inspire fear, as when the object of our affection is in a perilous state, or earnest desire, or sanguine hope. Some of these new passions and affections will arouse to action, as when the strong sense of an injury excites to revenge; others chill and depress the spirits, as sorrow and despair. Yet in the midst of all these diversities, the characteristic differences between Passions, fions, Emotions, and Affections, are equally obvious.

Confining ourselves therefore to what we deem the genuine import of the words, in opposition to the irregularities of custom, we shall as often as it may be necessary to observe distinctions, uniformly apply the term *passion*, to the violent impression made upon our minds by the perception of something very striking and apparently interesting; *emotion*, to the external marks, or visible changes produced by the impetus of the passion upon the corporeal system: and *affections*, to the less violent, more deliberate, and more permanent impressions, by causes which appear sufficiently interesting. The range of affection, may be from those stronger feelings which are proximate to emotions, to the mildest sensations of pleasure or displeasure we can possibly perceive.

Most Writers, on the Pathology of the Mind, agree to distinguish between Appetites and Passions. The former they refer to corporeal wants, each of which creates its correspondent desire; and the indulgence of this desire is termed gratification. The latter they ascribe immediately to the mind. In this the Moderns differ from the Ancients. The word *Appetitus*, from which that of *Appetite* is derived,

rived, is applied by the Romans and Latinists to desires in general, whether they primarily related to the body or not: and with obvious propriety; for the primitive signification, is the seeking after whatever may conduce either to gratification or happiness. Thus Cicero observes, " motus animorum " duplices sunt; alteri, cogitationis; alteri Appe-" titus, Cogitatio in vero exquirendo maxime ver-" satur; Appetitus impellit ad agendum." By two powers of action being thus placed in contrast to each other, and the one applied to thought simply, it is obvious that the other comprehends every species of desire, whether of a mental or corporeal nature. Metaphysicians also, who have written in the Latin language, use the word *Appetitus* in the same latitude.

But the modern distinction has the advantage of immediately pointing out a difference in the nature and character of the objects which interest us, according as they relate to the body or to the mind. Considering Appetites therefore, as confined to corporeal wants and cravings, we must still observe that they are as frequently the occasions of passions and emotions as other objects which are peculiarly adapted to the mind. Eager hope, joy, fear, anger, are daily manifested by the infant, whose desires are wholly confined to animal wants: and the keenest

sensations

sensations of anger, jealousy, envy, &c. are intimately connected with the carnal appetites of maturer age. Whatever is therefore beyond the mere instinctive appetite, becomes the province of the mind; and the influence which various cravings of nature have upon its ideas and conceptions, give rise to mental affections and passions. The subject of the present discussion obviously relates to these, without requiring particular attention to the existing cause.

SECTION II.

Plans of Arrangement examined.

So numerous and multifarious are the Passions, Affections, and Emotions, in their connections and ramifications, that it is difficult to propose a plan of Arrangement, that shall be in every respect unexceptionable. By preferring one method, we may be deprived of some advantages attending another; and in all it may be necessary to anticipate many things, which a rigid attention to order could not possibly permit. Some Writers on the Passions, have placed them in contrast to each other, as *hope* and

and *fear, joy* and *sorrow* :—some have considered them as they are personal, relative, social :—some according to their influence at different periods of life :—others according as they relate to past, present, or future time ; as sorrow principally refers to things past, joy and anger to present scenes, hope and fear respect futurity.

The Academicians advanced that the principal passions were *fear, hope, joy,* and *grief.* Thus Virgil :

Hinc metuunt, cupiunt, gaudentque, dolentque.

They included aversion and despair under the fourth; and hope, fortitude, and anger, under desire. But not to observe that this arrangement is much too general in some respects, and defective in others ;—that the characters of hope, and of anger are too opposite to each other, to be placed under the same head ;—that anger has no particular claim to be classed with desire, excepting when it excites a desire of revenge, which is not always the case ;—and that desire is so comprehensive a term as to embrace numberless other affections;—not to insist upon these objections, it is obvious that the passions enumerated cannot be primitive or cardinal, since some other affections or passions must be prior to them : We must *love,* or *hate,* before we can either desire, rejoice, or fear, or grieve.

Dr. Hartley

Dr. Hartley has arranged the Paſſions under five grateful and five ungrateful ones. The grateful ones, are *love, deſire, hope, joy,* and *pleaſing recollection;* the ungrateful are *hatred, averſion, fear, grief, diſpleaſing recollection.* The objections to this order are, that all theſe cannot be conſidered as cardinal paſſions. Nor do the diſtinctions themſelves appear ſufficiently accurate: hope is certainly a ſpecies of deſire; pleaſing recollection is a modification of love; averſion is only a particular manner of teſtifying hatred; and diſpleaſing recollections are ſometimes the renewal of grief, ſometimes of anger.

Dr. Watts divides the Paſſions into primitive and derivative. The primitive he ſubdivides into two ranks: 1. Admiration, love, and hatred; 2. The diverſe kinds of love and hatred, as eſteem, contempt, benevolence, malevolence, complacency, diſplacency. The derivatives are deſire, averſion, hope, fear, gratitude, anger, &c.

But the title of admiration to be conſidered as a primitive paſſion, does not appear to be ſo valid as that of the other two aſſociated with it. Love and hatred are in univerſal exerciſe; admiration is merely occaſional. The former indicate themſelves from the inſtant we have any powers of diſcernment, or the ſmalleſt degree of experience reſpecting the nature of objects: The latter is the reſult of ſome degree

gree of knowledge; it implies a spirit of inquiry and demands some portion of taste for particular qualities adapted to excite this emotion. Minds the most infantile, and uncultivated, will manifest that they love and hate, long before they have an opportunity of testifying their admiration. We might also observe that a subdivision of the primitive passions into two ranks creates a suspicion, if it do not fully indicate, that they cannot all be equally primitive; and the instances given under the second rank may justly be considered as different modifications of the two grand principles, and not as primitives of a distinct character. It is farther obvious that the Doctor's plan, makes no distinction between the Passions and Affections, which the nature of the subject not only admits, but requires.

Mr. Grove, adopting in part, the arrangement of Dr. Watts, reduces all the Passions to the three heads of admiration, love, and hatred; which he styles accordingly, the primitive passions. The others he denominates mixed passions; which he describes to be those which have admiration blended with them, and those compounded of the passions that fall under love and hatred. As the above remarks are no less applicable to this arrangement, I shall only observe that since Mr. Grove has defined admiration to be " that sudden surprise at the no-

"velty of an object, by which the soul is fastened down to the contemplation of it;" there seems to be a peculiar impropriety in *his* placing it among the primitive passions: and this impropriety is increased by another observation, viz. that "Admiration seems to be a more speculative passion, as being employed chiefly about the novelty or grandeur of objects;" for which reason he places the chief energy of this passion "in the *brain*," which he denominates "the grand instrument, or condition rather of thought and contemplation." He adds, "In the other passions, which respecting the good or evil of objects, proceed from a principle of self-preservation, the spirits agitated are in the *heart*, the fountain of life, and fittest residence of those motions of the animal spirits, which are intended for the benefit and preservation of life." *

These observations certainly increase the difficulty of admitting admiration among the primitive passions. It may also be justly doubted whether the author's ideas of the nature of admiration be admissible. But this is not the place to discuss that point.

The above comments upon the most material arrangements which have hitherto been followed, render some other classification desirable, which may be

* See System of Moral Philosophy; Chap. VII of the Passions.

exempt

exempt from similar objections. Perhaps the securest method to obtain this end, will be previously to recollect, what is the first and leading principle of our natures; and then inquire what are the necessary consequences of this principle in beings formed as we are; placed in various situations, and surrounded by an infinite variety of circumstances. By thus attending to the history of the human mind, and tracing the manner in which it is affected by various causes, a proper arrangement may present itself. We shall at least avoid those mistakes and embarrassments into which men of eminence have been betrayed by pursuing other methods.

It will be universally acknowledged, that it is essential to the nature of every sensitive and intelligent being, to be gratified with, or delight in *wellbeing*. This is so evident a principle, that the contrary cannot be supposed for a moment. Both reason and feeling unite to establish this axiom. We all feel the inestimable value of happiness, and we all know that to delight in misery, is a contradiction. It would be to annihilate misery. (See Note *C.*)

This well-being, or grateful state of existence, we unite to denominate an essential good; and its opposite an essential evil. Whatever promotes this state, we deem to be productive of good; whatever is an impediment to it, or occasions a state of uneasy sensation, we consider as productive of evil.

These ideas naturally lead us to esteem that as a *good* also, which is productive of this desirable state, and to characterize as an *evil* whatever is inimical to it. Cause and effect are so intimately connected in our imagination, that we not only substitute the one for the other, by a figurative mode of speaking, but we quickly learn to consider that as a *good in itself*, which appears uniformly to be the means or instrument of good; and to contemplate as an evil, whatever we suspect to have a pernicious tendency. Under the impression of this sentiment, we indulge a *predilection* for the one, and feel an *abhorrence* of the other.

It is impossible for the attentive and considerate mind, to view or contemplate objects so diametrically opposite as apparent good, or apparent evil either with total indifference, or with the same kind of sensation. We inevitably look upon what we deem to be a good, or conducive to happiness, with a *pleasant* sensation. We deem it desirable, and it inspires the affection of LOVE. Whatever occasions or threatens a privation of happiness, or inflicts positive misery, we view with displeasure, we consider it as injurious, or as an absolute evil, and it inspires the affection of HATRED: that is, we feel a strong

attachment

attachment of the *heart* to whatever may contribute to *well-being*, and we contemplate the reverse with feelings of displeasure, detestation, and abhorrence.

Although it may be said, without impropriety, that we all love to be happy, and hate to be miserable; yet this is such a self-evident truth, that it is very seldom uttered. The two expressions therefore, *Love* and *Hatred*, are almost entirely applied to the cause, means, or instruments of well-being or wretchedness; and we are habituated to love whatever is instrumental to our existing in a desirable state, and to hate its opposite.

SECTION III.

Love and Hatred; their Nature.

THESE two affections arise immediately and inevitably from our perpetual solicitude to *enjoy* the existence we possess. They are coeval with our ideas of good and evil. They are experienced by every one, in every situation, and in every period of life. They are inspired by every object which possesses some peculiarity, or is apparently endowed with some quality of a beneficial or a pernicious

nicious tendency: that is, by whatever is able, according to our conceptions, to promote or impede enjoyment or happiness, from the smallest gratification up to the most exalted felicity; from the smallest discomfiture, to the depth of misery. They are also the parents of every other passion and affection; and the history of the human mind is no other than a developement of their operations in the infinitude of situations and circumstances in which it may be occasionally placed. These characters will undoubtedly entitle them to the denomination of *primary* or *cardinal* affections. As no others are in the same predicament, they cannot deserve the same appellations; they can only be considered as derived from these.

We cannot therefore commence our minute inquiry into the passions with greater probability of success, than by paying previous attention to these two affections.

I. LOVE.

Love may be considered either as a principle or as an affection. As a principle, it may be defined " an invariable preference of Good; an universal " and permanent attachment to well-being or happi- " ness." In this point of view it has already been considered.

considered. It has also been remarked, that the love of good, and solicitude to procure it, is not only the ruling principle of every *sentient* being, but it meets with the full approbation of every *rational* being. For nothing can excel that which is good, and nothing can be valuable, but as it has a tendency to promote it. Hence when we speak of love abstractedly, we call it the *principle* of love: for it is the principle by which the whole tenour of our conduct is directed; and it retains that appellation, as long as we speak of it as a general principle of action.

When this principle is directed towards any particular object it becomes an *affection;* that is, the mind becomes well disposed or pleasingly affected towards that object: and whenever this love is more violent in its effects upon the system, it is even deemed a *passion*.

The affection will be diversified, and acquire various characters, according to the nature of the object, its relations, or the peculiar qualities it may seem to possess. It may relate to ourselves; to those with whom we are connected, by the closest bonds of nature or intimacy; to the whole of our species; to those beings of inferior order in the creation, which are rendered capable of possessing any portion of enjoyment; and even to things inanimate. When

When the affection of Love immediately relates to *ourselves* personally, it is called *Self-love*; and it marks the peculiar concern and solicitude we entertain for our own interest, prosperity, or enjoyment. The principle of self-love generally operates with the greatest force upon the mind; for every circumstance which affects our own happiness makes the most vivid impressions. This is naturally the source of many abuses, which have brought the term itself into disrepute. But self-affection, when it does not interfere with the claims of others, is not only an innocent affection, but it manifests the wisdom and benevolence of the great Source of good. By rendering every being active in the pursuit of his own happiness, the greatest *quantum* of general good is most effectually secured. As the largest communities consist of individuals, were each individual to seek his own welfare, without prejudice to his neighbour, the individual stock of each would render happiness universal. (See Note *D.*)

When our love or desire of good, goes forth to others, it is termed *Good-will,* or *Benevolence.* This operates with various degrees of force, according to our various connections and degrees of intimacy. It may possibly render the interests and happiness of those with whom we are more immediately connected, by the bonds of nature or friendship, equally dear to us as our own. It has in some instances been known to exert a more powerful influence. Of this truth, the love of parents towards their own offspring frequently presents us with striking instances. Admiration of personal excellencies, habits of intimacy, gratitude for benefits received, &c. may also increase our attachment to individuals, until it rival the natural influence of self-love.

All these powerful ties are usually characterized by the term *affection;* as the conjugal, parental, filial affections; and those who possess these attachments in an exemplary degree are termed *affectionate* parents, children, relatives, friends.

When love extends to the whole human race, it is termed *Philanthropy;* a principle which comprehends the whole circle of social and moral virtues. Considering every man as his neighbour, and loving his neighbour as truly and invariably as he loves himself, the philanthropist can neither be unjust nor ungenerous.

In its utmost extent the love of benevolence embraces all beings capable of enjoying any portion of good; and thus it becomes *universal* benevolence: which manifests itself by being pleased with the share of good every creature enjoys;—in a disposition to increase it;—in feeling an uneasiness at their sufferings;—

ings;—and in the abhorrence of cruelty, under every disguise, or pretext.

When these dispositions are acting powerfully towards every thing capable of enjoyment, they are called the *benevolent affections;* and as these become in those who indulge them, operative rules of conduct, or principles of action, we speak of the *benevolent principle.*

It has been remarked that predilection for good, as the *end,* enstamps a value upon the *means* productive of this end. This creates an affection for various qualities and propensities, which we pronounce to be good, when they possess the power, or indicate the disposition to promote happiness or enjoyment. If these be eminently good qualities, we call them *excellencies;* and if they be connected with the characters and conduct of moral agents, they are *moral excellencies.*

From the habitual pleasure which the contemplation of excellence inspires, without our adverting perpetually to the benefits which may accrue from it, we may be induced to imagine that we love things deemed excellent for their own sakes, abstracted from their power of becoming useful. But this is impossible. Every excellence contains a capability to possess or to communicate good. Nothing

thing which deserves the name, can be in its own nature *inert*. An *useless* excellence is a contradiction.

The propensity to love what is productive of good, extends itself much farther than to the powers and properties of moral agents. We naturally acquire an attachment to every object, animate or inanimate, which has been the habitual instrument of good to us, or is capable of contributing to our gratification or advantage. Their latent powers first induce us to value them as treasures in reserve; our opinion of their capacity to become serviceable, inclines us to place our affections upon them; and in process of time they will, by the association of ideas, excite pleasing emotions, although their powers of utility are not always in our recollection. (See Note *E*.)

II. HATRED.

HATRED expresses the disposition we entertain concerning, or the manner in which we are affected by, the contemplation of whatever we suppose to be an *Evil*. It is not confined to absolute suffering; it marks also our abhorrence of whatever exposes to the danger of absolute suffering, or the diminution

minution of that portion of good we enjoy, or wish to poffefs.

Hatred of mifery and its caufes, is a natural and neceffary confequence of our folicitude to poffefs good; and the affection of hatred is as naturally infpired by that ftate, conduct, difpofition, &c. which is productive of, or threatens to induce pernicious or difagreeable confequences, as the affection of love is attached to their contraries. Nor is our hatred at all times confined to that particular quality, or peculiarity of circumftance, which is immediately unfriendly to us. It is apt to raife unpleafant ideas, and create prejudices againft many things, which in themfelves are far from being the objects of hatred, and which may be highly advantageous, merely becaufe they have been difpleafing or injurious to us in particular inftances. As our predilection for whatever proves acceptable, will often prevent our difcerning its pernicious qualities, thus do we frequently extend our hatred far beyond the juft limits, until we betray our ignorance, or manifeft that we are under the dominion of invincible prejudice.

Perfonal hatred, or malevolence towards an individual, commences with fome circumftance, quality, or difpofition which is difpleafing to us, or with
fome

some species of injury committed or intended. It has these for its professed objects. But here also a quick and powerful transition is instantaneously made in our imaginations, from an incidental blemish, to the whole of character;—from a single act, we are prone to form unfavourable sentiments of general conduct;—and the lively sense of an injury annihilates too frequently every species of merit in the offender. This is obviously the source of hatreds, long and inveterate.

But notwithstanding these excesses and exaggerations of hatred and malevolence, yet they cannot possibly be so extensive in their operations as the principle of love. The affection of hatred has particular and partial evils alone for its objects, while the principle of love may embrace the universe. As nutritious aliments are infinitely more numerous than the substances which are of a poisonous quality, thus does the number of those things which are pleasing, beneficial, important in their nature, infinitely exceed those which are either in themselves comfortless, or detrimental, or calculated to foster a malevolent disposition. The true object of hatred is alone some particular and partial evil, which we experience or dread;—some incidental interruption to the usual tenour of our feelings;—or some pernicious quality which may threaten this interruption.

The

The objects of our fears, our anger, or our grief, are confidered in the light of robberies, or painful privations, and not as permanent caufes of the malevolent affections. They are not looked upon as ftreams perpetually flowing from one inexhauftible fource, but as interruptions to an ufual or defirable ftate, by adventitious caufes. Happinefs appears to be our birth-right, of which all the painful fenfations raifed by hatred, are the profeffed guardians. The wifh for happinefs is perpetual and unlimited, while our evil affections expire with the caufes which gave them exiftence. Nor can malevolence extend itfelf to every individual in the creation, in a manner fimilar to the contrary virtue. That happy cultivation of our natures which infpires a benevolence towards all animated beings, cannot poffibly have a perfect contraft or complete parellel in the moft uncultivated and brutalized. This would conftitute a ferocity of character which can fcarcely be found in the moft infane. When tyrants cruel and ferocious are diffufing mifery in the wantonnefs of their power, their conduct does not proceed from univerfal hatred;—but from fome low policy of felf-defence;—from an infernal fpirit of revenge for fuppofed injuries;—from inordinate felf-love, which creates an infenfibility to human woes;—from pride, vanity, and exceffive ignorance, which induce them to imagine that

that they shall be revered as deities, because they imitate the destructive thunder of heaven; and to dream that their favourite idol *Power*, can only be made known and established by deeds which excite consternation and horror!

Indeed the affection of hatred is of so unpleasant a nature, that the being who could hate every thing, would be his own tormentor. The only pleasure of which malevolence is capable, proceeds from the gratification of revenge; which can only be directed against particular objects. Nor is it merely bounded; it is irritating, unsatisfactory, and purchased by the sacrifice of all the enjoyments which flow from the contrary disposition.

SECTION IV.

Desire and Aversion.

WITH the affections of Love and Hatred, are intimately connected the affections of Desire and Aversion. That is, we constantly desire, and are solicitous to possess or accomplish, whatever is pleasing or beneficial; and we are averse from, and endeavour to shun, whatever is displeasing, or threatens to be pernicious. These two affections are therefore the necessary consequences of the preceding. They are accompanied with a certain eagerness of mind, either to obtain or escape, which is not so essential to the former. Love and Hatred may be inspired by a calmer contemplation of excellence or demerit, or any of the causes of happiness or misery, without our feeling an immediate interest in them;—as when we reflect upon beneficial discoveries or destructive errors. The one may approve of worthy conduct or respectable characters, from which we can expect no benefit to ourselves; and the other despise villanies by which we cannot be injured; whereas Desire and Aversion refer to particular objects, which have some relation to ourselves; and they are indicated by some effort of mind, either to possess the promised good, or to repel the impending evil. Desire and Aversion are to be considered therefore as *manifestations* of love and hatred; and the earnest *application* of these principles, in each particular instance of their excitement.

As love and hatred may be resolved into that one principle, the *love of well-being;* thus may the affections of desire and aversion be resolved into *desire:* although the use of both terms is in common language, necessary, in order to distinguish the objects

jects of our purfuit, from thofe we wifh to fhun. Strictly fpeaking, averfion is no other than a particular modification of defire; a defire of being liberated from whatever appears injurious to well being. The objects in our poffeffion, productive of this good, we defire to retain. We are confcious of this defire every time we appreciate the worth of the object, and it is neceffarily excited when we are under the apprehenfion of privation. If the good, or the means of good, be not in our poffeffion, we defire to obtain them; if a privation be unjuftly attempted by any one, and the paffion of anger be excited, the defire of preferving or recovering the object is connected with a defire to chaftife the aggreffor; if it be in danger from any other caufe, the fear of lofs is excited by the defire of fecuring; and if we be actually deprived, the hopelefs defire of regaining, is an effential ingredient in our grief for the lofs.

But although, in this philofophical fenfe, defire may feem to be equally extenfive with the affection of love, yet it is neceffarily more confined in its application. Love relates to all things which appear good and beneficial in themfelves, or to beings capable of receiving good. It comprehends the things enjoyed, and the ftate of pleafing exiftence in which thofe beings are actually placed, as well as the defirablenefs of fuch a ftate, and all the means and instruments of good. Desire mostly refers to the state in which we *are not*. It solicits some favourable change, and exerts itself to obtain it. Hatred also is universally applicable to whatever appears pernicious or displeasing in itself; aversion more immediately concerns whatever appears pernicious or is displeasing to *us*. These Affections may be considered as the satellites of love and hatred, perpetually accompanying them, and prompt to execute their orders. Wherever love or hatred direct their immediate attention, desire and aversion seek to appropriate or repel.

Thus it appears that the love of good and hatred of evil; the desire of possessing good and escaping evil, are the leading principles of our natures. The love of good commences with our existence, and the desire of good is coeval with our powers of discernment. Neither of them will leave us, until we cease to exist, or lose the consciousness of our own sensations and perceptions. Whatever diversity there may be in our situations, however various and opposite the objects engaging our attention, however versatile our humours, these remain the immutable principles of action. They pervade the animal system, as the electric fluid pervades the material; and though, like that, they may sometimes be latent,

latent, yet like that they may be instantaneously roused into vivid action, and manifest both their existence and their power by the effects they produce.

Our natures possess various sensitive and mental powers, to each of which an infinite diversity of objects is adapted: and as the gratification of each communicates pleasure, we are prone to estimate every thing as a good which is capable of contributing to these gratifications; and every thing as an evil which opposes them. However, a contrariety or opposition frequently takes place, between the higher and inferior pursuits of our natures; in consequence of which, the interests or gratifications of the one must yield to those of the other. As sensual objects, and things which administer to our immediate desires, are apt to make the strongest impressions, and captivate our attention, in preference to things less sensual and more remote, though of superior importance; thus do we frequently deem that to be a good, which is virtually an evil. We may also deem that to be an evil, which is virtually a good; as being productive of extensive, exalted, or permanent advantage. But notwithstanding these facts, we still pursue every thing as an apparent good; and we avoid every thing under the idea of its being an evil of greater or less magnitude. Our appetites, our particular propensities, our imaginations, our passions may spread deceitful charms over some objects; and our want of attention, our ignorance, our impatience of present restraints and inconveniences, or the perverseness of our affections, may render objects inimical in their appearance, which are beneficial in their tendency: yet our desires are alone excited by the idea of some enjoyment or advantage; and things are rendered objects of our aversion alone because they are disagreeable to our feelings, or threaten to endanger, some way or other, our well-being. (See Note *F*.)

SECTION V.

Objects of Love and Hatred; their Characteristics.

SHOULD it be asked, "In what do this good and this evil consist?" it would be difficult to give a satisfactory answer. To say that they consist in a certain consciousness of well-being, or of a comfortless existence, would be little more than to assert that happiness consists in being happy, and

misery

misery in being miserable. The following observations however will discover to us what we expect in the means of good, and what we deem to be the causes of unhappiness; and will indicate where these are principally to be found.

Creatures formed like ourselves, with different organs of sense, with various powers of mind, accompanied with quick perceptions and high sensibility; creatures endowed with great diversities of dispositions, tastes, propensities, must be variously affected by every thing around them. We are as it were plunged into the universe " tremblingly " alive all o'er," and we are rendered capable of receiving impressions pleasant or unpleasant, from every object that addresses our senses, from every thing we perceive, and from every thing of which we can form an idea. Nothing in this vast universe can at all seasons be totally indifferent to every person in it: nothing is so inert as to be incapable of exerting some influence in one connection or other, and of calling forth a correspondent passion or affection.

These effects are produced by our perception or supposition of certain powers, properties, or qualities in the different objects, by which ideas of an agreeable or disagreeable nature are excited within us. The diverse influences of these are to be ascribed to an apparent aptitude or correspondence in some objects with the frame and constitution of our natures, and to an inaptitude or want of correspondence respecting others; to a certain coincidence between properties and relations in objects and circumstances, with the appetites, powers, propensities of our natures, the gratification of which seems to promote our well-being; or, to the want of this coincidence, or the exertion of a contrary power, which constitutes our misery.

The diversity of attributes seated in different objects, and the no less diversity in our situations, and in circumstances surrounding us, render it difficult to make choice of such terms as may be universally appropriate. It may therefore be necessary to observe, that by *attribute, property, quality, &c.* is meant to express that peculiarity, whatever it may be, which exerts an influence upon us: and these terms are used, to indicate the distinguishing characteristics of various objects, as they are connected with some singularity in state, circumstance, or conduct; without the real or supposed existence of which, the passions and affections could not have been excited. (See Note *G.*)

The subjects possessing this real or apparent aptitude and coincidence, or inaptitude, relate to our animal natures, to the various powers and employments of our minds, to our state and connections as social beings, and also to the opinions entertained respecting

respecting our relation to a superior Being, or to a future state of existence.

The various objects soliciting our attention under these heads; the degrees of their suitability, excellence, importance, or the contrary; our ideas and mistakes concerning them; the facility or difficulty, with which some things are pursued, obtained, preserved, lost, dismissed; the uncertainty, dangers, contrarieties to which we are constantly exposed, respecting whatever may appear interesting, are perpetually engaging our affections, or exciting our passions, during the whole of our passage through life, from the cradle to the grave!

Thus is that love of well-being which is one and simple in its principle, most wonderfully diversified in its operations! Every object, every circumstance, every idea which can enter the mind, makes some impression upon us of a pleasant or unpleasant nature; contributes a something towards, or deducts from the good we seek. They all contain powers and properties, by which we are attracted towards the grand desideratum HAPPINESS, or are repelled to various distances from it!

CHAP. II.

Classification of the Passions according to their characteristic differences.

SECT. I.

The efficient Causes of the Passions, Emotions, and Affections examined.

THE Affections and Passions to which the above circumstances give rise are not only innumerable, but like their exciting causes, so connected, and intermixed, that to arrange them in a lucid order, would be almost as impracticable as to form a regular path through the Hercynian Wood. Very few of the passions or affections are perfectly simple; some are extremely complex: their complexities are so various, that it is almost impossible to restore each to its appropriate place; and the most opposite affections are so intermixed, that it is very difficult to assign to each its due share of influence.

In this labyrinth, an attention to the following facts may perhaps furnish us with something of a clue.

Some of our passions and affections are inspired by circumstances which more immediately relate to *Ourselves*, and to our own personal interests: that is, they belong to the principle of *Self-love*: some of them belong to the *Social principle*, and refer to our connections with our own species, or to all animated natures.

In some of our Passions and Affections, the ideas of *Good* are obviously predominant, in others the ideas of *Evil*.

The passions and affections, which relate to self-love, and are excited by the idea of a good, may either refer to the good which is *actually in our possession*, and communicate various degrees of enjoyment, from simple gratification to ecstasies: or

The good we love *may not be* in our possession; but it may appear attainable, and become the object of our *Desire*: or

Though it be not in our possession, circumstances may appear highly favourable to our *attaining* it, and it may thus inspire *Hope*.

The state in which *Evil* is the predominant idea, referring to ourselves, may relate:

To the *loss* of that good which we possessed, or to *disappointments* respecting the good we desired, and hoped to obtain; inspiring *Sorrow*, with its various modifications: or

We may be *apprehensive* concerning the loss of what we possess, concerning the approach of some positive evil, or concerning the accomplishment of our desires, which introduces the family of *Fear*.

The cause of both sorrow and fear may be some *agent*, whose designed conduct, or even whose inadvertency, may threaten or produce injuries, and thus excite *Anger* in various degrees.

The causes and excitements of our passions and affections respecting *Others*, may also be arranged under the predominancy of good, or evil in our ideas.

Under the former head may *Benevolence* be placed, which will indicate itself either by *good Wishes*, or *good Opinions*; each productive of a large diversity of affections and passions, according to contingent circumstances.

The predominance of evil in our ideas will shew itself in actual *Malevolence* of disposition concerning another; or in a *Displacency* and disapprobation of conduct.

The above sketch seems to indicate a plan of investigation which, upon the whole, is the least confused and embarrassing. It is founded upon the remarks which have been made concerning the grand propensity of human beings to seek felicity;

upon

upon their ideas of good and evil, either relating to themselves or others; and it seems to comprehend most of those contingent circumstances which surround us.

That the idea of *good* is most prevalent in the diverse kinds of gratification, in the pursuit of various objects of desire, in the indulgence of hope, and in *benevolent* dispositions, no one will dispute; and that the idea of *evil* is prevalent in *malevolence* and *displacency* is no less evident. It will also be obvious upon a moment's consideration, that as the love of good may produce hatred to what is inimical to it, thus in the affections and passions correspondent with this principle, the primary and influential idea is that of *suffering*. In *sorrow*, when we grieve for the loss of what we love, it is the *privation* which immediately presents itself to the mind, and the hatred of this privation is the efficient cause of sorrow. In *fear* the apprehension of *impending evil* takes the lead in our minds, though this evil may virtually consist in being deprived of some good. In *anger*, the evil intended or perpetrated is the direct incitement to wrath, and we expatiate with so much eagerness upon all the circumstances of aggravation, that we cannot allow ourselves, at the first instant, to dwell upon the attributes or qualities of the good thus endangered or destroyed. These instances manifest that the perception of an evil

evil from privation in every inftance is ftronger, than our eftimation of the intrinfic value of that which occafions the painful emotion.

But although thefe obfervations may fuffice to juftify the Order propofed, yet it is acknowledged that they are not comprehenfive enough to embrace every thing relative to the paffions. There is a clafs of emotions, in which diftinct ideas of good or evil are not prefent to the mind, and which in fact may with equal propriety enlift themfelves under each divifion. They are vivid impreffions, productive of effects which ftrictly fpeaking, neither belong to the paffions nor affections; and yet their prefence frequently conftitutes the difference between an affection and a paffion.

This enigma will beft be explained, by our attention to the manner in which our ideas of thofe influential and operative qualities, exciting paffions and infpiring affections are obtained.

SECTION II.

Introductory Emotions.

WHEN the attention is stedfastly fixed upon any quality or number of qualities apparent in an object, whether they be good or bad, some impression is made, or certain sensations are produced. These may dispose the mind to dwell yet longer upon the subject; and the qualities they exhibit may be contemplated with all their relations and connections. Their former and their present influence, future consequences, &c. may thus be placed before us. Numberless correspondent ideas will present themselves, each producing its particular effect, until strong affections either of love or hatred, desire or aversion, will be excited; and these may gradually arise to the most violent passions and emotions. In this manner have persons been known to *work themselves up* into ecstasies, or into phrensies; and the mind has been so completely

pletely occupied by its subject, that it has totally lost the power of self-command; nothing foreign being able to gain admission, and divide the attention.

But on the other hand, whatever presents itself in a sudden and unexpected manner, has in most cases, a much greater effect upon us, than subjects of very superior importance for which we have been gradually prepared. The more *sudden*, that is, the greater the improbability of its appearing at that instant; and the more *unexpected*, that is, the greater distance the train of thought was from the expectancy, the more violent will be the first percussion; and this circumstance will give peculiar energy to the exciting cause, whatever its peculiar complexion may be. The strong impulse is given by the very mode of its appearance, previous to our being able to acquire a distinct knowledge of its nature. This impulse is the emotion we term *Surprise*.

Another circumstance which frequently attends the cause of any specific emotion, and produces its own characteristic effects in subjects of seeming importance, is that of *Intricacy*; in which the mind is thrown into an *embarrassed* state concerning the particular object, or something material relative to it. This embarrassment also gives an additional impetus to the characteristic passion, whether it be of a pleasing or a displeasing nature, and is distinguished by the name of *Wonder*.

A third adventitious effect is produced by an inftantaneous perception of the *magnitude* or *extent* of the fubject which calls forth any of the paffions and affections. It feems to poffefs fomething immeafurable, unfathomable, beyond the utmoft ftretch of comprehenfion. This we call *Aftonifhment*.

It now appears that fome of our emotions may be excited, before the fubject can poffefs leifure to contemplate the good or evil feated in the exciting caufe! Yet even in thefe cafes, Good or Evil are not excluded. For thefe emotions are moft intimately connected with the idea of fomething peculiarly *important;* but we can deem nothing important unlefs it poffefs a power of producing good or evil. Their peculiar ftrength is even occafioned by the vivid idea of importance, while the emotions themfelves manifeft our *ignorance* of its fpecific nature.

Thefe emotions therefore are excited by the confufed idea of fomething peculiarly interefting in the caufe, and they are manifeftly intended to awaken and direct the attention to this caufe, that its nature and character may be afcertained. Surprife, like a watchful centinel, is equally alarmed at a fudden approach, whether it be of a friend or an enemy. Wonder is excited by a curiofity which induces us to inveſtigate the character of the intruder with peculiar keenneſs: and although Aſtoniſhment is almoſt overwhelmed with the ſubject, yet it is irreſiſtibly attracted towards it, with a force proportioned to its magnitude. At the inſtant in which we feel our imbecillity the moſt, we are the moſt eager to inveſtigate thoſe qualities which we acknowledge to exceed our comprehenſion!

The above characters aſcribed to them plainly indicate that theſe emotions cannot be conſidered ſtrictly ſpeaking either as *paſſions* or *affections*, which are always inſpired by the idea or perception of ſome ſpecific Good or Evil, but merely as *introductory* to theſe: and it is very ſingular, that common language, without the ſuſpicion of its being founded on philoſophical inveſtigation, uniformly characterizes them by the term *Emotions*. We never ſpeak either of the *paſſion* or *affection* of ſurpriſe, or of wonder, or of aſtoniſhment; but conſent with one voice to denominate them *emotions*. It is alſo agreed that they are very diſtinct from the permanent calmneſs of an affection, and that they are common to the moſt oppoſite paſſions.

The moſt violent paſſions of every kind are well known to proceed more frequently from the impulſe of the moment, than from deliberate thought. There is ground therefore for ſuſpicion that this impulſe is to be aſcribed to one or other of the above emotions, and that it is their influence which constitutes the difference between a passion and an affection. This is certain, that they are equally excited by subjects of a pleasing or displeasing nature; that they are the precursors of many passions, and are able to communicate an energy to all.

Thus we perceive that the passions,—using this term in a generic sense, may proceed both from our *Ignorance*, and from our real or supposed *Knowledge* of the nature and qualities of objects. As the excess of cold operates upon the corporeal system, with a stimulating power like the excess of heat; thus the opposites of expectancy, of knowledge, of comprehension, become powerful stimulants to the awakened mind, and communicate a painful energy which is peculiarly instrumental in removing their cause. This effect is manifestly produced by the power of the imagination, which immediately creates alarms, forms numberless conjectures, and expands itself to the utmost, that it may equal if possible the vastness of the object.

Surprise, Astonishment, Wonder, being excited by something *novel,* something *embarrassing,* or something *vast* and *incomprehensible* in the objects, without any reference to its peculiar nature, and exerting their influence indiscriminately in passions of the most opposite characters, they may with strict propriety be contemplated as *introductory* to those

those subjects which upon a minuter investigation seem calculated to exert their own specific influence. We shall therefore term them *Introductory Emotions.*

When the nature of the exciting cause is more accurately ascertained, it will be found to respect either the *Selfish* or the *Social* Principle. Hence arise two important distinctions, forming two different CLASSES.

In each Class the predominant idea of a *Good*, and the predominant idea of an *Evil*, will constitute two different *Orders*.

The leading passions and affections under each order, point out the *Genera*.

The complicated nature of some of the passions, and other contingent circumstances, may be considered as constituting *Species* and *Varieties* under each characteristic *Genus*.

These distinctions were suggested to the Author, by an attention to the natural progress of our passions and affections, from the first exciting cause to all the ramifications and diversities of which they are susceptible. The Reader will doubtless perceive a striking coincidence with the classification, which Nosological and Botanical Writers have found it expedient to adopt.

The *Introductory Emotions* from their nature and influence, demand a prior investigation.

I. SURPRISE.

We have described Surprise to be the strong emotion excited by something which presents itself in a sudden and unexpected manner, when the mind was totally unprepared for it; something we presume to be highly important, and yet the kind or extent of this importance may not be ascertained. It is the apparent *novelty* of the subject, or of some peculiarity relative to it, or the *unexpectedness* of its introduction, at a particular time, or in a particular manner, contrary to probability or expectancy, which produces the effect; and whenever these circumstances take place, surprise may be equally excited by things agreeable or disagreeable; by objects of our love or hatred, admiration or horror.

The primary or natural effects of surprise, are to rouse the mind, to force it out of that train of ideas with which it was occupied, and compel it to advert to the novel object; which is afterwards to exert a characteristic influence, according to its nature. The secondary effect of Surprise, is to add an impetus to the exciting cause, whatever that may be. It renders pleasing sensations more delightful; and gives an additional keenness to the unpleasing ones. This effect is evidently produced by the force of an awakened and active imagination; which preceding either deliberate attention, or the exercise of judgment, magnifies the apparent good or the apparent ill, as soon as their specific natures are obscurely perceived. In Surprise, the mind is totally passive. It can neither be produced nor prevented by any exertions of the will. Nor is it its immediate province, either to reflect or investigate. Its pathological effect is that of a simple stimulus, whose sole object is to arouse the attention. Sudden startings, earnest looks, extension of arms and hands, strong exclamations, are the characteristic signs of the emotion; and when the violence of surprise excites an alarm, which is oft-times the case without the actual presence of danger, the whole body is instantly placed in an attitude of defence.

II. WONDER.

WONDER expresses an *embarrassment* of the mind, after it is somewhat recovered from the first percussion of surprise. It is the effect produced by an interesting

teresting subject, which has been suddenly presented to the mind, but concerning which there are many intricacies, either respecting the cause or manner in which any event has taken place, motives of extraordinary conduct, &c.

In Wonder the mind begins to re-act, but its ideas are in a state of confusion. It attempts to examine and investigate, but it seems engaged in a fruitless inquiry. It rapidly collects together various circumstances, from which to form conjectures, but rejects them as unsatisfactory, as soon as they are formed. Whenever the desired discovery is made, Wonder ceases, and gives way to the impression which is correspondent to the nature of the discovery, and to those circumstances which are perceived to belong to the exciting cause; whether they be productive of joy or grief, admiration or abhorrence, hope or fearful apprehension. As in this emotion the mind begins to exert its active and discriminating powers, so is it able to prolong or to shorten the effects of the emotion, either by dwelling upon the subject, and deliberately following its intricacies, or by diverting its attention to other objects. Being introduced by surprise, and partaking of its indefinite nature, the pathological indications of Wonder are very similar. They are however less violent; and they are intermixed with stronger marks of mental embarrassment. The eyes are

sometimes

sometimes fastened upon the author or narrator of something wonderful; sometimes they are directed upwards, to be more detached from every surrounding object, which might distract the attention; sometimes they roll about, as if they were in search of some object that may be equal to the explanation; and the half-opened mouth, seems eager to receive the desired information. In very intricate and important concerns, total abstraction from every thing external, and depth of thought marked by countenance and posture, indicate how busily the mind is employed in searching out the mystery.

III. ASTONISHMENT.

Astonishment is the kind and degree of wonder introduced by surprise, which as it were, overwhelms or petrifies the soul. The mental powers are in a stupor, in a state of stagnation. High astonishment is the *incubus* of the mind, which feels nothing at the instant, so much as its inability to act. This emotion always relates to things of the highest importance, to things which appear too vast and extensive for the grasp of intellect, rather than to intricacies. When it relates to human conduct, astonishment is excited by great undertakings, or
extensive

extensive projects; by the accomplishment of plans which appeared more than human, whether beneficial or destructive; or to some excess either of virtue or of vice.

The Body marks, in a striking manner, the singular state of the mind. That also becomes immoveable; *petrified* as it were, or *thunder-struck;* which are the favourite expressions in almost every language. The eyes are firmly fixed, without being directed to any particular object; the character of countenance which was formed by the habitual influence of some predominant affection, is for a time effaced; and a suspension of every other expression, a certain vacuity, strongly notes this singular suspension of mind.

Wonder and astonishment are expressions which, in many cases, may be used synonimously; as both causes and effects are very analogous: for the intricacy attending an important subject, may be connected with its vastness; and sometimes occasioned by it. When these are introduced by surprise, that is, when subjects of the kind are *suddenly* and *unexpectedly* forced upon the attention, their united effects are extremely powerful; and they give an infinite momentum to their causes, whether they be of a pleasing or displeasing nature.

According to the above view of the emotion, it may obviously be connected with the causes either

of

of happiness or misery; causes which inspire the pleasing sensations, which so often accompany the perception of things sublime and stupendous, or excite painful sensations from things we deem horrible. It may introduce the excess of joy, or the excess of fearful apprehension; call forth the most exalted admiration, or inspire the deepest indignation and contempt.

The term *Amazement*, which is sometimes employed, seems to express a medium between wonder and astonishment. It is manifestly borrowed from the extensive and complicated intricacies of a labyrinth; in which there are endless mazes, without the discovery of a clue. Hence an idea is conveyed of more than simple wonder; the mind is *lost* in wonder.

Though all these emotions have, generally speaking, the greatest power in things which unexpectedly arrest the attention; yet they may also proceed from contemplation. When the subject is complicated, the more we discern concerning it, the more will unexpected novelties present themselves, and successively become the causes of surprise. These novelties may be of such a nature, as to amaze and confound the understanding. We may also be the more deeply penetrated with a conviction of the vastness and incomprehensibility of

the

the subject, so as to be worked up into *astonishment*. The powers of the soul may become petrified as it were, or paralized by their fruitless attempts to comprehend what is far beyond their reach, and to fathom that which is unfathomable!

SECTION III.

Classification of the Passions and Affections, as they respect the Selfish or the Social Principle.

WE are now prepared to contemplate the immediate effects of those particular qualities, supposed to be seated in the subjects themselves; which the emotions of *Surprise, Wonder,* and *Astonishment* may have forced upon our attention, or which may have been discovered by calmer observation.

According to the order proposed, we shall first attend to those which are the most interesting to *Ourselves,* or which relate to the principle of SELF-LOVE.

CLASS I.

On the Passions and Affections, which owe their Origin to the Principle of SELF-LOVE.

THESE may be divided into two distinct Orders; that in which *Love,* and the *Idea of Good,* that is, something either beneficial or pleasing are more immediately present to the mind; and that in which *Hatred,* and the *Idea of Evil* are most impressive.

ORDER I.

The Passions and Affections founded on SELF-LOVE, *which are excited by the Idea of Good.*

THESE are of two Kinds: the one relates to Good in *Possession,* the other to that in *Expectancy.*

That in *Possession* inspires the following passions and affections.

JOY.

JOY.

Joy is the vivid pleasure or delight inspired on the immediate reception of something peculiarly grateful, of something obviously productive of an essential advantage, or of something which promises to contribute to our present or future well-being. This delight may be communicated by our liberation from fearful apprehensions, or from a state of actual distress,—by obtaining some new acquisition, some addition to our stock of enjoyment,—or by the full assurance of this without any mixture of doubt.

The various degrees of *Impetus* produced by this passion, will depend upon the sensibility of the subject, his supposed ignorance of the object, the sudden and unexpected manner in which it has been communicated, and the contrast formed between the preceding and the present state. A sudden and instantaneous translation from extreme anxiety or the depth of distress, to an exalted pinnacle of happiness, constitutes the highest possible degree. In this case, *Surprise, Wonder, Astonishment*, take possession of the soul; and though they may at first confound, they afterwards are productive of unutterable transports.

On

On the first impulse of joy, we are perfectly passive. No effort of the will can check the sensation itself; and where the joy is excessive, it is not in the power of resolution to suppress every external sign. The state of passive impression is succeeded by the exertions of a vigorous imagination, which, with rapid confusion, runs over the many supposed advantages to be derived from the welcome treasure: and these it is disposed to multiply and aggrandize far beyond the bounds of reason or probability. This pleasing, I had almost said, *intoxicated* state of mind, produces correspondent effects upon the system. A brisk and delectable flow of the animal spirits diffuses a pleasurable sensation over the whole frame. Every species of torpor is subdued; an exhilaration succeeds, indicating itself by emotions, which not only manifest the influence of the passion to spectators, but solicit their participation. The subject feels himself too much animated to remain in a tranquil state. Unusual vivacity in the eyes, and smiles upon the countenance, are accompanied by joyful acclamations, clapping of hands, and various other lively gestures. Where the mind is strongly agitated, and under no restraint from a sense of decorum, or solicitude for character, loud laughter, jumping, dancing, and the most wild and extravagant gestures, indicate the frolicksomeness of the heart.

Intense

Intense meditation upon some supposed good, the contemplation of its intrinsic worth, and of the happy consequences which are expected to flow from it, have sometimes raised the mind to transports, over which reason has lost its controul. But these instances seldom occur; as they require the union of strong conviction, lively imagination, and a warm heart. The transports of joy usually proceed from sudden impulse; and of consequence, ecstasies will sometimes be great, from very trivial causes.

Gladness is an inferior degree of joy; it may be excited by incidents agreeable or desirable in themselves, which are not of sufficient moment to raise the ecstasies of joy; or it may consist in that lively flow of spirits, which immediately succeeds to the transports of joy.

Cheerfulness is an emotion of still gentler influence. It is often inspired by very trivial circumstances in persons of a lively disposition, and free from anxious care.

Mirth is a higher degree of cheerfulness, generally excited by things facetious, or ludicrous; and greatly augmented by the power of social sympathy. Thus it frequently becomes noisy and boisterous, from causes not able to communicate the smallest emotion to an individual in a solitary state.

When the mind is more compofed, and we are able to reflect with a degree of calmnefs upon the good received or anticipated, we become varioufly affected,—according to the value we place upon the object,—according to its apparent fuitablenefs to our ftate and fituation,—and according to its correfpondence with our previous defires and expectations: and if the good be not tranfitory or evanefcent, we remain under the influence of *Contentment, Satisfaction,* or *Complacency.*

Contentment expreffes the acquiefcence of the mind in the portion of good we poffefs. It implies a perception that our lot might have been better, or that it is inferior to what others enjoy, or that it does not fully anfwer the expectations we had formed. An effort of reafon or of prudence is neceffary to produce it. We compare our prefent with our former fituation; or with the inferior lot of others; and thus learn to acquiefce in the degree of advantage obtained.

Satisfaction denotes a pleafing ftate of mind exceeding that communicated by fimple contentment. The good obtained is duly appreciated; is found to be correfpondent to our defires, and adequate to our wifhes. The word Satisfaction is frequently employed to exprefs the full accomplifhment of fome particular defire; which always communicates a temporary pleafure, whatever may be the nature of that desire. This affection by no means implies, that felicity is complete, as it chiefly refers to particular objects; and when it respects our state and situation, it admits that greater good might have been our portion, though we are more than contented, we are *well-pleased* with what we possess.

Complacency is full and continued satisfaction connected with a considerable degree of approbation. It has intrinsic value, or some species of *worth* for its object;—some mental excellencies, or advantages accruing from them;—some sentiment, disposition, acquirement, conduct, performance, either of ourselves or others with whom we are immediately connected, which upon close examination, we deem deserving of esteem or applause. Complacency may be enjoyed as the reward of our own conduct, or of the purity and benevolence of our motives: it may be inspired by a review of conduct, acquirement, disposition, on which we can pronounce that it *was well done,* or *well-intended.* Complacency may also relate to the approved conduct, sentiments, attainments, dispositions of others, for whom we are deeply concerned. In this case, the affection may be inspired, by their conduct and dispositions towards ourselves; or by the interest we take in whatever contributes to the promotion of their own honour and happiness.

The *Satisfaction* produced by Complacency, indicates

dicates that we have, in some respect or other, a personal interest in the object of it; which distinguishes the affection from that high gratification we may enjoy when we contemplate and applaud the sentiments, dispositions, and actions of great and respectable characters, with which we can have no immediate concern.

The *Approbation* which accompanies Complacency, distinguishes its object from the more common causes of satisfaction. These may arise from whatever quadrates with our wishes and desires, without paying attention to their intrinsic merit. A Suitableness to the occasion is the only requisite to inspire satisfaction; but the *Approbation* implied in complacency, conveys the idea of some kind of *Excellency*. The term has never been profaned by the application of it to guilty pursuits, dishonourable success, or unworthy sentiments, however they may flatter our vanity, or be the completion of our wishes. Nor are things of a trivial or transient nature deemed worthy of this affection. It is not said of a mere spectator, that he takes complacency in a ball, a concert, or at a theatrical exhibition; however highly he may be delighted and satisfied with the performance.

Nor can the term be applied with propriety to any beneficial acquisition, which has been purely accidental. The highest prize which the wheel of fortune

tune may have thrown into our laps, may be received with joy, delight, and satisfaction; but the terms approbation and complacency would be equally improper to express our feelings.

It may refer to some parts of the inanimate creation, in which we have an immediate concern, and which communicate pleasure on the review. Works of art well executed, may be contemplated with complacency; certainly by the *Artist*, if he has succeeded to his wishes; and the *possessor* will enjoy something of a similar pleasure, if the performance be calculated to recal pleasing ideas, or if he should have manifested either taste or address in the purchase of it. (See Note *H*.)

The above instances will evince that, in strict propriety of language, *Complacency* is alone applicable to that species of good, which originates from some mental or moral excellence; where there is an indication of propriety, ingenuity, wisdom, address, or dignity in sentiment, design, execution; or of rectitude and benevolence in the motive.

It is obvious that the affection of complacency, will possess different degrees of strength, according to the various kinds and degrees of excellence discernible in the exciting cause. The highest degree of complacency can alone be inspired by the obvious use of wise and pertinent measures from beneficent motives, which are, or promise to be, productive

tive of the moſt deſirable ends: or by laudable diſ-poſitions, and powerful exertions, crowned with the ſucceſs we moſt ardently deſired. When the means have been as wiſe as the nature of the thing would admit, the motives the moſt noble and generous, when the execution indicates ſkill, and the reſult proves as ſucceſsful as could have been wiſhed, Complacency, reſpecting that object, is complete.

High Complacency is the moſt grateful of all the Affections. It poſſeſſes an elevation and a ſuavity peculiar to itſelf. It is permanent ſatisfaction, enjoying the full approbation of reaſon; and conſequently it ſuffers no alloy from the ſtruggle of contending paſſions, or oppoſite deſires. When it is inſpired by our own conduct, it is accompanied by ſelf-approbation, or the teſtimony of an applauding conſcience, enlivened perhaps by the voice of gratitude, and enriched by the eſteem of the worthy. If it proceed from the conduct of others, it augments the pleaſures of affection, friendſhip, and gratitude.

According to the above view of the affection, may a virtuous and comprehenſive mind, contemplate things in themſelves of a diſpleaſing nature with complacency; ſuch as difficulties, which are introductory to benefits, and ſufferings, which may be requisite for the production of the most essential good.

But the affection of Complacency has its counterfeit. Being more complicate than either of the preceding, and the approbation of the mind forming a constituent part of it, an erroneous opinion of ourselves may change the nature of this sublime affection, and render it the parent of vice and folly. Thus false conceptions of our own talents, acquirements, conduct, may inspire *Pride, Vanity, Haughtiness,* and *Arrogance*.

Notwithstanding these affections are evil in their nature and tendency, yet as they are the illegitimate offspring of Complacency violated by Self-love, and have the appearance of great good for their object, they demand a place in this arrangement.

Pride is that exalted idea of our state, qualifications, or attainments, which exceeds the boundaries of justice, and induces us to look down upon supposed inferiors with some degree of unmerited contempt.

When this elevated idea of ourselves becomes a motive to avoid and despise any thing mean and unworthy, its impropriety is overlooked; and as it leads to worthy conduct, it is honoured with the appellation of *laudable* Pride.

It sometimes consists in exaggerated ideas of the superiority

superiority of our own country; of merit in our relatives or intimate connections, whose character and conduct reflect some rays of honour upon ourselves;—such as the pride of family descent,—that of children whose parents may have acquired celebrity,—or of parents in the accomplishments of their children, or particular honours conferred upon them. This proceeding from the excess of affection, where affection is natural, is called a *pardonable* Pride.

When Pride is manifested by an ostentatious display of wealth, station, or accomplishments, it is deemed a *vain* Pride.

When it is indulged to such an excess, that it looks down with disdain upon others, but little inferior, perhaps equal, possibly much superior in real merit, it is branded with the title of *insufferable* Pride. (See Note *I*.)

Vanity is that species of Pride, which, while it presumes upon a degree of superiority in some particular articles, fondly courts the applause of every one within its sphere of action; seeking every occasion to display some talent, or supposed excellency. Generally speaking, it is the foible of superficial and frivolous minds, that think much more of their attainments, than of their remaining deficiencies. Yet it may be founded on the excessive love of praise, in those who possess no inconsiderable share of merit.

Haughtiness is an overt act of Pride, manifested by some conduct or expression, indicative of unmerited contempt of others. It may be deemed in this case, the swelling of Pride into an emotion.

Arrogance indicates itself by some particular claims to precedency, or marks of distinction and respect from those whom Pride considers its inferiors in station and character; or by impertinent pretensions to an equality with superiors.

These indications of false complacency in their mildest influence, may be placed with strict propriety among the *affections*. Upon sudden occasions they rise into *emotions*; and sometimes, particularly when connected with anger, from a supposed insult or neglect, they possess every characteristic of *passion*.

Having considered the Passions and Affections immediately connected with the *Possession* of Good, we shall proceed to the Passions and Affections which are excited by the contemplation of Good when it is *not* in our possession, but of which the attainment is deemed possible. Which constitutes our second division under the present *Order*. These are *Desire* and *Hope*.

DESIRE.

The general nature of Desire has already engaged our attention. It has been described as that influential effect which the perception of good or evil produces within us, in consequence of which we seek to obtain the one and avoid the other. Our plan demands that we now contemplate Desire as it is excited by particular objects, conducive of some kind of good, either of benefit or pleasure, which we have not yet obtained.

According to the common acceptation of the term, Desire may be considered as an eager longing for some apparent good, centered in particular objects, situations, or circumstances.

This description is made as general as possible, in order to comprehend two different acts of the mind concerning such objects; which are signified by the terms *Wish* and *Desire*.

Lord Kaims expresses this difference in the following manner: " Desire, taken in its proper sense,
" is that internal act which by influencing the will,
" makes us to proceed to action. Desire in a lax
" sense respects also actions and events that depend
" not on us; as when I desire that my friend may
" have a son to represent him; or that my country
" may flourish in arts and sciences: but such inter-
" nal

" nal act is more properly termed a WISH than *de-*
" *fire*."* Though this obfervation does not fully
mark the difference, it plainly indicates there is
one.

We will therefore firft confider the defire which
is influential to action; and then advert more particularly to the characteriftic diftinctions between that
and a *Wifh*.

In the firft fenfe, Defire may be defined, that
uneafy fenfation excited in the mind by the view or
contemplation of any defirable good, which is not
in our poffeffion, which we are folicitous to obtain,
and of which the attainment appears at leaft *poffible*.

Defire is in its nature reftlefs. Mr. Locke juftly
remarks that " it is the uneafinefs it occafions,
" which excites the mind to purfue its object, and
" roufes it from its natural ftate of apathy and inac-
" tivity." Thus it is founded on fome fpecies of
difcontent; for were we perfectly contented and fatisfied with all our fenfations, and with every circumftance furrounding us, all defire muft ceafe.
It relates to fomething which is not immediately in
our power, and which requires either our own exertions or the agency of others, over whom we poffefs fome influence. It implies therefore that fomething

---

* Elements of Criticifm, vol. 1. p. 42.

thing is to be done, before the end can be obtained: and this necessarily implies also that there is a possibility of success attending the attempt. It is not always discouraged by difficulties; but our most active desires are never so ardent as to attempt known impossibilities.

Desires are either excited by the wretchedness of our present situation,—by periodical wants, which demand gratification,—by comparing the defects and imperfections of our own state, with the preferable state of others,—or by the perception of some pleasing and useful quality in objects which we wish to appropriate.

When desire is excited by wretchedness itself, it looks forwards towards *Good;* towards liberation from this state, and the enjoyment of a better. Relief, and the means of relief, are the predominant ideas accompanying Desire. In this case, the idea of a good is immediately engrafted on the stock of evil. The desires excited by periodical wants belong to the appetites exclusively. When the comparison of our own state with that of others, implants desires, they proceed from the discovery of new sources of enjoyment, to which we were strangers, united with a conviction that there is a possibility of attaining them. The recent perception of pleasing qualities in objects, has a similar influence. Our natural love of good inspires a wish to possess
whatever

whatever promises an augmentation of our welfare.

Hence it appears, that our ignorance is often the parent of contentment. We must acquire some knowledge of stations and qualities before we can desire them. The enlargement of our ideas becomes a copious source of discontent with our present possessions, and inspires ardent desires after new objects. Nothing can injure the good we possess, so much as the idea of a something better; and the superlative is equally injurious to the comparative.

The objects of desire are infinite, and infinitely diversified. They relate to whatever is essential to our existence and welfare, and to every thing which may strike the fancy; that is, to all our natural, and all our artificial wants. They refer also to all our social connections, and all our mental pursuits. These desires acquire such a diversity of character according to their origin, the degrees of their strength, and other circumstances, as to render a minute analysis impossible. We shall therefore confine ourselves to a few remarks.

It is observable that many of those desires which are common to all men, and without which the usual offices of life could not be discharged, are of the mildest and most permanent natures: such as the

desire

desire of preserving health, a desire of procuring a competency suitable to our station, to provide for our families, &c. Desires of this class are not distinguished by any particular epithet; nor are they denominated either affections or passions, though they obviously belong to the former. But when any extraordinary and unusual desire presents itself, which exceeds the common tenour of disposition; or when the object of desire is something peculiarly striking and important, it is distinguished by some discriminating epithet, and frequently assumes the character of an *affection, emotion,* or *passion.*

Thus, the moderate and legitimate gratification of the sensual appetites, is not marked by any particular appellation; but inordinate desires, which transgress the bounds of sobriety and decency, are stigmatized by the names of *Gluttony, Drunkenness, Debauchery, Lust, &c.* When we expatiate upon such a character, we remark that the person to whom it belongs, is *passionately* fond of good eating, or of his bottle; that he is led by his *passions,* &c. An exemplary command over these excesses is honoured with the title of *Temperance,* and *Chastity.* These, consisting in the love of moderation in conduct, and purity of mind, deserve to be placed among the affections; though from the mildness of their perpetual influence, they are simply

termed

termed dispositions. The moderate desire of wealth has no particular name; but when the desire becomes excessive, when it consists in amassing riches, without applying them either to utility or enjoyment, it is termed *Avarice*. This also is denominated a *passion*; not from the violence of any emotion, but from its permanent effects, and from the passive and abject state of the person who is under its influence. When riches are eagerly pursued, in defiance of justice and humanity, the conduct is termed *Rapaciousness*. The wish to improve in any valuable qualification or to acquire esteem, when moderate, has no distinguishing character, but an eager desire to equal or excel others in any particular accomplishment, is called *Emulation;* and to seek pre-eminence in office, title, or station, is *Ambition.* These desires are frequently so inordinate, as to require the name of passions: thus the *ambitious passions* is a familiar expression. (See Note *K.*) The exemplary desire of regulating our thoughts and pursuits, by right principles, constitutes *Virtue;* and all the duties which are performed with warmth and feeling are deemed the result of virtuous *affections*: the opposite propensities and conduct, constitute *Vice,* whose characteristic consists in depraved affections, and ungoverned passions. The desire of yielding obedience to the divine command, and habitual solicitude to obtain the divine favour, is *Religion*. This under its mildest influence is termed, a disposition or character. When a religious temper is indicated by prayer and meditation, which warmly interest the *affections*, it is called *devotion*. If any one imagines that the divine favour is to be obtained, by a scrupulous attention to frivolous ceremonies, he is considered as *superstitious*. Superstition is deemed a principle of action rather than an affection. It is in fact, a consecrated self-interest, devoid of love or regard to the supposed duties it enjoins, or to its object. A tenacious reverence for unimportant sentiments, with a censorious disposition towards those whose opinions are opposite, is the province of *bigotry*; which if it deserve the title of an affection, certainly does not belong to the benevolent class. An earnest desire, and unremitted endeavours to propagate any particular sentiment, or to enforce a particular rule of conduct, either out of love of truth, or of those we wish to become proselytes, or in order to recommend ourselves to some Principal, by our assiduity, is denominated *zeal*; which is deemed an *affection*. When some particular object gains the ascendancy over every other, and occupies the greater portion of our attention, it is occasionally termed a *passion*; as a passion for music, &c. in what sense, and with what propriety has already been considered. Such an invincible predilection for any subject as shall occupy the choicest of our thoughts, and incite to the most vigorous exertions with such an ardour and constancy, as to brave difficulties and danger, is termed *enthusiasm;* which has a place among the *Passions.*

The very *Motives* by which we are actuated, and the choice of means in order to effectuate our purpose, form various species of desire, sufficient to characterize the prevailing disposition. These constitute integrity, honesty, industry, honour, &c. or artifice, deceit, cruelty, &c. according as the prevailing desire is under the influence of worthy or base and unworthy principles and dispositions.

It should also be recollected, that a particular desire may, in certain circumstances, become the parent of various other affections and passions. Of this the Passion of Love presents us with striking instances; which in its progress is so frequently productive of hope, fear, joy, grief, and tormenting jealousies. In short, every pursuit, which primarily respected the gratification of our senses, may become the occasion of hope, joy, fear, anger, sorrow, envy, &c. according to the impediments or aids received from others, or according to our success or disappointments.

The *Novelty* of an object will frequently elevate desire

desire into a passion. This doubtless proceeds from the force of imagination, which greatly enhances the value of those qualities of which the object may be possessed, and is very prone to supply defects. Love at first sight illustrates and confirms this idea. Those charms which had seized the mind by surprise, become both unrivalled and irresistible to an heated imagination.

Impediments to our desires, if they be not sufficiently powerful to subjugate them, redouble their ardour. The affections being once engaged, desires being once enkindled, we are placed in a very different state of mind, from that we experienced previous to the excitement. We know that the disappointment of our wishes will not leave us in the former state of tranquillity, but will become a source of unhappiness; we therefore redouble our energy not to suffer a disappointment. This also is strongly exemplified in the passion of Love. Pride, anger, &c. are sometimes called in as powerful auxiliaries; and they exert all their impetuosity in support of our pretensions. Inordinate ambition abundantly illustrates this fact. It engenders a thousand evil passions, which like the Imps of Sin in *Milton*, yelp around it. Where it meets with obstacles, it is not scrupulous about the means of opposing them. Success increases its powers; and contrary to every other monster, it is rendered more insatiable and ravenous

ravenous by being fed. In either state, therefore, it becomes the terror and scourge of the earth.

Mental pursuits seem to be the most remote from every thing passionate and turbulent. An affection for science is, in general, the most productive of a pleasing serenity of mind. Yet even here no small diversity is observable, according as the memory, the reasoning powers, or the imagination are employed. The knowledge of interesting facts, and the examination of the relation of things to each other, are generally of the calmest nature; though the latter may justly be deemed of a more elevated character than the former. It is sometimes also rewarded with the transports of joy, inspired by the surprise of some new and important discovery. The creative powers of the mind, are as various in their effects as they are unlimited in their operations. They are the sources of lively amusement, and they may excite ecstasies. Where the imagination is the most vivid, its pleasures are the strongest; but they are of short duration: whereas the pursuits of knowledge furnish a temperate perpetuity of gratification, sufficient to comfort and support the indefatigable student in his most arduous researches.

The *Motives* to study are accompanied with various effects upon the mind. When science is pursued simply from the pleasure which knowledge affords, that pleasure is placid and mild. When the primary

primary motive is to benefit mankind by useful communications, the pursuit itself has self-complacency for its companion. When the object is personal advantage, either of fortune or of reputation, adventitious passions will arise according to the prospects of success, or the actual accomplishment of our desires; according to apprehensions entertained, or to disappointments experienced. When high ambition is the primary object, the passions proceeding from disappointment, uncertainty, rivalship, renown, disgrace; such as joy, vexation, hope, fear, jealousy, &c. will agitate the mind.

The desires respecting our social connections, are for the reasons given above, and according to the plan proposed, referred to a distinct class.

Desires, inspired by religious principles, are of all others the most diversified, both in kind and degree; according to the notions we entertain of religion, and the stronger or weaker effects of these notions upon our feelings. The most extensive signification of the term *Religion*, that which comprehends the greatest diversity of opinions, and meets the ideas of most philosophers, seems to be the following; *An impressive sense of the irresistible influence of one or more superior Beings over the concerns of mortals, which may become beneficial or inimical to our welfare.* It is evident, that a great diversity of the most opposite principles may be included

cluded under this general definition; and it is no less evident, that these principles, as often as they become influential, will be productive of effects correspondent with their natures; will form the temper and implant desires, most congenial with themselves, but the most opposite to each other. Zeal and enthusiasm are common to them all; but their indications will be correspondent with the supposed characters of the Powers they revere, and the methods supposed to be necessary to conciliate their favour, and avert their displeasure. Fear, terror, bigotry, superstition, cruelty, may thus be engendered; every evil propensity and atrocious vice may thus be consecrated, however inconsistent with the genuine dictates of religion, or the feelings of humanity. (See Note *L*.)

When, on the contrary, the mind is inspired with the most exalted conceptions of Deity, and correspondent sentiments of moral obligation, religion may cherish the purest dispositions and affections,—moderate and restrain inordinate desires,—elevate the mind by the contemplation of perfection in character, and by a warm desire to imitate. It may inspire love, joy, hope, gratitude; correct impatience and discontent; foster the principles of universal benevolence, and of every social virtue. Thus may religion, according to the ideas formed of its object and duties, be rendered capable of exciting the

the moſt deſpicable, or the moſt noble affections; and of forming the moſt abject, or the moſt elevated of characters!

Mr. Hume has remarked, that Religion is the fulcrum, which Archimedes required, to enable him to move the world. He might have added, that according to the manner and addreſs exerciſed in applying the lever of opinion to this fulcrum, will the world be raiſed up to the heavens, or depreſſed down to the abyſs.

A WISH is an inactive deſire. It is the reſult of that longing after happineſs ſo natural to man, in caſes where no expectations can be formed, no efforts can be made. It is the breathing after ſomething deſirable, where the means to obtain it are not in our power; or where the opportunity may be for ever loſt. It is excited by the contemplation of a ſomething, which if it could poſſibly be obtained, might augment our portion of good; or by reflecting upon a ſomething, which, had it been poſſeſſed, performed, or avoided, might have proved highly advantageous. Thus we may wiſh for impoſſibilities, which cannot be the objects of our active deſires. The *beggar* may wiſh to be a *King*, who cannot ſeriouſly *deſire* it. We may wiſh that we could fly, even without wings, and pay a viſit to some of the planets; though we know that the wish will be in vain.

A Wish may refer to *past* scenes, where Desire is totally inapplicable. The essence of repentance consists in wishing that we had conducted ourselves in a different manner.

These instances abundantly confirm the remark of *Lord Kaims*, that we may wish for things not in our power; and they shew that the range of our wishes is of an infinite extent, comprehending impossibilities, which refer to the past, present, or future. (See Note *M*.)

Hope is the encouragement given to desire; the pleasing expectancy that its object shall be obtained. Without this affection, desire would sink into despondency; like a simple wish it would remain inactive, and prey upon itself; producing perpetual uneasiness, destitute of any advantage. Hope is so pleasing, and so invigorating an affection, that it is emphatically styled the *Balm of Life*. It preserves the mind from stagnating in its present possessions, corrects the uneasiness of desire, and animates it to struggle with the difficulties it may have to encounter. Hope possesses the happy secret of *anticipating* the good we desire. By the pleasing sensation it communicates, we already taste the pleasures we seek. Where the object has not been of the first importance,

importance, the pleasures of hope have frequently been experienced to surpass those of actual possession; for the imagination is, in this affection, solely occupied by the supposed advantages and eligible qualities of its object, without attending to any of its imperfections. In its general operation, the indulgence of hope is mixed with certain portions of doubt and solicitude; but when doubt is removed, and the expectation becomes sanguine, hope rises into joy, and has been known to produce transports and ecstasies, equally with the full accomplishment of ardent desires. Thus, according to the degrees of force with which it affects the mind, it may be considered either as an affection or a passion.

It also appears that joy and hope are perfectly similar in their natures; and that the pleasing sensations they inspire, are perfectly correspondent. The difference consists in the degree of uncertainty, which intervenes before possession, and checks the ardour of hope; and as the object was in expectancy, the pleasure is not so powerfully quickened by the influence of surprise. Yet where the object has been highly valued, and the anxiety great concerning its attainment, a release from this anxiety has communicated a delectable elasticity to the mind, and rendered its sensations as vivid as those excited by more unexpected causes.

As the above Passions and Affections are inspired by the contemplation of Good, thus are most of them of a *pleasant* nature. This is obviously the case with *Joy*, and all the affections connected with it. *Hope* is also uniformly, a pleasant affection. *Desire* will vary according to its object, degrees of strength, and the different passions and affections so frequently arising from it. Although in its mildest state, it possesses a degree of restlessness, which serves as a stimulus to exertions, yet its immediate attendants give a preponderancy in its favour. Desire, as defined above, has always some species of Good for its object, which is always a *pleasant* object; and it is encouraged in its attempts by the possibility or probability of *attainment*. These two circumstances united, more than compensate for the degree of restlessness it in general occasions. The sportsman, who delights in the chace, who endures cold, hunger, and fatigue, with more than patience, inspired by the hopes of exercising his skill, and carrying home the triumphant, though trifling, reward of his assiduity, is a just emblem of the state of our minds, in the pursuit of objects we deem of superior importance. Desires are not only comfortless, but approach to *misery*,—when they are impetuous and ungovernable,—when hopes are frequently checked by disappointments,—when patience is wearied

ried out by procrastinations,—and when desires are borne away by the whirlwind of turbulent passions, which they have excited.

The *Wish*, which characterizes the benevolent heart, is of a pleasing nature. When it refers simply to the amelioration of our state, not being supported by hope, it subsides almost as soon as it is formed. It is most painful, when it is excited by our own improper conduct, or by the neglect of advantages which are never to return.

ORDER II.

WE proceed to consider those Passions and Affections operating upon the Principle of *Self-love*, in which the idea of EVIL is immediately present to the mind.

These are distinguished into *three Kinds*: the *first* relates to actual losses and disappointments; the *second*, to evils of which we are apprehensive; and the *third*, to the conduct which seems to deserve reprehension. They inspire the passions of *Sorrow*, *Fear*, and *Anger*, with their different modifications and combinations.

It is obvious from this general description of each, that they must be frequently blended together. Partial evils inspiring *sorrow*, are frequently the harbingers of others which alarm our *fears;* and both the evils we lament, and those we dread, may be occasioned by a conduct calculated to excite our *anger*. It is in consequence of these combinations, that many of the affections under this

class

class become so complicated, as to render it difficult to give them a specific arrangement.

Those which are the least complex demand our first attention.

I. SORROW.

It is scarcely necessary to observe, that Sorrow is the direct opposite of Joy. It expresses a mental suffering under the privation of some good which we actually possessed; or concerning which we entertained a pleasing expectation. The one we term loss, the other a disappointment. When the loss or disappointment has been very great, and we feel it as a privation of something which was deemed essential to our felicity, or upon which our affections were strongly placed; when the event arrived in a sudden and unexpected manner, so that the mind was not able to collect itself or prepare for it; this passion produces extreme anguish. Surprise, Wonder, and Astonishment exert their powerful influence, and greatly augment the pangs of sorrow. The senses are troubled; the soul is overwhelmed, and sometimes sinks into a painful stupefaction. This state marks the *Passion* of Sorrow, according to the distinctions noticed in the preceding pages; for it is here that the mind is perfectly passive. As soon as it is able to collect its powers, it wanders over and exaggerates every distressing circumstance and possible disadvantage, that may be consequent upon the loss, until tumultuous emotions are excited, bordering upon phrensy. Violent agitations, and restless positions of the body, extension of the arms, clapping of the hands, beating the breast, tearing the hair, loud sobs and sighs, manifest to the spectator the inward agony of the soul. Such are the *Emotions*, which indicate the nature and strength of the *Passion*. Sometimes a flood of tears relieves these pathognomonic symptoms. Universal lassitude and a sense of debility succeed, with deep dejection of countenance and languor in the eyes, which seem to look around, and solicit in vain for assistance and relief. Every thing, which used to communicate pleasure and inspire vivacity appears frivolous, or becomes indifferent to the mind. The only delight which is now enjoyed, is to contemplate the cause of its affliction; to enumerate all the excellencies and advantages of that which was once possessed, or might have been possessed; and fondly to dwell upon each. Thus the *Emotions* gradually sink into permanent *Affections*.

Grief is sometimes considered as synonymous with Sorrow; and in this case we speak of the *transports*

sports of grief. At other times it expresses more silent, deep, and painful affections, such as are inspired by domestic calamities; particularly by the loss of friends and relatives; or by the distress, either of body or mind, experienced by those we love and value.

When the mind is very deeply impressed with a sense of calamity, for a continuance, and the attention cannot by any means be diverted from it, the subject is in a state of *Melancholy*.

This affection manifests itself by dejection of spirits, debility of mind and body, obstinate and insuperable love of solitude, universal apathy, and a confirmed listlessness, which emaciate the corporeal system, and not unfrequently trouble the brain.

It is a striking characteristic of deep Sorrow, that it is of a tacit and uncommunicative nature. In this also it is the opposite to Joy. After the violent effusions of the mind in the first emotions, it subsides into a pensive and reserved state. It attempts concealment, even from the bosom of a friend; like Viola in Shakespear,

    Who never told her love:
But let concealment, like a worm in the bud,
Feed on her damask cheek.

This disposition may proceed from some peculiar delicacy

delicacy in the cause of grief,—from that indolence, which is the reverse both of the vivacity and loquacity of joy,—from the apprehension that the many will not sympathize with the sufferer,—and from a reluctance to afflict the few that will.

The above remarks refer to Sorrow, excited by more simple causes, and unconnected with any other affection: but it is very frequently blended with other affections, by means of which it is greatly diversified. Sometimes it assumes the appearance of *discontent* and *dissatisfaction*. The first is mostly inspired by a comparison of our situation with that of others, and the discovery of an humiliating inferiority. The other principally refers to the disappointment of our desires, or a partial and imperfect accomplishment of our ardent wishes. In disappointments, where the affections have been strongly placed, and the expectations sanguine, particularly where the agency of others is concerned, sorrow may degenerate into *vexation* and *chagrin;* which are still higher degrees of dissatisfaction. They all imply an *irritated*, as well as *sorrowful* state of mind.

Impatience is also a mixture of sorrow and anger, under the immediate sensation of something irksome; or at the causes of delay, where any desirable object is in expectancy.

Repining

Repining is sorrow united with a degree of resentment against some superior agent, where the mind dares not to break forth into strong expressions of anger.

Sympathetic sorrow is that species of sorrow we participate with others, in consequence of our social connections, or the general benevolence of our natures. These will be more amply considered hereafter.

Of the virtuous affections inspired by Sorrow, which are personal, the most conspicuous are, *Patience*, *Resignation*, and *Humility*. These by their habitual influence often form the disposition and character.

In the exercise of *Patience*, the mind has wisely determined to render the evil as light as possible, by counteracting the usual effects of sorrow or vexation. It endures actual sufferings with composure, or waits for expected blessings, without a culpable restlessness. In short, patience is a calm acquiescence in a state, of which we perceive the evils and discomfiture: by this it is sufficiently distinguished from *insensibility*.

Resignation superadds to patience a submissive disposition, respecting the intelligent cause of our uneasiness. It acknowledges both the power and the right of a superior to afflict. It is usually connected

nected with a confidence in his justice; and indulges a hope also in some future exemption. Thus it opposes a fretful repining temper of mind.

Humility is a degree of habitual sorrow, or painful apprehensions,—by which it is connected with fear,—concerning our deficiencies in intellectual or moral attainments. It is inspired either by comparing ourselves with others, who appear to be our superiors in these excellencies; or by the contemplation of their intrinsic value, importance, extent, and the obstacles which we have suffered to impede our progress. (See Note *N.*)

We have considered the principal cause of sorrow to be *privation;* because the loss of some good is in most instances the prevalent idea. Pecuniary losses, the loss of relatives and friends, of their good-will and affection, are obvious privations. Sickness is the privation of health; imprisonment the privation of liberty; and the hardships endured in prison, the privation of accustomed indulgencies; calumny and disgrace are the privations of a good character. Yet it is acknowledged, that being in the habit of considering these things as essential to comfort and happiness, we view this privation in a positive light; and if we attend simply to the effects, the idea is doubtless pertinent; for all misery, whatever be the cause, is a positive sensation. In bodily

bodily pains or corporeal sufferings, the evil endured is uniformly considered as of a positive nature; nor does the idea of a loss present itself to the mind. It would be an affectation of philosophic precision, to consider the agonies of the torture as a privation of former ease. Perhaps the reason of this distinction is founded in our claiming an exemption from pain, as our natural and only inheritance. Every thing besides is an acquisition, either as a gift, or the purchase of our own labour. The following peculiarity confirms this idea; the term sorrow cannot with any propriety be applied to our bodily sufferings. We should smile at any one, who asserted that he was *sorry* because he had a fit of the gout, or suffered a public flagellation; though in fact, the body cannot suffer without the participation of the mind. Hence it appears that the prevalent cause of Sorrow is privation, though the effects are positive misery.

II. FEAR.

THE second effect produced by the hatred of Evil that we shall mention, is FEAR.

Fear is a painful sensation produced by the immediate *apprehension* of some impending Evil. This evil may consist in being deprived of what we at present enjoy, in being disappointed in what we expect, or in the infliction of a positive misery.

The passion of Fear is still more painful than that of Sorrow, which notwithstanding its severity has, when calmed into an affection, something soothing in its nature. Fear produces an agony and anxiety about the heart not to be described; and it may be said to paralyze the soul in such a manner, that it becomes insensible to every thing but to its own misery. Inertness and torpor pervade the whole system, united with a constriction of the integuments of the body, and also a certain sense of being *fettered*, or of being rendered incapable of motion. The eyes are pallid, wild, and sunk in their sockets; the countenance is contracted and wan; the hair stands erect, or at least this sensation is excited, which every child experiences as often as he is terrified by stories of ghosts, witches, &c; the bowels are strongly affected, the heart palpitates, respiration labours, the lips tremble, the tongue faulters, the limbs are unable to obey the will, or support the frame. Dreadful shrieks denote the inward anguish: these are often succeeded by syncopies, which, while they manifest that the sufferings are greater than nature can sustain, afford a temporary relief.

Such are the external signs which indicate the wretched state of mind under this horrid passion.

Since

Since torpor, debility, and painful conſtrictions, frequently accompany fear more than any other paſſion, the *Emotions* will of conſequence be leſs vivid. Inſtead of violent tranſports, a deep depreſſion and numbneſs, as it were, both of body and mind characterize the paſſion; though theſe may be viſible to the attentive ſpectator, and are not leſs expreſſive of inward anguiſh.

When the effects of fear operate powerfully, without any mixture of hope, theſe paſſive impreſſions are predominant: but where there is a poſſibility of eſcape, the mind re-acts with wonderful energy. Abject depreſſion is changed into violent agitations; collected force takes place of debility; and tremendous exertions ſucceed to a ſtate of torpor and immobility. When a perſonal attack is apprehended, momentary and trembling ſtrength is thrown into the muſcles;—the body inſtinctively places itſelf in the attitude of defence;—a mixture of fierceneſs and wild horror is expreſſed in the countenance, well adapted to alarm and terrify the enemy. If eſcape be attempted, an unuſual energy is thrown into the limbs, enabling the ſufferer to precipitate his flight, by exertions that would have been impracticable in a more compoſed ſtate of mind.

Conſternation. This ſpecies of fear is a ſtrong foreboding of tremendous evils, which are likely to follow misfortunes that have already taken place. It may seize an Individual, when surprised by the arrival of some dreadful disaster; or at the instant of his being made acquainted with the event. But it chiefly refers to alarms of a more extensive nature; to those excited by some general calamity, which threatens evils beyond the power of calculation. Earthquakes, volcanic eruptions, inundations, conflagrations, the sudden approach of an incensed and powerful enemy, are of this kind. Here the danger is widely diffused. Fear is rendered contagious, and by the influence of social sympathy, the consternation becomes universal, without having any particular tendency, or being directed to any particular object. When calamities of this nature arrive in a sudden and unexpected manner; particularly where the ideas of perfect security had been indulged, and perhaps were triumphant and insulting; surprise, wonder, astonishment manifest their powers, by the augmentation of misery, while a troubled imagination aggravates every possibility of horror. In all these cases the expressions of fear are wild and frantic. Beating the breast, tearing the hair, loud lamentations indicate the agony of the soul.

Perhaps the panic which has sometimes seized a whole army, flushed with victory, will illustrate the preceding observations. Rapid success had excited the arrogant idea of *invincibility*. An unexpected defeat,

defeat, has not only subdued this vain conceit, but given an opposite direction to the active imagination, and has transferred the idea of invincibility to the *enemy*. The troops now think that it will be in vain, any longer to resist a power which has shewn itself superior to their own wonted prowess; and where resistance is supposed to be absolutely in vain, it never will be attempted. The force of superstition either in depressing or animating courage, is well known. This has made the most valiant tremble at shadows; and consecrated banners have secured victory over an host of enemies. Thus the warlike Achilles, who was the bulwark of the Grecian cause, and whose sole delight was in the tumults of war, trembled at the sudden appearance of Minerva.*

Abject Fear, which is accompanied by the more silent symptoms of depressed spirits, seems to be inspired chiefly by the idea of an *irresistible* power in its cause. This also is the faithful companion of superstition. It is easily excited in feeble minds by every tale of horror. It is very observable in those who are led into captivity, or to prison; in those detected in the commission of a crime, which exposes them to the severity of the law; in those who are under the expectation of immediate punishment:

---

* Θαμβησεν δ' Αχιλλευς. See Homer. Iliad. A. l. 199.

that is, in cafes which admit of no efcape or redrefs.

Terror is that fpecies of fear, which roufes to defend or efcape; producing the violent agitations which have been already noticed.

So painful is the paffion of Fear, that the evil can fcarcely exift which induces anguifh equal to its feelings. Innumerable are the inftances in which the fear of a calamity of the greateft magnitude, has greatly exceeded the miferies it brought with it; and the mind has refumed a tranquillity under misfortunes, which, in the profpect, appeared infupportable. Bufy imagination always magnifies the evil, and cafts the darkeft fhades over every poffible concomitant. It will not fuffer the fuppofition that any circumftances of alleviation can be attached to a ftate fo much dreaded. But when the dreaded evil is arrived, an immediate releafe from the agonies of fear, is of itfelf a fpecies of confolation. In the worft of circumftances, fear yields its place to *forrow;* which is certainly fome mitigation of fuffering:—habit reconciles to many things, which were at firft repugnant to our nature:—experience in a fhort time points out many comforts, where they were leaft expected:—in moft cafes, as foon as we ceafe to fear, we begin to *hope;* for there are few fituations situations so completely dark and gloomy, as to exclude every ray of consolatory hope.

The union of such cases sufficiently explains the reason why, in numberless instances, the agony of actual sufferings, is not so great as the dread of their arrival. (See Note *O.*)

The *Affections,* that is, the more permanent impressions of fear, unaccompanied with external signs to characterize emotions, are principally the following:

Dread. This is a degree of permanent fear; an habitual and painful apprehension of some tremendous event, which may be too remote to excite any of the preceding passions. It keeps the mind in a perpetual alarm; in an eager watchfulness of every circumstance that bears any relation to the evil apprehended.

It is obvious, that this strong and painful affection cannot be the result, or the residue of fear, in the same manner as satisfaction may be the result of joy, and melancholy of the transports of sorrow; because it is not susceptible of a retrospect. When the evil is arrived, the dread of that evil is removed; though the affection may become attached to some pernicious consequences, which may possibly follow. (See Note *P.*)

Despair.

Despair. This is a permanent fear of losing some valuable good, of suffering some dreadful evil, or of remaining in a state of actual misery, without any mixture of hope. It generally succeeds to ineffectual efforts, which have been repeatedly made; and of consequence is excited where no means can be devised equal to the magnitude of the supposed evil.

Remorse has already been placed under *Sorrow;* but whenever it is connected with a fear of punishment, it deserves a place under this passion also, which greatly increases its agonies. When remorse is blended with the fear of punishment, and arises to despair, it constitutes the supreme wretchedness of the mind.

Cowardice, considered as distinct from the occasional panic mentioned above, is that habitual temper and disposition, which disqualifies from opposing the dangers and difficulties it is our duty or interest to combat. Every indication of cowardice, is an indication of culpable and unmanly fear.

Pusillanimity is a feebleness of mind, still more disgraceful; by which it is terrified at mere trifles, or imaginary dangers, unauthorized by the most distant probability.

Timidity, though similar, is not so reproachful. The term is chiefly used, where there is some apology,

logy, from sex, tender years, or feebleness of frame.

Doubt, considered as an affection, and distinguished from simple deliberation of the mind, is a comfortless state occasioned by the uncertainty of an event, and the predominancy of fearful apprehension concerning it, though a degree of hope is still indulged. (See Note *Q*.)

Irresolution represents the mind as fluctuating between hope and fear, between fits of courage and painful apprehensions, in cases where it ought to determine. It is suspended between probabilities of success, and apparent dangers of disappointment.

Shame is a painful sensation occasioned by the quick apprehension, that reputation and character are in danger; or by the perception that they are lost. It may arise from the immediate detection, or the fear of detection in something ignominious. It may also arise from native diffidence in young and ingenuous minds, when surprised into situations where they attract the peculiar attention of their superiors. The glow of shame indicates, in the first instance, that the mind is not totally abandoned; in the last, it manifests a nice sense of honour and delicate feelings, united with inexperience and ignorance of the world.

Modesty may be deemed an habitual concern and solicitude not to offend against any species of decorum;

rum; either by unsuitable behaviour, in which it is opposed to indelicacy; or by too exalted an opinion of our own good qualities, in which it is opposed to vanity. It sometimes manifests itself by resenting indecencies in speech or conduct; in this case it is united with anger.

Fortitude, Courage, Intrepidity are affections and dispositions opposed to fear. They are virtuous affections, excited alone by exposure to those evils, which are usually productive of that emotion: and therefore they deserve to be mentioned in this connection.

Fortitude expresses that firmness of mind, which resists dangers and sufferings. It is founded on a resolution of the will to counteract or surmount those cowardly impressions, which terrific objects will infallibly make upon inferior minds. It is secretly supported by hope, and greatly invigorated by some portion of the angry affections.

Courage is active fortitude. It meets dangers, and attempts to repel them.

Intrepidity, according to its etymology, proceeds yet farther; it expresses a courage perfectly undaunted, a superiority to the very sensation of fear; boldly impelling the mind forwards to meet the greatest dangers, to which a sense of obligation may expose it.

III. ANGER.

III. ANGER.

This is the third strong effect produced by the immediate perception of evil.

Anger has been confidered as a paffion, directed againft the real or fuppofed caufe of our danger or our fufferings. In the firft tranfport of the paffion, a fenfe of perfonal evil unjuftly inflicted is the primary idea; and thus from the *effect*, the mind makes an inftantaneous and powerful tranfition to its *caufe*. The primary idea entitles it to a place among the paffions excited by Self-love; but many of the effects derived from it properly belong to the focial affections, and conftitute no fmall portion of malevolence and difplacency. The paffions of Sorrow or of Fear do not immediately or neceffarily direct the attention to their caufe, fo as to have an influence upon their fpecific characters: that of Anger does. Thus it becomes as it were the connecting medium between ourfelves and others; exciting painful and irritating fenfations, which relate to both. We fhall therefore confider in this place the general nature of the paffion, as excited in confequence of a keen fenfe of perfonal injuries,

without

without paying particular attention to its objective cause; and refer its influence over the social affections to the Order assigned them.

Anger is the strong passion or emotion, impressed or excited, by a sense of injury received, or in contemplation; that is, by the idea of something of a pernicious nature and tendency, being done or intended, in violation of some supposed obligation to a contrary conduct. It is enkindled by the perception of an undue privation of that to which we thought ourselves, in some degree or other, entitled; or of a positive suffering, from which we claimed an exemption. These are obviously the exciting causes; though our ignorance, or inordinate self-love, may suggest erroneous ideas respecting our claims, or render the resentful emotion very disproportionate to the offence. The pain we suffer from the injury, the unexpectedness of the offence, our wounded pride, &c. are so apt to disturb our reasoning and discriminating powers, that we are at the first instant prompted to consider every injury received, as an injury intended. Nor are there wanting numerous instances, in which an heated and irritated imagination attributes *design* to the irrational and inanimate creation, in order to gratify the passion of resentment.

Anger viewed as a passion, that is, as referring to the first impression in which we are passive,—or the impression

impression preceding the external signs, which constitute the emotion,—may be considered as a painful sensation of a heating and irritating nature. It is an irksome stimulus, by which the animal spirits are troubled and violently agitated. Yet the sensation is not so painful as in the excesses of sorrow or of fear. When the injury appears great, totally unprovoked, too recent or sudden for the mind to call up motives of restraint;—when surprise at receiving an offence from a quarter the most remote from expectation,—or astonishment at base and ungrateful returns for benefits conferred, accompany the first impulse of passion, an ardent desire of *revenge* is immediately excited. The imagination runs over every circumstance of aggravation; depicts the offence as a crime of the most atrocious nature; and vengeance is denounced against the aggressor, as an indispensable obligation of justice, and as a retribution due to the violated laws of morals, of honour, or of gratitude. The emotions strikingly correspond with this state of mind. The corporeal system immediately assumes attitudes and appearances, calculated to inspire the offender with terror, and preparatory to the infliction of the chastisement, he is supposed to have deserved. The countenance reddens, the eyes flash indignant fire, and the aspect speaks horror; muscular strength is abundantly increased; and powers of exertion are

acquired,

acquired, unknown to cooler moments. This new appetite for revenge gains the ascendancy, not only over every consideration of compassion, but of personal safety, and impels to dangerous encounters, totally regardless of the danger. In some instances, an apprehension of dreadful consequences, a kind of presage of the mischief that may possibly ensue, and become the subject of future regret, intermixes fear with the paroxysms of anger; and a pallid tremour unites with symptoms peculiar to wrath, or accompanies the first tokens of revenge.

Anger is deservedly placed among the most violent emotions. From its ungovernable excesses, it has almost appropriated to itself the term *passion*. When the paroxysms of anger are excessive, the subject is deaf to the most cogent reasons, or to the most pathetic representations of the mischief it may occasion; and being worked up to a degree of phrensy, he fully vindicates the adage *Ira brevis furor*. While under the influence of this turbulent emotion, the incensed person often imagines that he is solely actuated by the purest love of equity, and ardent desire to administer justice; though at the instant he may be violating the dictates of compassion, in the perpetration of the most atrocious deeds.

It is observable, that Sorrow and Fear, though they may be the result of culpable conduct or even criminality,

criminality, are calculated to excite our compassion. The anguish manifested by the subject, calls aloud for our sympathy: but Anger, though it is a painful emotion, seldom excites our sympathy, unless we suppose the subject to be insane. In those cases where we acknowledge the provocation has been very great, sympathy is chiefly transferred to the object of resentment; prompting us to act as mediators, and exert all our influence to mitigate or avert the punishment to which he is exposed.

Anger in the excess of its violence, when it is excited to a degree of phrensy, so that the mind has totally lost self-command, when it prompts to threats and actions extravagant and atrocious, is termed *Rage*.

Wrath is violent and permanent anger; and as such it may be deemed an *affection*. This may be seated in a breast possessing too much self-command to will the infliction of punishment, though it notices and dwells upon every circumstance of aggravation; and though it should resolve to punish, it is capable of being appeased by the concessions and penitence of the offender.

Resentment is a lesser degree of wrath, excited by smaller offences, or by offences committed against less irritable minds. It is a deep reflective displeasure against the conduct of the offender.

Indignation is a resentment against a conduct that appears

appears peculiarly unworthy; some atrocious violation of the principles of gratitude, or something which appears peculiarly despicable and base.

But we are now trespassing upon the affections which properly belong to another Class, and which will demand our attention under the article of *Displacency*.

Anger, and its principal ramifications are generally directed against the conduct of others, and almost universally with superior degrees of violence; however they are sometimes directed against ourselves, when our conduct has been either negligent or criminal. In *Repentance*, *Contrition*, and *Remorse*, Self-reproach, and even *Indignation* are largely intermixed with the affection of Sorrow.

Vexation, *Chagrin*, *Impatience*, do not relate to persons, so much as to particular circumstances of a teazing nature. They are chiefly excited by disappointments, and tedious delays to the accomplishment of our wishes.

Peevishness may be considered as a slighter degree of anger, perpetually recurring to irritable persons from trifling causes. It is such a soreness of temper, that it can scarcely suffer the touch of the gentlest hand; and it resents upon the most Innocent, the vexations that have been excited by causes with which they had no concern.

Although

Although *Fortitude, Courage, Intrepidity* have been considered under the article of *Fear*, as they are virtuous resolutions which oppose themselves to the objects of our fear, or to the dangers which threaten us; yet they might with no impropriety have been placed under the passion of *Anger*. If we advert to the physiological, or rather pathological effects of anger, we shall perceive that it rouses the mind, increases muscular strength, braces the system for action, and renders the subject heedless of danger; and these are the effects produced by fortitude and courage. Though that strong irritation of mind peculiar to anger, may not be sensibly felt by generous spirits, and self-command may calm the agitations natural to this passion, as well as those peculiar to terror, yet some modifications of it obviously remain. Where courage is merely instinctive, it is manifestly quickened by anger, though cultivation and noble principles may suppress the appearance and almost the sensations, in minds endowed with the virtues of fortitude and magnanimity.

It may perhaps be asserted with justice, that some degree of anger is naturally excited by every object of hatred. Though privation or danger be the predominant ideas in Sorrow or Fear, yet these are mostly, it may be said *always* accompanied with a sense of injury, in minds not influenced by moral restraints. In sorrows inflicted by a Power against which we dare not to murmur, the irritations natural to a wounded mind, may be subjugated by motives of virtue and piety; but without these, it would be strongly disposed to burst forth into frantic and impotent rage. This may be explained by the strength and quickness of our painful feelings, which at the first instant dispose us to impute blame where no blame can be attached. History makes us acquainted with many curious instances in the heathen world, where the images of their deities have been very roughly treated, and even suffered public flagellation, for not having averted the calamities which had been deprecated; and the repinings of those who have been better instructed, manifest a similar temper, though it may be somewhat checked by awe.

It is an indication of no inconsiderable progress in reason and in resolution, always to distinguish with accuracy between an evil endured and its inculpable cause; and to support the calamity without the least mixture of resentment. Nor are these observations confined to the occasions of Sorrow; in the passion of *Fear*, the first object being safety, every other consideration may be suppressed for the instant: but in the emotion of *Terror*, not only some degree of courage, but a very considerable portion

portion of anger is perceptible: the rage of a coward despairing of escape by flight, is proverbial.

The most accurate distinctions therefore which we have been capable of making in the above Analysis of the Passions, have been to mark the leading characteristics of each. The primary idea exciting Sorrow is that of loss, or painful privation; that of Fear is danger; and the genuine idea appropriate to Anger is that of injury, or some species of injustice. These are very distinct in themselves, though inordinate self-love so frequently confounds them together.

We have thus endeavoured to trace the various Passions and Affections, which are of a personal nature; and which are more immediately excited in consequence of the principle of SELF-LOVE.—A principle implanted in every breast; seated in every individual of our species, from the most ignorant to the most intelligent; from the capricious infant, to the sublimest philosopher. All who are able to discern, or *think* that they discern, things conducive to their happiness or enjoyment, are occasionally placed in situations which expose them to the influence of one or other of the above Passions,

Emotions, and Affections, in their individual capacities.

The Passions and Affections, which belong to the *social* Principle, next demand our attention.

CLASS II.

CLASS II.

On the Passions and Affections, derived from the SOCIAL PRINCIPLE.

IF our connections with the *inanimate* creation expose us to be differently influenced by various powers and properties discernible in every part of it; if many things around us call forth our passions and affections, by sustaining certain relations with our corporeal and intellectual natures, it is to be expected that a still more intimate connection with the *animated* creation, should implant within us various dispositions correspondent to those higher qualities and properties belonging to it. The *animated beings* around us not only excite certain Passions and Affections, arising from the principle of Self-love, in common with other parts of nature, but they also are rendered capable of *enjoying* or of *suffering*, equally with ourselves; and we possess the power of administering to their well-being, or of proving injurious to it.

Rational and intelligent agents being furnished with certain rules of conduct, which respect both themselves and others, are subjected to various degrees of approbation or censure, according as they act conformably to such rules, or in violation of them.

These peculiarities introduce a train of Passions and Affections, very distinct from those which are excited by the selfish principle alone. Self-love confines its attention to certain qualities and properties, merely as they have an influence upon our own personal welfare; and we deem these qualities good or bad, solely as they produce certain effects upon *Ourselves*. The Social Principle extends its regards to the state, the conduct, and the character of *Others;* and it operates according to the degrees of their connection with us,—to their powers of communicating or receiving from us either good or evil,—to their actual enjoyments or their sufferings,—to their prospects of future good, or exposure to evil,—to their occasional or habitual deportment,—and to the degrees of merit or demerit attached to their dispositions and conduct as conscious and intelligent agents.

Numberless are the Passions, Emotions, and Affections proceeding from these different causes; and they vary in their complexion and character, according to the peculiarities of their excitements. Yet they

they are all reducible to the two grand diftinctions which have been already pointed out. They may be placed under the Cardinal Affections of *Love* and *Hatred*, in which *Good*, or *Evil* are the predominant ideas. Nor can there be a difpofition in this clafs of objects, or of ourfelves towards them, which may not, in one point of view or other, be ranged under thefe general heads.

It is obvious that thefe affections primarily relate, either to the *perfons* or the *characters* of their objects. The *good* refers to that which we behold in them, or wifh them to poffefs; and the *evil* to the fuppofed depravity of their characters, or the malevolence of difpofition we may entertain towards them. The predominant ideas therefore of good and evil refpect thefe alone. The affections of love and hatred are excited, by the immediate intereft we take in their merits or their welfare, or by the refentments indulged againft them; without immediate reference to concomitant circumftances. Thus the love and defire of good refpecting their *perfons*, may often be connected with the contemplation of the evils that furround them; and malevolent difpofitions may, in fome cafes, be implanted by the contemplation of the good they poffefs, or have the profpect of enjoying. In the focial affections, for example, which are infpired by the diftreffes of our fellow-creatures, a compaffionate heart cannot contemplate

template their situation, without contemplating their misery. This necessarily fixes the attention upon the *evils* to which they are exposed; yet as it is the benevolent principle which induces us to direct this attention towards their sufferings, and as an ardent wish is inspired that they may be rescued from them, the love of good respecting them, is evidently the predominant principle.

On the other hand, it is very possible for us to be more displeased with the conduct of others than with our own; to entertain very *different* ideas of their characters, from those we should entertain of our own, were we precisely in their situation; and also to wish to another much greater evils, than we shall ever wish to ourselves. These peculiarities may inspire personal hatreds, which shall indicate themselves not merely by malevolence, or actually wishing them evil, but also by deep resentment at the good they actually enjoy. In this case, malevolence is predominant even in the act of contemplating good.

No one general term is adapted to all those passions and affections which belong to the social principle. Dr. Hartley, however, has comprehended them all under the name or character of *Sympathy*. This he divides into four Classes: rejoicing at another's happiness; grieving at his misery; grieving at his happiness; and rejoicing at his misery.

But

But the word *sympathy*, whether we advert to its genuine import or common usage, is ill adapted to the two last divisions. The usual idea of sympathy is that of *suffering with* another; which is the most opposite possible to grieving at his happiness, or rejoicing at his misery: the last is not suffering, and the other is suffering in a manner directly contrary.

These two opposite dispositions are usually expressed by the opposite terms *Benevolence* and *Malevolence*; the first referring to kindly dispositions towards its objects, and the other to the reverse. But should they be the best terms we are able to employ, yet they are not entirely unexceptionable; as they do not always convey ideas perfectly correspondent with the various differences comprised under these general heads.

Benevolence signifying *good-will*, might, according to its etymology, be considered as applicable to *Ourselves* as well as to others; yet in its usual acceptation the idea of *Self* is totally excluded; and it expresses a disposition directly opposite to the *selfish* principle.—This good-will does not indicate itself in all those affections which are ranged under Benevolence. We may warmly commend some particular conduct, and admire peculiar excellencies, in those for whom we entertain an indifference, or a degree of *ill-will*.—Some characters inspire us
with

with the deepest reverence and awe; which affections, though they do not exclude benevolence, are not immediately inspired by it. Notwithstanding these slight objections, the word appears to be more deserving of being employed as a *generic* term, than any other that can be adopted.

Were we more familiarized to the signification given to the term *Passion* in our introductory Chapter; were it confined to the idea of *passiveness*, whether the cause be of a pleasing or displeasing nature, then might we with the strictest propriety use the term *Sympathy* to express a *fellow-feeling* with another, both upon joyful and mournful occasions. It would be applicable to every coincidence of sensation, sentiment, and disposition, comprehending our good wishes, good opinions, and that benignity which rejoices in their prosperity.

But even in this case, *Sympathy* can only be applied to incidental indications of benevolence, and is not to be substituted for the word itself. It will have the same relation to the benevolent principle as *desire* has to that of *Love*. The principle of benevolence pre-disposes to these social virtues, and sympathy engages in particular acts of benevolence. To this sense its etymology necessarily confines it; for we can neither suffer with another, nor have any kind of sensation in common with him, until he be

placed

placed in certain situations, with which we are become acquainted.

There are much stronger objections to the word *Malevolence* as a generic term, than to the preceding. It always conveys the idea of *ill-will* to a considerable degree: but hourly instances of displacency, and even of anger and resentment, present themselves, without any mixture of that ill-will it describes. In some cases, painful resentments may be excited by the purest *good-will;* as in the anger of a parent towards his child, on account of conduct prejudicial to his welfare. Even the momentary ill-will indulged by a passionate man, seeking revenge for injuries received, deserves not to be stigmatized by the odious name of malevolence, which conveys the idea of permanent ill-will.

For the above reasons, and from a reluctance to use a term so malevolent in its complexion and character, more frequently than absolute necessity demands, I beg leave to substitute *displacency* as a generic term. Its superior propriety will be manifest from the consideration, that every instance of *malevolence* is an indication of *displacency* to a high degree, although the latter is not at all times an indication of the former.

The

The Reader will not be disposed to censure as superfluous these minute investigations, respecting the signification of terms, when he recollects that the want of precision has been the grand source of confusion of ideas even among philosophers. The least difference in our conceptions respecting the force of words may direct to very different conclusions; the smallest deviation from the requisite point of the compass, will in a short time steer the vessel into an improper latitude.

In the prosecution of our Analysis under this Second Class, or in tracing the Passions and Affections which belong to the *social* Principle, I shall according to the plan proposed, divide the subject into two Orders; the first belonging to the principle of *Benevolence*, in which the idea of *Good* is the more immediate and predominant idea; and the second to *Displacency*, in which the idea of *Evil* prevails.

The *benevolent* principle may refer to *good Desires* and *Dispositions*, and to *good Opinions*: which form two distinct kinds or genera. *Displacency* may also be divided into two kinds; *Malevolence*, properly so called; and *disfavourable Opinion*, or *Displacency* according to its usual signification.

ORDER I.

ORDER I.

Passions and Affections excited by Benevolence, in which GOOD *is the predominant Idea.*

I. Those which respect *Benevolent Desires* and *Dispositions*.

IN our general remarks concerning *Love* as a Principle, we inevitably anticipated some things which properly belong to this branch of our Subject. It was then hinted, that our benevolent dispositions may be directed towards those who are connected with us in various degrees of relation or intimacy; to the whole human race indiscriminately, in which it is termed *Philanthropy;* and to all beings rendered capable of any portion of enjoyment, or *universal benevolence,* according to the most extensive sense of the expression.

It will not be necessary, in the process of our investigation, to have the distinction between the rational

tional and irrational creation always in our view. The dispositions towards each are similar; though rational beings, from their superior importance, are the most interesting, and the diversity of their situations admits of a greater variety of correspondent affections. Both may be comprehended under the title of *general benevolence.*

It will however be proper to remark, that the benevolence which respects our most intimate connections, approximates very closely to the principle of *Self-love.* It considers every thing belonging to its immediate objects, as belonging also to ourselves, and thus constitutes one common interest. Of this kind are all those connections which form the intimate relations of life, and create so large a portion of its happiness or its misery. Such are the *conjugal, parental, filial, fraternal* relations, various degrees of consanguinity, and particular friendships. Here the habitual attachments, and benignant dispositions which the mind experiences, assume the character of *affections,* by way of pre-eminence. For it is in these relations that the kindly affections manifest the greatest warmth and constancy. The general objects of our *philanthropy* may possess a portion of our *good-will,* without particular interest being habitually taken in their welfare. The *operation* of this principle is confined to particular cases and situations, in which they may be incidentally placed.

placed. Those animals to which we are the most strongly attached, or that we may have appropriated to ourselves, are considered as sustaining an occasional, and accidental connection; and when they are the most requisite for our use and comfort, we chiefly value them as the instruments and means of our convenience and pleasure. Their influence is chiefly temporary. They are transferred with little regret. The mind may become versatile and changeable towards them, without the imputation of cruelty or injustice. But in the social relation, the kindly affections *dwell* with the well-disposed mind, and are *perpetually* operative.

These social affections may arise from various causes, which give them their distinguishing characteristics, and possess various degrees of strength, which in most cases is regulated by the degrees of their utility. Some are deemed instinctive; that is, originally implanted in the breast without the conscious aid of reason, or reflection. The love of parents for their offspring is adduced as an evidence of instinctive affection. This is observable in persons who seem to have eradicated every other social affection. They still retain a solicitude for their young, after they have rendered themselves strangers to every other virtue; and indulge a fondness *here* amidst the greatest animosities against those around them. But whatever ideas we may affix to

the

the word *instinct*, self-love seems to form its basis. Parents manifestly contemplate their children as *scions* from the stem; and the selfish affections accompany them not only as being their own representatives, but as *second selves*. The superior strength of affection natural to the female breast, which receives a daily increase by unremitted habits of care and attention, gives the appearance of a much stronger instinct to the *maternal*, than to the *paternal* affections.

Some of the social affections arise from the perception or persuasion of amiable qualities personal or mental, for which a strong predilection is formed; as in the *conjugal* relation. This predilection having also a *sexual* influence, may become a *passion* the most impetuous and ungovernable. The sexual passion is rendered remarkable for its contrarieties. It may be considered as the most generous and the most selfish;—at once the most interested, and the most disinterested:—it is ready to sacrifice every thing, even life itself for the beloved object;—but it is anxious to appropriate the beloved object entirely to itself.

Where the impetuosity of passion is not succeeded by indifference, it gives place to the milder and more permanent joys of *conjugal* affection.

Filial affections, if they do not originate from, are closely connected with an early sense of superiority,

ority, united with a conviction that this superiority is exercised in perpetual cares and acts of kindness.

Fraternal affection owes much of its strength to the closest habits of intimacy, the perception of one common interest, and an impressive sense of the inestimable value of domestic harmony.

The *friendly affections* are inspired by the contemplation of pleasing qualities, and the perception of a similarity in dispositions. They are always cherished by reciprocal acts of kindness.

All these connections may be said to relate most intimately to *Self*. They manifest an *adoption* of others into our hearts. They blend and intermix interests so completely, that the ardent desire of good towards the particular objects of these affections is not considered as a branch of *disinterested* benevolence. All the Passions and Affections which have been enumerated under the preceding Class, as primarily belonging to the *selfish* principle, may be excited by the state and situation of those we love, with equal, and sometimes with superior vigour. In events incidental to them, Joy, Desire, Hope, Sorrow, Fear, Anger, become as quick and impetuous as in cases where our own interests are exclusively concerned: and wherever the Universal Parent has constituted us the agents, or the guardians of the good fortune of others, we enjoy the affections of Satisfaction, Contentment, Complacency, &c. according to the degrees of their prosperity, or the value of circumstances contributing to it, as if this good immediately pertained to *Ourselves*.

To the good-will which extends itself beyond the circle of personal attachments, and with which our own permanent welfare is not so intimately connected;—to the good-will which is often exercised towards *strangers*, and which is sometimes exercised by generous minds towards *enemies*, is the title of *Benevolence* usually applied. Because it is here that the innate benignity of disposition appears the most conspicuously. In these instances of good-will nothing *selfish* appears. The benevolence acquires the character of being *pure* and *disinterested*.

Considering this benevolence as a principle constituting a pre-disposition, or a readiness of temper to act in a manner correspondent to the particular situation of the object, the direct operation of this principle will manifest itself by emotions and affections to which the term SYMPATHY seems to be peculiarly applicable.

According to the observations already made upon *Sympathy*, it may be considered as an inward feeling, which is excited by the particular and extraordinary

traordinary situation of another; or which harmonizes with the condition and feelings of its object. Sympathy indicates a mind attuned to correspondent vibrations, whether they be of the pleasing or displeasing kind. Consequently it operates with various degrees of strength, according to the degrees of danger to which its objects may be exposed;—to the misery they suffer, and the aggravating circumstances attending it;—to the good fortune with which they are surprised and delighted;—and to their capacities of receiving good. It also disposes the mind to accommodate itself to the tastes, dispositions, and manners of others in the social intercourses of life.

In this enlarged sense of the term may sympathy be considered as a *passion*, an *affection*, and a *disposition*.

In some urgent and extraordinary cases, sympathy rises into an emotion, which yields not in strength and exertions to the most violent of the *selfish* passions. When its object is suddenly exposed to some instantaneous and tremendous danger which demands immediate aid, the whole soul is devoted to the sufferer. *Danger* and *relief* are the thoughts which occupy the mind, to the total exclusion of every other. Impelled by this irresistible emotion, the sympathizer plunges into the ocean and braves its billows, or rushes into the midst of flames regardless of their horrors, to snatch a wretched victim from destruction. He is insensible to personal danger where it is the greatest. I will not say that he does not listen to the suggestions of prudence, as prudential thoughts are not suggested. There is no passion, excepting anger approaching to madness, which resembles the heedless impetuosity of this emotion. Rage, eager to punish an offence or revenge an insult, will also rush into danger, and expose its own life in order to glut its passion; but its pallid countenance and the tremour of its limbs, indicate that *Self* is by no means forgotten. The impulse of sympathy renders the generous mind completely courageous. It is a stranger to *personal* fear; all its anxieties are transferred to the perils of the object.

When the evil is less sudden and alarming; when it is apparently of a permanent nature, sympathy with distress becomes an *affection*.

Sympathetic affections are distinguished into various species, and discriminated by various appellations, according to the peculiarities attendant upon their cause, or the particular state of their object.

They may be divided into those which respect *Distress, Prosperity, Imitation*.

Of those which respect *Distress*, the following are the principal.

Compassion.

Compassion. Compassion is that species of affection, which is excited either by the actual distress of its object, or by some impending calamity which appears inevitable. It is a benevolent sorrow at their sufferings or approaching misery. The etymology of the word expresses this idea with strict propriety; as it signifies *suffering with the object.*

Compassion is always connected with a disposition to relieve, and will always prompt to vigorous exertions, wherever there is a possibility of success; unless some important considerations should render the endeavour improper or unjust.

Compassion has no necessary connection with the *character* of its objects. Their *distress* is a sufficient excitement. It is frequently exercised upon the unworthy, whose reiterated imprudences or vicious conduct, may have been the cause of their wretchedness. From the great extent and universality of this affection, it may justly be considered as a generic name, comprehending several other affections which have a more specific application; as *Mercy, Commiseration, Pity, &c.*

Mercy is the most exalted branch of compassion. It particularly refers to that state of mind, which induces us to exercise our compassion upon persons whose fate is in some respect at our disposal. It induces us to relinquish demands, which, if enforced to the utmoſt, would render us the immediate agents of miſery. It is peculiarly applicable to unworthy or criminal behaviour towards ourſelves, which would inevitably involve the offender in diſtreſs, were we to be tenacious of our rights. In a word, it is that dignified compaſſion which induces us to ſuppreſs reſentment, to pardon offences, or mitigate puniſhments as far as diſcretion may admit.

Commiſeration. Although this term ſeems ſynonymous with the preceding, yet in its general uſe it is ſomewhat different. It is always preferred when we wiſh to expreſs our ſympathy for misfortunes, which it is not in our power to remove; or for which there is no apparent remedy. Commiſeration ruminating upon the ſtate and ſufferings of others, induces a permanent concern. In ſuch caſes it may be ſaid that we *commiſerate* the unfortunate ſufferer, rather than that we *have compaſſion* upon him. But although this is a more helpleſs, it is not an uſeleſs affection. It ſooths the mind of the afflicted, and greatly alleviates their ſorrows, when every other conſolation fails.

Condolence is the expreſſion of our commiſeration.

Pity is alſo ſimilar to the two preceding affections, but it is more frequently applied to particular circumſtances in the ſtate and ſituation of the object, rather than his immediate *feelings*. Thus we
often

often pity thofe who have no pity upon themfelves; whofe difpofitions and conduct are leading them into evils, of which they entertain no apprehenfions, or concerning which they are not folicitous. The decrepit and infirm alfo are the objects of our pity, though they may fuftain their infirmities with an enviable cheerfulnefs. Children rendered deftitute of worthy and affectionate parents, and expofed to future calamities of which they are unconfcious, are deemed peculiar objects of pity. Nay, their ignorance of their misfortunes augments the force of our fympathetic feelings.

Generofity is the difpofition which prompts us to beftow favours, which are not the purchafe of any particular merit. It has not, like mercy, any immediate relation either to imprudences or criminality. It is compounded of benevolence with a degree of fympathy with fome peculiarities in the ftate or circumftances of another, which demand our aid, either in the remiffion of pecuniary claims, in voluntary grants, or in donations and benefactions to affift their indigence. It generally relates to fome conceffions, facrifices, or peculiar exertions that have been made in the exercife of the benevolent principle. The extent of generofity is meafured by the advantages and pleafures which have been relinquifhed in favour of another; or according to the troubles and difficulties which have been encountered by the benefactor on the one hand, and the slender pretensions of the object to these benevolent offices, on the other.

Liberality has sometimes a similar import with generosity. Sometimes it has a particular reference to the largeness of pecuniary or other donations. In the present day it is frequently applied to *sentiments* respecting another. It is used in opposition to a narrow contracted mode of thinking, or to a censorious disposition inspired by a difference of opinion. It expresses a freedom from the bias of prejudice or partiality. The man who is disposed to think well of, and act with kindness towards persons whose religious or political creed differs materially from his own, is deemed *liberal-minded*.

Thus may liberality be considered as a species of generosity, which usage chiefly applies to free donations, or to subduing unfavourable pre-possessions respecting the opinions of another. It is a liberation from the confined manner of acting, or thinking, which characterizes either the parsimonious, or the bigot.

Charity in its original import is synonymous with Love. In its application it is sometimes used to express a disposition to entertain a favourable opinion of the moral character or conduct of others, in opposition to unfavourable reports, until the strongest evidences implant conviction; at other times it signifies

nifies giving of alms, and doing good to inferiors. Benevolent interference in behalf of the wretched, or the oppressed, are deemed acts of charity.

Condescension is that species of benevolence, which designedly waves the supposed advantages of birth, title, or station, in order to accommodate ourselves to the state of an inferior, and diminish that restraint which the apparent distance is calculated to produce in him. It greatly enhances the value of every other species of benevolence.

From the above Analysis we perceive that Mercy, Commiseration, Pity, Liberality, &c. are different branches of Compassion adapted to the peculiar situation and exigencies of its objects. While compassion relates to distress in general without minute distinctions, its ramifications respect *criminality* of character or conduct,—the *permanency* of distress,—*state* and *situations* which strike us as peculiarly unfortunate,—*minuter exigencies*,—*reputation*, —and *inferiority* of station. It is not always requisite to give to each species of compassion its appropriate term; yet the diversity of misfortunes, and the diverse alleviations of each, have imperceptibly introduced a correspondent phraseology, which in particular cases, manifests its peculiar propriety.

Another important branch of Benevolence consists in partaking of the *good fortune* of others; in the participation of their joy, upon the accession of good, or liberation from evil.

If the term sympathy be employed in this connection, it will denote a pleasurable sensation excited within us, similar to that enjoyed by the primary participant of good.

It is observable that no particular terms are appropriated to this species of sympathy. There are no nice discriminations which indicate the different kinds of good, or the circumstances relative to it, in a manner correspondent with those which have been traced under sympathetic sorrow. Freedom from distress, or the increase of actual enjoyment, produce, as it were, one simple effect upon the mind of the benevolent sympathizer, without those various and more complicated sensations which a diversity in misfortunes may occasion. These pleasing sensations can only be expressed by the general terms of *joy, gladness, happiness, &c.* We *rejoice* at the fortunate event which has made another happy; we are *glad* to hear of their success; are *happy* to be informed of their welfare, &c.

In some instances this species of benevolence becomes a very lively emotion, and the sudden impulse of joy may emulate that inspired by our own good

good fortune, although the object should be almost a stranger to us. When, for example, our minds have been previously and deeply affected with the knowledge of his distress;—when a prosperous change has *suddenly* taken place;—and particularly when this change has been accomplished by the triumph of the party over cruelty and oppression. In such cases, we enjoy this sudden transition from painful to pleasing sympathy, and we participate in that exultation over tyranny or injustice, to which every man entertains an hatred, unless it be his own act.

But excepting upon extraordinary occasions of this nature, our sympathies with the good fortune of others, are much inferior in strength to those we experience from their distress. Various reasons may be assigned for this difference. The influence of many blessings newly acquired may not be so extensive and important, as the influence of a single calamity;—it is scarcely possible for any one to be elevated to the pinnacle of happiness, in so rapid a manner as he may be plunged into the depth of distress;—good fortune, to whatever state or circumstances we may apply the term, is generally of slower progress, is accumulated by almost imperceptible degrees, and therefore is not calculated to make a vivid impression at any one period of its progress;—the object may be more deeply afflicted in his relative

tive and social connections by the misfortunes or irregular conduct of an individual, than he could feel himself benefited by their prosperity; consequently were we to sympathize with him in a manner correspondent with his own feelings, joyful events could not make an impression upon us equal to his afflictions;—those distresses which call forth our sympathy of sorrow are generally promulgated to a considerable extent, while recent acquisitions of good, with all the striking circumstances attending them, are mostly confined to the narrow circle of relatives and friends.—To these incidental causes, we may justly add the wise constitution of our natures as the *final* cause. Sympathy with the distresses of another is infinitely more useful than rejoicing in his prosperity. It is an incentive to administer relief, to annihilate this distress, and to restore the sufferer to the pristine state of ease and comfort; and therefore is it rendered, by the Great Source of Benevolence, more powerful in its influence and operations, than the sympathy of joy in their welfare; which cannot be productive of equal good. The different kinds of sympathetic sorrow are admirably adapted to the particular state of its objects, in order that each may receive its correspondent benefit. These considerations will explain the reason why an insensibility to the misfortunes of any one,

is

is much more opprobrious than an indifference to his actual enjoyments.

The immediate *expressions* of our joy are termed *Congratulations.*

All the affections excited by the contemplation of good or evil which relate to others, are manifestly compound. Sympathy with sufferings, is composed of benevolence and *sorrow;* and cordial congratulations are the effusions of benevolence and *joy.*

It is observable that in the benevolence we are now contemplating, the affection of Love is not necessarily placed upon the object personally, on account of any excellence of character, or peculiar amiableness of disposition. It loves the welfare of another, unconnected with his virtues. The capacity of enjoyment is a sufficient motive for attempting to impart it; and a state of distress is a sufficient incitement to attempt relief. In its noblest exertions benevolence indicates itself by the communication of good, in opposition to evil deserts, and in a strong propensity to protect from misery, which the bad conduct of the offender has not been able to subdue. It becomes a desire of promoting happiness too ardent to be extinguished, by injury itself.

Sympathy

Sympathy is also applicable to the sociableness of the human character; to the nature of man as formed to live in society. This is manifested by the reciprocal pleasure and satisfaction we experience in our daily intercourse;—by the eagerness with which we receive and communicate tidings that interest our fellow-men;—by the love of imitation, and the readiness with which we conform to the custom, manners, and dispositions, and acquiesce in the opinions of others, without attention to the higher authority of propriety or impropriety, or weighing motives and arguments in the balance of reason. In short, it respects every act, habit, and sentiment, of which to participate in common is gratifying to our natures, and constitutes so large a portion of the enjoyments and seductions of life.

This sympathetic imitation brings us by imperceptible degrees to our Second Division.

II. The Affections derived from *Good Opinion*.

In this Class of Social Affections the operations of the Benevolent Principle are not so immediate. Though benevolence is associated, it is not the primary

mary agent: it is rather a consequence than a cause. It is not our benevolence which inspires us with these favourable opinions, but their good qualities which awaken and direct our benevolence. Our affections are drawn forth by an impressive sense of some species of excellence in character; and they may be placed upon objects, whose situations do not require either our sympathetic joys or sorrows. These are most properly expressed by *complacential regards*; for they consist both in the approbation of the mind, and feelings of the heart; they relate to conduct and qualities, concerning which our judgment pronounces that they possess merit, while they are rendered interesting by virtue of our social connections.

The nature of Complacency, as it refers either to ourselves, or to our most intimate connections, has already been considered.* I shall only observe in this place, that when we are rendered participants of good from those qualities which are the proper objects of complacency; or when we contemplate peculiar marks of mental or moral excellencies in others with whom we are conversant, our *approbation* is accompanied with various degrees of affection for them, although they may not be within the sphere of our intimacy.

* See Page 66, passim.

Of these affections the following are the most conspicuous.

Gratitude. Gratitude is a pleasant affection excited by a lively sense of benefits received or intended, or even by the desire of being beneficial. In its strength it is the powerful re-action of a well-disposed mind, upon whom benevolence has conferred some important good. It is mostly connected with an impressive sense of the amiable disposition of the person by whom the benefit is conferred, and it immediately produces a personal affection towards him. When the affection operates according to the natural course of influence, it will be correspondent to the importance of the good obtained,—the distance in station between the recipient and his benefactor,—the smallness of his claims,—perhaps the consciousness of deserving very opposite treatment. These circumstances unite to warm the heart into raptures. The grateful mind is impatient of a silent and passive reception of the blessing. It cannot be restrained from acknowledging its obligations, either by expressions or deeds. It considers every return in its power as an act of the strictest justice; nor is it deterred by difficulties or dangers from making the attempt. The term most familiarly employed was originally suggested by this idea. The *obligation* is perceived, and felt; and the person benefited considers himself as *bound* in honour

and

and justice, either to repay or acknowledge the debt, by a bond that cannot be cancelled.

We shall not wonder at the peculiar strength and energy of this affection, when we consider that it is compounded of *love* placed upon the good communicated, *affection* for the donor, and *joy* at the reception. Thus it has goodness for its object, and the most pleasing, perhaps *unexpected* exertions of goodness, for its immediate cause.

Thankfulness refers to verbal expressions of gratitude.

Admiration. Although there is scarcely a word in more familiar use than the term *admiration*, yet much ambiguity attends its precise signification; nor have authors of the greatest celebrity been uniform in the sense they have affixed to it. Sometimes it has been deemed synonymous with Surprise; sometimes it is used to express Wonder; sometimes it is applied to subjects, as a mark of degradation; at others, as expressive of excellencies.

In Milton's Paradise Lost, it is more than once employed to denote *wonder*.

———Let none *admire*
That riches grow in *hell.*———

BOOK I. L. 690.

In the following passage of Shakespear, it obviously

ously signifies *wonder* and *astonishment*. Lady Macbeth says to her husband, terrified at the sight of Banquo's Ghost,

You have displac'd the mirth, broke the good meeting, with most *admired* disorder.
MACBETH.

Mr. Pope has used it to express the indiscriminating applause of ignorance:

For FOOLS *admire*, but Men of Sense *approve*.

Mr. Grove defines admiration to be " that sud-
" den surprise at the novelty of an object, by which
" the soul is fastened down to the contemplation of
" it." He also asserts that " according to the differ-
" ent characters of its object, it is called *esteem* or
" *contempt*."

These significations have doubtless been given in conformity to the Latin words *miror* and *admiratio*, which are equally expressive of surprise, wonder, astonishment, and that vivid pleasure which the sudden perception of something extraordinary is calculated to produce in the mind.

But in the most pertinent and appropriate use of the terms to *admire* and *admiration*, they are manifestly deviating from a generic to a specific sense; and in proportion to our advances in precision and accuracy,

accuracy, we feel not only the advantage, but the *necessity* of applying them to some kind of *excellency* exclusively; otherwise we shall be destitute of words to discriminate the finest feelings of the soul, from those which are common to the most ignorant and uncultivated. Even Idiots may be surprised, the most Ignorant may wonder, and frequently do wonder the most; but neither of them are susceptible of that impression which is best expressed by *admiration*.

If we adhere stedfastly to the rule, that no two words are perfectly synonymous, which cannot be used with equal propriety in every possible connection; we shall find that admiration is as superior to surprise and wonder simply considered, as knowledge is superior to ignorance: for its appropriate signification is that act of the mind, by which we discover, approve, and enjoy some unusual species of excellence.

The authority of Poets is of little weight, when we aim at philosophical precision. Their object is to produce some striking effect; and this must be accomplished by other means than by dividing and subdividing ideas into their component parts. Their subjects frequently borrow strength from foreign auxiliaries, which they claim a licence to press into their service, as often as they require their aid, in direct violation of primitive rights. As the ancient

Poets, by the personification of attributes and characters, have peopled both Worlds with innumerable deities, which reason has found it very difficult to expel; thus have Poets in general, by the use of tropes and figures, by availing themselves of resemblances and affinities of every species, given energy to their thoughts, by inspiring false ideas, which philosophical precision finds it difficult to eradicate. They have represented things which *are not*, as if they *were;* and thus imposed a severe task upon philosophy, to discriminate the differences which they have confounded.

Our best prose writers, whose subjects demand an attention to just distinctions, generally apply admiration to some degree of excellency.

"When we have those elevated ideas of nature," says Mr. Dryden, "the result of that view is *admi-* "*ration,* which is always the cause of pleasure." Mr. Addison observes, that "neither Virgil nor " Horace would have gained so great reputation " had they not been friends, and *admirers* of each " other." In the following passage, Archbishop Tillotson gives a full and satisfactory explanation of the term. "There is a pleasure in admiration, and " this is that which properly causes admiration, " when we discover a great deal in an object which " we understand to be excellent: and yet we see " we know not how much more beyond that which

" our

" our underftandings cannot fully reach and com-
" prehend." (See Note *R*.)

That excellence which is the fubject of admiration, may either confift in the intellectual powers of mind, or difpofitions of the heart. Admiration may be excited by the contemplation of greatnefs and extent of genius, by indications of fuperior talents, by plans and projects which difcover great ingenuity in contrivance and invention, or unufual fkill in the execution. It is often excited by extraordinary exertions of benevolence; fuch as dangers encountered to protect and fave a friend, a ftranger, or an enemy; the greatnefs of the facrifice made to mifery, and the compaffion that excites to extraordinary acts of mercy. In fhort, the objective caufe of admiration is whatever indicates a fuperior degree of wifdom, ingenuity, good fenfe, or benevolence. To fuch qualities it is properly confined. *Power* abftractedly confidered is not the object of admiration; though the dignified or benevolent exertions of power to the production of good, may excite the higheft degree of admiration, and place it among the ftrongeft of our emotions.

It is obvious that the range of admiration is from the fimpler approbation of the mind up to the moft lively fenfation, according to our conceptions of the extent of excellence, and the degrees of our intereft in its effects. It is alfo blended with various other emotions, according to different circumstances attendant upon the passion. It is frequently introduced by *Surprise;* when for example, the discovery of these excellencies is sudden and unexpected; and then it becomes a vivid emotion. It is generally connected with some degree of *Wonder;*—as we are so frequently ignorant of the causes which enabled any one greatly to excel ourselves or others: but as it is always excited by the real *discovery* of some qualities, it is not to be confounded with an emotion that proceeds from ignorance and embarrassment, previous to the discovery.

When the evidences of wisdom and goodness exceed our utmost comprehension, or proceed far beyond the usual extent of excellence itself, they may excite *Astonishment*.

Whatever is good, or productive of good, is the proper object of love; Excellence must of consequence be peculiarly calculated to excite the affection in a superior degree: hence the pleasing and intimate connection between love and admiration. When these are united with gratitude, they constitute the happiest and sublimest affections of the soul. When the object manifests extraordinary benevolence;—when immeasurable extents of wisdom and goodness direct power to execute their purpose;—when incalculable advantages are the issue of their united operations, admiration swells into delectable astonishment,

aſtoniſhment, and our conſcious incapacity to fathom is an augmentation of enjoyment.

Eſteem is the value we place upon ſome degree of worth. It is higher than ſimple *approbation*, which is a deciſion of the judgment. Eſteem is the commencement of affection. It is a degree of love entertained for others on account of their pleaſing qualities, though they ſhould not immediately intereſt ourſelves; by which it is diſtinguiſhed from *gratitude*. The term is peculiarly applicable to virtuous and amiable diſpoſitions of the heart, ſuch as honeſty, integrity, patience, kindneſs, gentleneſs, &c. which have no neceſſary connection with the underſtanding. Thus may we entertain an eſteem for perſons of merit, although they are at a remote diſtance from our intimacy: we eſteem the character of a perſon merely from the report of his good qualities.

Reſpect is that favourable impreſſion which the goodneſs of a character has made upon the perſon contemplating it, united with a ſhare of *good ſenſe*. An union of both theſe qualities is requiſite. Goodneſs alone is not ſufficient to create reſpect. For ſhould it be ſeated in a mind that indicates extreme imbecility, it cannot be deemed reſpectable. On the other hand, ſuperior ſenſe in a mind deſtitute of goodneſs, will not inſpire reſpect. It will either waste itself in idle speculations, which renders it indifferent to us; or it may degenerate into low cunning, which renders it hateful. Should it be connected with power in a wicked and perverse mind, it will excite horror and dismay; which are very remote from respect.

This affection is always connected with a cautious disposition not to disoblige its objects; inspiring a solicitude to obtain their good-will.

Veneration is a higher degree of respect; in which the mind seems to be more forcibly struck with *wisdom*, connected with the sterner virtues. Hence we speak of characters which are more *venerable* than amiable. The term is chiefly applicable to wisdom matured by years, or connected with some peculiar dignity of title or office, and indicated by integrity and uprightness. Thus we speak of venerable ancestors, venerable parents, magistrates, &c. from a presumption of their superiority in wisdom.

Awe is the impression made upon us by the lively idea of power; a power which would inspire distressing fear or terror, were it not modified by other circumstances and qualities suggesting the idea of safety. It may be inspired by things inanimate, where the perception of irresistible power is united with a confidence of safety. Thus lofty mountains, steep precipices, deep caverns, the tempestuous ocean,

ocean, inspire the mind with awe, in situations where they cannot injure us. When the emotion is inspired by *character*, it acknowledges a power, restrained from pernicious exertions, either by justice, or benevolence.

Reverence is the veneration paid to superior sanctity, intermixed with a certain degree of awe. It is the high respect paid to the sacred character of its object, attended with a conscious inferiority in moral worth. Esteem and respect may be inspired by the qualities observable in our *equals*, and the former more particularly in our *inferiors*; but veneration, awe, and reverence imply various degrees of *superiority* in their objects.

It is manifest from the above Analysis, that the qualities which influence our favourable opinions, are various degrees and modifications of *Goodness*, *Wisdom*, and *Power*; that some of our complacential affections are inspired by the predominance of one, some by the predominance of another; and in some there is almost an indistinguishable union. *Gratitude* refers to goodness indicated by our reception of benefits. *Esteem* refers to goodness in its feeblest indications; therefore it is that we frequently express our esteem for the good qualities of the heart in any one, more than for the soundness of his understanding. *Respect* and *Veneration* refer to various degrees of wisdom, or intellectual power united with goodness; and *Awe* may relate either to physical or intellectual power, which becomes impressive without inspiring dread. *Reverence* relates to superiority in moral endowments, connected with awe at intellectual powers, and a consciousness of our own deficiencies upon a comparative view. *Admiration* may refer to an unusual display of either of these qualities, separately; or to the union of them in an extraordinary degree.

As self-complacency has its counterfeit in pride and vanity, thus are the complacential affections liable to abuse, and give rise to the following imperfections.

Fondness. Though this affection is frequently pardonable, and sometimes amiable, yet it is an acknowledged weakness. It indicates an attachment to whatever belongs to us, or is immediately connected with us, far beyond its intrinsic merit. Sometimes it is inspired simply by the idea of its being our own property;—sometimes it is contracted or strengthened by habit;—sometimes it is the excess of love, where love is most natural, which indicates itself by infantile manners, or culpable indulgences;—and sometimes it is the degree of affection manifested

manifested to inferior animals, to which their superiors have a much better claim.

Partiality. This is such an excess of personal attachment as obscures the judgment, or corrupts the heart. It inclines to a favourable opinion of the motives, conduct, and general merit of its object that is inconsistent with the justice due to others.

When any of the social and sympathetic affections are very strong, they rise to emotions, and produce some correspondent tokens in the countenance. Complacency indicates itself by ineffable smiles; the countenance becomes animated, and the eyes sparkle with delight. Sympathetic joy manifests itself by the indications characteristic of joy. Sympathy with distress retains something of the benignant smile, mixed with marks of dejection, of deep concern, or inward anguish. When admiration rises into transport, all the symptoms peculiar to surprise are sometimes mixed with marks of complacential love, and sometimes checked by veneration and awe, in which some portion of fearful apprehension, free from absolute dread, becomes an ingredient.

In all these sympathetic affections, the Eye is the most expressive. It is properly termed the *Index of the Soul.* Particular attitudes and gestures, and the various forms and plaits of the features may be counterfeited by the unfeeling heart: but it cannot so easily imitate the brisk suffusions of joy, the sympathetic tear, the deep veneration and awe, and the eager admiration, which real feelings transmit immediately from the heart into that wonderful organ.

ORDER II.

Passions and Affections excited by Displacency, *in which* Evil *is the predominant Idea.*

THE reason for preferring the word *Displacency* to *Malevolence* as a generic term, has already been given. Malevolence is rejected, as not being so applicable to every branch of that displeasure, we may possibly indulge against others; whereas *Displacency* comprehends those various kinds of discontent to which we are exposed in our social intercourse. Displacency may indicate itself by dispositions exceedingly inimical to its objects, or it may

may confift in warm difapprobation of their conduct. In the firft fenfe, it is oppofed to the operations of the benevolent principle; and in the other, it is the reverfe of complacency, which indicates various degrees of affectionate approbation.

I believe that the word difplacency is folely applicable to our intercourfe with the human fpecies, and is not employed to exprefs difcontent or uneafinefs from any other fource.

Difplacency divides itfelf alfo into two kinds. It may be indicated by *malevolent defires* and *difpofitions* towards the object; or by *unfavourable opinions* and *difapprobations*, without any mixture of malevolence.

I. The difplacency which is indicated by *malevolent defires* and *difpofitions*.

Thefe may be either of a permanent nature, or merely occafional. The former relates to that malevolence or ill-will which is conftant and uniform in its influence; the other to the paffion of anger, and its various modifications, which have fome particular acts of an unpleafing and irritating nature for their immediate objects.

The

The first species of malevolence is a branch of that general principle of hatred, which has already occupied our attention. (See Ch. i. Sect. iii.) It originates from various incidental caufes, fuch as reiterated injuries, and vexations;—from juft or exaggerated reprefentations of the temper, defigns, motives, conduct of another, which are unpleafant or pernicious;—from the partialities fo intimately connected with our focial intimacies and affections, which give rife to violent prejudices againft thofe who appear inimical to their interefts;—from a fpirit of envy and jealoufy, which connects hatred of the perfon with repining at their good fortune. Clans and claffes of enmity may thus be formed, which, augmented by the power of focial fympathy, will finally become inveterate and implacable. Malevolence therefore commences with fome idea of evil, belonging to and connected with the object; and fettles into a permanent hatred of his perfon, and of every thing relative to him.

The principle thus formed gives rife to the following malevolent affections.

Malignancy or *Malignity*. Both thefe words exprefs a difpofition that cherifhes inveterate hatreds, and maintains implacable war againft its object; a difpofition which deliberately plans fchemes of mifchief,

chief, and employs every means that power, mental or physical, can furnish to the prejudice of another. These words are nearly synonymous. In some connections *malignity* seems rather more pertinently applied to a radical depravity of nature, and *malignancy* to *indications* of this depravity in temper and conduct, in particular instances.

Both may be manifested by the perversion of power, whether physical or intellectual; and our dread of the disposition will be proportioned to our conceptions of the magnitude of this power. Hence the terror inspired by the idea of demons and wicked spirits, or beings of an higher order, who are supposed to be devoid of every thing that is good, and replete with every thing that is evil. So that

> To do ought good never can be their task,
> But ever to do ill, their sole delight.
>
> MILTON.

To such beings we ascribe malignancy to an infinite extent.

Malice, on the other hand, is more frequently employed to express the dispositions of inferior minds, to execute every purpose of mischief, within the more limited circle of their abilities. It often shews itself by little incidents; such as,—by thwarting the favourite purposes of another;—by refusing the good that might be communicated without personal

sonal injury;—by encouraging unfavourable reports;—by raising unjust suspicions;—by perverse misrepresentations, &c. This temper is sometimes expressed by *spite*, or by *having a spite* against any one. In a word, if we ascribe Malignancy to beings of a superior order by way of pre-eminence, *malice* and a *malicious* disposition, may with peculiar propriety be reserved for the minor agents of mischief, whose power of doing evil is not proportionate to their inclinations.

Envy. This is a painful sensation excited by the view of something desirable in the state and situation of another, which self-love wishes to appropriate. To envy, is to repine at the good conferred upon another, or possessed by him. Thus it is a perfect contrast to the sympathy which rejoices at their welfare. Envy entertains a degree of *sorrow* that the good contemplated should escape ourselves, and of *anger* that it should fall to the share of another. The inordinate self-love which excites to envy, naturally induces the envious person to imagine that he is more deserving than the object who has been favoured. He contemplates his own supposed merit, in opposition to the supposed demerit of the more happy object, until he becomes fully convinced in his own prejudiced judgment of the injustice of the distribution; and feels a spirit of resentment

ment arising against the possessor, and every cause of his enjoyment.

Thus is envy that species of malevolence, which is inspired by the conjoined influence of pride, sorrow, and anger.

Envy is denominated a passion, together with many other of the malevolent affections; partly because it may be very strongly excited by particular incidents, and partly in consequence of that singular law of usage which assigns the word *Affections* to the benevolent feelings, and *Passions* to the powerful influence of vicious dispositions. (See Ch. 1. Page 3.)

Rancour is that degree of malice which preys upon the possessor. His heart is torn with vexation when he contemplates the happiness of another, or when he is foiled in his evil purposes towards him.

Cruelty. A *cruel* disposition respects the particular temper manifested in the contemplation or infliction of absolute misery. It has various degrees. Sometimes it is expressive of that hardness of heart, which is able to look upon extreme distress without any sensations of humanity. Sometimes cruelty is indicated by the voluntary and unnecessary infliction of misery: and in its highest state it rejoices and triumphs in the diffusion of horrors; in the wanton shedding of blood, and spreading desolation.

tion. It is gratified with the convulsions of agony; groans and lamentations are music in its ears.

This fiend-like temper may proceed from a natural insensibility, strengthened by a perverse education;—from envy;—from a spirit of revenge for supposed injuries;—from cowardice, resenting the panic it feels;—or from insatiable ambition, which wades through torrents of blood, and renders the mangled bodies of the slain, stepping-stones to that pre-eminence of station after which it aspires.

Censoriousness is a disposition to find fault with the conduct, sentiments, or dispositions of another, deeming every action improper, or ascribing it to improper motives.

Prejudice is the reverse of *partiality*. This inclines to the *favourable* side in judging or vindicating of conduct more than reason, or charity demands; *prejudice*, on the contrary, is that degree of malevolence which disposes us to *pre-judge* the character, conduct, or motives of another to his *disadvantage*, without having the proper evidences before us. It is obvious that the partiality indulged for one person, may excite, or greatly increase our prejudice against another.

It is observable that the common use of each of these terms is not entirely correspondent with their original import. Partiality properly signifying a partial and imperfect view of the evidence, is in itself

self applicable to an undue bias of opinion or disposition, whether it be *favourable* or *disfavourable* to the object; and *prejudice* as it originally signifies *pre-judging*, is in itself equally applicable to a precipitate decision *for* or *against* any one; but custom applies the term *partiality* to a disposition in *favour*, and *prejudice*, without an expletive, to a disposition *against* another.

There is a personal hatred, which has no specific name. It consists of an habitual dislike against some particular object, without being connected with *ill-will*, or a desire of his being unhappy. It avoids social intercourse with the party, or renders social intercourse irksome. It is sometimes the residue of anger which *forgives*, as it is frequently expressed, but does not *forget*. It is sometimes inspired by unfavourable reports and misrepresentations, constituting insufferable prejudices; and not unfrequently, by some very disagreeable peculiarity of manners.

Ingratitude cannot be termed either an affection, or a disposition. It is the negative of a virtue, which a feeling heart places among the first of obligations. It is an insensibility to benefits received, either arising from stupidity, culpable inattention, or innate pride, that annihilates the idea of a favour, and considers every service rendered, as the discharge of a debt.

Apathy is a singular stagnation of all the social feelings.

feelings. It professes neither to love nor to hate; it affects an indifference to which it cannot possibly attain, as it terminates in a disgust of life and all its objects. Apathy is a kind of gangrene affecting the social principle, which like a mortified limb in the corporeal system, is an incumberance to the patient, and a nuisance to others.

Neither dislike, ingratitude, nor apathy, are absolutely chargeable with *malevolence;* but as they are the disgraceful negatives of every social affection, and are much more prepared to hate than to love, this seems to be their proper department.

The second species of Malevolence relates to those occasional and more transient fits of ill-will, which are excited by particular provocations, and which are not totally repugnant to the benevolent affections. These are indicated by *Anger,* and its various modifications.

Anger has already been considered as the passion which is excited by a quick sense of injury; and it has been described as having a double relation; the one immediately respecting *ourselves,* the other respecting the *offender.* To the first we directed our thoughts under the *selfish* passions; where the influence of anger upon our personal feelings, and effects upon the corporeal system, were particularly considered. We shall now confine our attention to the

the changes produced in our minds respecting its *object*.

As long as we are under the influence of anger, considered either as a passion or an affection, we experience a temporary suspension of our usual complacency, and even of our good-will and general benevolence towards the object of our displeasure. Under the impulse of the first emotion, we are conscious of a desire that the offender should suffer, in some degree proportionate to this recent instance of his demerit; we are prompted to imagine that justice itself demands a punishment adequate to the offence; we feel ourselves much inclined to become the ministers of justice, and are impatient of delay in the execution of her commands.

When the provocation arises from the conduct of any one, with whom we are intimately connected, our habitual love of their persons and regard for their welfare, may restrain the passion within the bounds of justice, and the explosion which gave vent to the passion may restore the calm. When it arises from the misconduct of a person, for whom we are particularly interested, and when this misconduct endangers his welfare, the very principle of benevolence converts our complacency into its contrary. In this case, being such an expressive indication of our displeasure as to inspire terror, it is admirably calculated to strike the offender with awe and reclaim his conduct. As soon as passion is able to attend to the united voices of reason and affection, they will frequently join to palliate the offence, by ascribing it to some incidental cause, to the common frailties of our nature, to the strong impulse of particular circumstances, &c. and the offender becomes re-instated in our favourable regards. But reiterated provocations being indubitable marks of culpable inattention, disrespect, or depravity of disposition, will entirely change our opinion of character, and inspire us with indifference or permanent displeasure against the cause.

Rage has been described as the *madness* of anger.

Revenge is an insatiable desire to sacrifice every consideration of pity and humanity, to the principle of vindictive justice. It renders the demands of that terrific giant paramount to every other claim. It is a propensity to retaliate evil, too fervent to be cooled by time, too deep and inveterate to be obliterated by concessions and entreaties. It anticipates joy in the contemplation of sighs and groans, and the only moment of transport is the instant of inflicting misery.

We see that this disposition approaches very near to permanent malevolence of the most despicable character. The abstract idea of justice, however, forms a partition between them; for to this malevolence

lence has no rightful claim. But its more honourable distinction consists in that repentance which humanity excites in the mind that is not totally obdurate, after the gratification of this dreadful passion. The avenger feels, too late, that he has sacrificed realities to a phantom; and that to inflict misery, is in no case, the path to happiness.

Wrath is a deep and irritating sense of an injury. It is deliberate anger; being chiefly inspired by the contemplation of various aggravating circumstances attendant upon the offence. The desire of retaliation is not a constituent part of it; by this it is distinguished from revenge. But it occasions a ferment in the spirits incompatible with the indulgence of complacency.

Resentment. This affection has been described to be a deep reflective displeasure against the conduct of an offender. We may now observe, that resentment is chiefly excited by some personal offence committed against the laws of social intercourse, of friendship, or of gratitude;—by some affront, that wounds our self-love, it may be, our *pride*;—by some reprehensible inattention to our minuter claims;—or by the want of respect and affection, to which we imagine that the tenour of our conduct towards the object, has given us an undoubted right. It may terminate in indifference, and

and, in weak minds, in malice; but it is generally appeased by concessions and acknowledgments.

Suspicion. This is a comfortless state of doubt concerning the conduct and character of another. The mind is greatly embarrassed respecting the degree of esteem, cordiality, or friendship which is due to the object. Suspicion may be excited by some kind of accusation, not supported by evidence sufficient for conviction, but sufficient to trouble the repose of confidence. When exercised towards *Intimates*, it is an anxious suspension of mind between complacency and displacency; between that respect we were accustomed to entertain for them, and the painful apprehension that they no longer deserve it. We feel an incipient anger and resentment, which we dare not to indulge, and cannot suppress.

Jealousy is a species of suspicion that relates to conduct, which still more intimately concerns ourselves. A painful apprehension of rivalship, in cases that are peculiarly interesting to us. It will of consequence increase in strength, according to the value we place upon the object, and to the degrees of danger to which we imagine it may be exposed. It is the inseparable companion of the ambitious, who view every competitor, and every one capable of becoming a competitor, with a jealous eye. It is sometimes engrafted upon *pride*, which is deeply wounded by appearances of neglect. It is a frequent

quent attendant upon love; and in a milder sense of the term, it may be considered as an anxious solicitude least we should be supplanted in the affections of those we most highly esteem. The passion is sometimes excited in weak minds, by the very excess of affection; for this excess is prone to be perpetually upon the watch, and torment itself with groundless fears. Jealousy, in the extreme, contains a complication of the most tremendous passions that can agitate the human breast. Though it has love for its basis, yet it suffers the united torments of every painful emotion. It finds equal danger in the most opposite appearances. Every token of innocence is interpreted into proofs of guilt; and every instance of affection, as a mark of insulting hypocrisy.

> It is a green-ey'd monster, which doth *make*
> The meat it feeds on.————
> ————————Trifles light as air
> Are to the jealous, confirmations strong
> As proofs of holy writ.————
>
>   SHAKESPEAR'S OTHELLO.

Under the influence of this baneful passion the mind becomes, at intervals, the sport of transporting hope, and wild despair; is alternately tormented by fits of rage, and the depth of contrition for excesses committed in its transports. In a word, uniting the extremes of dreadful hatred and passionate fondness, it entertains most cruel suspicions of the object it most adores; and is tempted to destroy that which it dreads to lose!

The class of evil passions under permanent malevolence are indications of the depraved character and dispositions of the subject in whom they are seated, not having any immediate reference to the character of their object. Those which are now described as the modifications of anger, respect the impressions which occasional deviations from the usual tenour of conduct, make upon the mind of the person most interested; in which, both the feelings and indications of ill-will are of a more transitory nature; so that they deserve not to be confounded with permanent hatred.

We shall now proceed to consider those emotions and affections which are inspired by the contemplation of Evil, and in which neither malevolence, nor any of the selfish affections, are necessary ingredients.

II. The Displacency which is indicated by *unfavourable opinions* of conduct and disposition. This gives rise to the following emotions and affections.

Horror.

Horror. Horror is that very strong and painful emotion, which is excited by the view or contemplation of something peculiarly atrocious in the conduct of another; by some vice which exceeds the usual extravagance of vice; enormities that surpass the bounds of common depravity;—such as impurities too gross to be named, profligacies too shocking to be repeated, and cruelties that make us shudder at the recital. It may also be excited by the extremes of agony mental or corporeal, by sufferings and punishments at which our natures recoil.

This passion may be deemed the antipode of admiration. The one is inspired by the contemplation of surpassing excellency; the other by the excess of vice and wretchedness. As that is one of the most pleasing sensations we can possibly enjoy, this is among the most painful we can possibly suffer. Scenes of the above description excite a tremour upon the mind; a species of terror scarcely equalled by the most lively apprehensions of danger.

Indignation expresses a strong and elevated disapprobation of mind, which is also inspired by something flagitious in the conduct of another. But it does not always suppose that excess of depravity which alone is capable of committing deeds of horror. Indignation always refers to culpability of conduct; and cannot like the passion of horror be extended to distress either of mind or body. It is

produced

produced by the violation of some indispensable obligation, connected with circumstances peculiarly aggravating;—by acts of treachery, the abuse of confidence, base ingratitude, &c. which we cannot contemplate without being provoked to anger, and feeling a generous resentment: though we should not be interested in the consequences of the conduct we condemn. Indignant emotions are always excited by particular incidents.

Contempt. This is a more calm and deliberate affection of the mind. It directs its chief attention to the *character* and *disposition*, which is capable of committing unworthy and disgraceful actions. Its objects are radical baseness, and radical imbecility where it ought not to exist. Thus we despise the man who is capable of fraud, deceit, falsehood, and every species of moral depravity which indicates an extraordinary degree of meanness. The man who makes great pretensions to more exalted powers and better qualities, than he really possesses, renders himself also an object of contempt; and the man who vainly boasts of much more than he can perform, or courts our admiration of accomplishments of which he is destitute, or which he possesses in a very inferior degree.

Thus the characters which are sunk below the common level of humanity, and those which arrogantly

gantly and impotently attempt to rise above it, are universally deemed the proper objects of contempt.

Both indignation and contempt are accompanied with a certain elevation of mind. The observer feels and enjoys a conscious superiority when he compares himself with the offender. This sense of superiority is more strongly marked in *contempt*. When it rises to a certain height it indicates,

Disdain. Disdain is such a degree of contempt as precludes any commerce with the party despised. It considers him as totally unworthy of our notice;—even of our *reprehension*, which always supposes a possibility of reclaim. It feels as if there was something so repulsive in the character of the aggressor, that he is no longer entitled to the rights of social intercourse.

Contempt and disdain are often accompanied with a satirical smile, which strongly insinuates that baseness and meanness are also intermixed with large portions of *folly*.

Irrision. This term is employed to express an affection inspired by any peculiarity in sentiment, disposition, or conduct, that we deem an offence against some acknowledged law of congruity, some standard of propriety universally received and respected; but which is not of sufficient magnitude to excite anger, or any of its ramifications. It chiefly refers to something odd, whimsical, absurd, that is
calculated

calculated to excite laughter, rather than incur our difpleafure. Various miftakes, and egregious blunders which indicate culpable ignorance, inattentions, and extravagances, are the proper objects of irrifion.

The above feem to be the principal emotions and affections that are infpired by the contemplation of conduct and character. They are ftrong marks of difplacency, which does not arife from malevolence in our difpofitions, but on the contrary from the warm love of beneficent virtue. Nor are they neceffarily connected with perfonal injuries, though a fenfe of injuries will infallibly impart great energy to each emotion.

As anger is the guardian of our own perfonal interefts, thus is the prefent clafs of emotions and affections deftined to be the guardians of virtue, decency, and propriety in general. It is remarkable that the mind is affected by tranfgreffions againft thefe, in exact proportion to the degrees of culpability obvious in the offence. *Horror* roufes within us fuch a degree of refentment, as becomes the fevereft reproof to the enormities at which it fhudders; and when excited by deeds of cruelty it calls up a laudable fpirit of revenge, and renders the mildeft and meekeft difpofitions folicitous for a power of retaliation. *Indignation* is always directed against the violation of some sacred law, that is respected by every man who is not destitute of virtue and honour. *Contempt* is the punishment directed against that meanness of character, and perverseness of conduct, which sink a man below the level of social intercourse, and disqualify him for decent and respectable society. *Irrision* and *ridicule* are the protectors of order, decency, and propriety in the lesser departments; against which the transgressor is thus made to feel his offence. He is taught to perceive that it is inconsistent with common sense, and to suspect that he is in danger of being ranked in the opprobrious class of fools.

The visible tokens of emotion under each species of displacency are characteristic of its nature. Those painful sensations which are peculiar to the most malevolent passions legibly inscribe their marks upon the countenance. The deep sunk eye, the pallid anxiety of Malice and Envy, indicate the inward torments of the mind; and the ineffectual attempts to smile in transient gleams of satisfaction at misery, only serve to render horror more horrid. Fear and dread have been considered as the most painful emotions inspired by the selfish principle; and their pathological symptoms manifest an insuperable anxiety and depression; malignity has adopted these feelings with their external marks; intermixing them with

with the irritations of anger; which however it attempts to repress from bursting forth into emotions, through the apprehensions of detection.

The displacency of anger manifests the tokens descriptive of anger already noticed; which, according to the degrees of their violence, strike terror into great offenders, or inspire the thoughtless and inattentive with respect and awe.

The *horror* excited by the excess of wickedness or of misery approaches to *terror*, both in sensation and in external marks. *Indignation, contempt,* and *disdain* paint upon the countenance a singular mixture of dignified superiority and deep disapprobation. A certain elevation, becoming the majesty of insulted virtue, is united with a lively sense of the depravity and meanness of the offender; and a contrast is instantaneously formed between exaltedness of character, and the state of degradation into which he has fallen. The satirical jocularity accompanying contempt in *irrision*, throws into the countenance marks of exultation over the imbecility or absurdities of the person ridiculed. Without subscribing to the hypothesis of *Mr. Hobbes*, that pride is the efficient cause of laughter, it must be acknowledged that this species of laughter, is always accompanied with an insulting consciousness of superiority.

In the above Analysis we have attempted to trace
the

the origin of the Paffions, their exciting caufes, their immediate objects, and their numerous ramifications. We have contemplated the infinite diverfity and contrariety of effects, which proceed from that one principle the *Love of Good*, in Beings formed as we are, ftationed in a world where every furrounding object is able to produce its own fpecific impreffion; Beings whofe individual, and whofe focial interefts, are fo many, various, and complicated.

But this Analytical Survey does not terminate the hiftory of the Paffions. There are various other points of view in which it is proper to contemplate them, in order to increafe our acquaintance with the rudiments of felf-knowledge, and enable us to draw thofe moral and practical inferences, which may prove moft conducive to the improvement of our natures.

Thefe are referved for the Second Part of our Treatife.

END OF PART THE FIRST.

PART II.

PHILOSOPHICAL OBSERVATIONS

AND

INQUIRIES,

Founded upon the Preceding Analysis.

PART II.

PHILOSOPHICAL OBSERVATIONS
AND
INQUIRIES,

Founded upon the Preceding Analysis.

CHAP. I.

Observations respecting the Laws of Excitement.

OBSERVATION I.

Surprise the efficient Cause of PASSION.

IN different parts of our Analysis of the Passions, the influence of the introductory emotions, in quickening affections of the most opposite nature into a passion, has fully appeared. It has been shewn, that whatever strikes us in a sudden and unexpected manner, generally makes for the instant, a more vivid impression, than things and circumstances of much greater consequence, with which we have been familiarized, or which have been more slowly and progressively introduced to our notice. It has been rendered obvious, that wonder is compounded of surprise and the impression made upon the mind by the idea of intricacy;—and that astonishment unites the perception of *vastness* with surprise;—we have remarked that these are, by universal suffrage, emphatically termed *emotions;*—and we have seen the influence of these introductory emotions in passions of the most opposite characters.

These considerations united make it highly probable, that the essential and characteristic difference between a *passion* and an *affection* depends upon the superaddition of surprise, to the natural effect produced by the real or supposed quality of an object;—that this emotion, conjoined with the specific nature of its *exciting* cause, is virtually the *efficient* cause of a passion; the percussion of surprise rendering the affection visible by characteristic signs, correspondent with its specific nature.

Thus, for example, in *Joy*, the pleasing part of the impression owes its origin to the possession, or undoubted expectancy, of some desirable good. This, in its lowest influence, produces some degree of change in the corporeal frame. It is a sensation, and must be felt somewhere. The vividness of the impression, occasioned by the impetus of surprise, renders this sensation more vivid, diffuses its effects over the whole system, and occasions a delectable and ungovernable flow of spirits, which becomes
conspicuous

conspicuous to every spectator. But as Novelty is the exciting cause of surprise, in proportion as the *novelty* of the good subsides, surprise gradually diminishes, and leaves the mind under the influence of an *Affection*, more proportionate to the real value of the object.

Thus we may suppose the *passion* of *Anger* to consist of that disagreeable sensation, which a sense of injury will always occasion, quickened by *surprise* into an ungovernable emotion. The reluctance with which we part with any thing contributing to our benefit or enjoyment, will be quickened by surprise into the *agonies of Sorrow*; which is also able to convert painful apprehensions into the *excess of Fear*.

Nor does the acknowledged fact, that our passions are sometimes excited by deliberate contemplation, militate against this opinion. This can only take place in affairs of high importance; and in such cases, the more deliberate survey consists in examining and reflecting upon every circumstance relative to the nature of the exciting cause, which necessarily produces a variety of new and unexpected combinations, each of which will be attended with a proportionate degree of surprise; and although there will not be in any one circumstance, that *quantum* of novelty which so powerfully strikes the mind, in cases that are sudden and totally unexpected,

pected, yet, the combined influence of the aggregate number of novelties, may finally produce the most extravagant passions. Thus may the mind calculate the variety of benefits accruing from some prosperous event, until it be *transported with joy;* —enumerate the evils of privation until it becomes *frantic with sorrow;*—dwell upon the number and magnitude of provocations which aggravate an injury, until resentment shall be converted into *rage;* —and by ruminating upon the extent of danger, it may be driven into *despair.*

If this conjecture be admitted, it will give a beautiful simplicity to the theory of the Passions. It shews that they may be decomposed into the simplest elements; while it indicates the manner by which the combination of these elements may be productive of such an infinite variety, both in nature and strength. It shews that the different degrees of force in the quickening agent, or of its reiterated influence, are calculated to give various degrees of momentum to each particular affection.

OBSERVATION II.

Passions and Emotions are of a transitory nature; the Affections alone are permanent.

ACCORDING to the diftinctions which have been made between Paffions, Emotions, and Affections, it clearly appears that the two former are in their nature tranfient, and that the affections are capable of much longer duration. The paffions have been reprefented as vivid fenfations, paffively or involuntarily, produced by fome ftrong idea excited in the mind; and emotions as the external marks of thefe. But as this paffive ftate of mind is tranfitory, fo are its external marks; and as both gradually fubfide, they give place to fome correfpondent *affection*, which remains as long as our opinion, and the intereft we take in the object, fhall continue. It neceffarily follows from thefe facts, that we are not to look to the paffions and emotions either for permanent well-being, or for permanent wretchednefs.

wretchedness. They must either die away and leave no impression, as in cases where the imagination was deceived respecting the value or importance of the exciting cause, or they are the harbingers of some more durable affections; and it is the influence of these affections which has the permanent effect upon our well-being. Thus, when we give ourselves over to the delectable tumults of Joy, the joy is incidental. It is hastily introduced by the sudden perception or impressive sense of some acquisition, that we deem important to present or future welfare; of a something which we expect to be more or less durable in its nature, or to diffuse its beneficent influence to a considerable extent. These advantages are concentrated, as it were, in the imagination at the instant of joy. They operate upon the mind as the solar rays collected in a focus dart upon the surface of a body; and though the pleasures of joy are often greater than those derived from its causes, yet we naturally expect much more than the momentary well-being introduced by the emotion itself.

In the first impulse of Sorrow, the magnitude of the loss is the most impressive idea. As the mind becomes more intimately acquainted with the nature and extent of the privation, the agonies of sorrow will either subside into indifference, from the perception that the loss was not of that importance as
had

had been imagined, and that it has been amply supplied by some valuable and unexpected blessing; or the vivid impression will be effaced by time, which always places before us a variety of objects new and interesting; or finally, the transports of sorrow will gradually give way to habitual grief and melancholy.

Thus Fear is inspired, and becomes agonizing from the apprehension of some species of calamity; and the influential idea, at the instant, is, that by the expected calamity we shall be lastingly deprived of some good we wish to retain, or that it will be introductory to some durable evil; though the fear itself may be much more painful than the evil we dread. Anger is roused by an immediate sense of injury committed or threatened; that is, by the apprehension of some robbery of the good to which we have a claim. Here again the mind, comparing the present with the past, or looking forwards to the future, perceives or apprehends a disagreeable change of circumstances or of state; and is incensed against the offending cause. When the first impulse subsides, it is succeeded by the affections of *grief, resentment, indignation, &c.* according to the nature of the insult suffered, or the aggravations of the offence; and these become durable as the idea or perception of the injury received.

Nor does the transition which is sometimes made from affection to passion invalidate these remarks.

It has been observed, that when the object possesses many complicated and interesting circumstances, these by being placed before the memory, and distinctly examined, may gradually warm the imagination, and increase the strength of the affection, until the party be worked up into violent emotions. But when the passions are excited in this manner, they are also of short duration. The preternatural state of mind demands too great an expenditure of animal spirits, to render the passion lasting, and it soon relapses into the kindred affection. In cases deemed peculiarly interesting, and in persons of quick and lively feelings, gushes and fits of passion may be frequently excited by the same cause, and the mind may be placed alternately under the influence of the passion and affection; but wherever passions and emotions are permanently vehement, it becomes an indication of *infanity*, as it is a complete token that reason has totally lost its controuling power.

The permanent affections are therefore to be considered as constituting that habitual state of mind, into which the primary passion impelled it. Our ideas, and with them our affections, concerning the object are now changed. Instead of our former indifference, we contemplate it with some degree of pleasure or pain, become habitually attached to it, or indulge an habitual aversion respecting it.

Thus

Thus it is obvious that none of the leading passions and emotions constitute our permanent welfare, or the contrary. They simply manifest the first impression which the sudden change of our state has made upon us. The lasting effects, in consequence of this change, are to be learned from the *Affections.* If the good introduced by joy prove itself to be a lasting good, though it may be partial and incomplete, it may inspire Contentment. If it be the completion of an ardent desire, it communicates Satisfaction. If it meet with approbation, and be reflected upon as the result of a plan well-intended, wisely formed, and successfully executed, it becomes the source of Complacency. Fear sinks into permanent dread, or unmixed with any particle of hope, into lasting despair; Sorrow into confirmed melancholy; and Anger into resentment and displacency.

OBSERVATION III.

Relation of the Passions and Affections to each other.

IT has frequently been remarked, that the influence of any particular passion or emotion, disposes the mind to be subjected to some other that is of a similar nature and tendency; while it places the disposition at a remote distance from the affections of a contrary complection. *Dr. Hartley* has observed, correspondent to the grand division of the passions which he had adopted, that " the five " *grateful* passions, Love, Desire, Hope, Joy, " and pleasing Recollection enhance each other; as " do the five *ungrateful* ones, Hatred, Aversion, " Fear, Grief, and Displeasure." *Addison, Hume, Lord Kaims* have made similar remarks, and have adduced the association of ideas as the cause. Whether this be the *only* cause or not, the fact cannot be disputed, that the temper of mind produced by one affection,

affection, pre-difpofes to the affection which is moſt analogous, though it may not be immediately dependent upon it.

Thus, according to the diviſion which has been adopted in this Treatiſe, not only are gladneſs, cheerfulneſs, mirth, contentment, ſatisfaction, complacency, &c. the offsprings of joy, but while the mind is under their pleaſing influence, it is difpoſed to every affection of the pleaſing kind, which may be inſpired by very different cauſes, or by circumſtances too trivial to excite either of theſe emotions or affections in its calm and uninfluenced ſtate of mind. Let us ſuppoſe, for example, the exciting cauſe to conſiſt in ſomething merely perſonal; yet the pleaſing ſenſation produced, inclines at the moment, to the affections of generoſity, charity, ſympathy, compaſſion, and mercy: nay, at ſuch ſeaſons it is difpoſed to expand, that it may embrace all mankind; and the humbler acts of virtue, with which we might have been contented, at another period, will now appear contracted and unſatisfactory.

Upon this principle in our natures is the cuſtom manifeſtly founded, of making valuable preſents to the meſſengers of welcome tidings, or rewarding them with ſome peculiar marks of complacency: a cuſtom which has been practiſed in every age and nation. The overflowings of joy inſpire a generoſity fity of temper, which abfolutely requires an object; and none can immediately appear more meritorious, than the perfon who has been the inftrument, as it were, or the inftrumental caufe of joy. The delectable fenfation communicated to the mind of the principal participant, immediately excites in his breaft a grateful affection for the perfon, whofe communications have been the caufe of it; though he may have merely acted in an official capacity; and poffibly, contrary to his fecret inclinations. The liberation of captives, and prifoners of various defcriptions, upon acceffion to the throne;—the inftitution of fports and paftimes, that joy may be diffufed among the multitude upon events apparently replete with much future happinefs, as on births, marriages, and on the arrival of a young heir to the poffeffion of an ample fortune;—the pleafing incitements of illuminations, fire-works, diftributing good cheer to the populace, are univerfally felt as harmonizing with the exhilarated ftate of mind, which welcome tidings of a private or public nature are calculated to excite. In like manner does the luftre of great actions infpire us with a certain refpect for thofe moft intimately connected with the agent, whom we confider as the parent ftock, productive of merit in every ramification; or as able to fhed defert over every connection. Under the influence of thefe grateful and liberal principles, we are induced

duced to imagine that children are entitled to share the rewards due to their parents. Hence those hereditary honours which too frequently irradiate the Unworthy, and demonstrate that the generous inference is not always conclusive.

From these associating affections it proceeds, that the perception of good qualities centered in the Mind of any one, disposes to an attachment to their Person. Favourable impressions inspire an inclination to cultivate friendship; and friendship between the sexes has a powerful tendency to inspire love. That love, which in delicate minds appears to be at the remotest distance from every thing sensual, will finally excite the stronger and warmer passions. Nor are we without many instances of these becoming most impetuous, from their being founded upon sentimental refinements.

As the passion of Sorrow proceeds from the loss of what we have loved, it may imperceptibly dispose,—in persons whose passions are strong but very transient,—to the affection of Love towards the object commiserating our loss. No one can appear so worthy of the transfer, as the friend who sympathizes deeply with the affliction. The Poet has justly observed that "*Pity is akin to love.*" In these moments, the commiserator forgets every fault, even where he knows that they exist; he brings forward every good quality, which in his opinion renders the afflicted less deserving of their sufferings. We may also add that the gratitude which this pity inspires, is accompanied with the most favourable sentiments of the humane disposition, and has a tendency to produce a predilection for the person of the sympathizer. In short, whatever gives birth to any of the kindly affections, may be productive of personal predilections, and terminate in love, both as an affection and a passion. Othello says of Desdemona,

> She lov'd me for the dangers I had pass'd,
> And I lov'd her that she did pity them.

Nor can the dramatic Writer be accused of exaggeration, who represents the beautiful and accomplished Zemira, passionately fond of the generous monster Azore, whom she at first viewed with horror and detestation.

To this pleasing association is it also to be ascribed, that we are so prone to be blind to the faults of those we love. We are eager to represent to ourselves those persons who have taken possession of our esteem, as being entirely worthy of it. We dwell upon every good quality; forget, or discover apologies for, every defect.

It has been remarked more than once, that whenever an amorous temper has taken a religious turn, it excels in the warmth and fervour of its devotion. We might urge in its vindication, that what appears excellent can alone be the object of love; and where the mind is peculiarly susceptible of excellence, it will evince the warmth and strength of its affection, whether it be placed on our own species, or on beings of a superior order.

These two causes united may serve to explain a fact which has been noted by *Rousseau* and many others, that the language of religion and of love is so very similar. The lover also has his *idol*, *adores* her perfections, calls her *angelic*, talks of *altars, prostrations, vows, sacrifices, &c.* That is, what is *human*, in the warmth of his affection he contemplates as *divine;* and the person who has some striking accomplishments, he pronounces to be perfection itself.

The connection between the disagreeable passions and affections is not less obvious. The various affections originating from the idea of Evil, whether it be past, present, or apprehended, are so closely united, that they can scarcely be considered as illustrations of the subject. We are, for example, disposed to be angry at whatever occasions sorrow, and there is a vindictiveness in fear, which may render it dangerous to its most innocent cause. But pre-dispositions to the indulgence of unpleasant affections,

fections, are generated in cases where the connection is not so immediate. Disagreeable feelings produced by their proper object, are productive of other disagreeable affections where, strictly speaking, there is no proper object. Whatever irritates, renders the mind impatient, peevish, quarrelsome; disposes it to magnify trifles into real grievances, and to imagine a just cause of offence, where perhaps approbation has been merited; it engenders suspicions and jealousies, and disposes to envy the peace, tranquillity, or good fortune of another. In this state of mind, a transition is also made from things to persons, and some degree of guilt is imputed to the latter, in consequence of the evil passions stirred up by the former. It is upon this principle that tyrants have been known to sacrifice, in the impetuosity of their vexation and rage, the innocent messengers of evil tidings. Thus has Homer, that faithful historian of nature, represented Agamemnon as pouring out a torrent of invectives against the harmless and venerable priest, who was compelled, by virtue of his office, to utter unwelcome truths.

The Prophet spoke: when with a gloomy frown,
The monarch started from his shining throne;
Black choler fill'd his breast that boil'd with ire,
And from his eye-balls flash'd the living fire.

Augur

> Augur accurst! denouncing mischief still,
> Prophet of plagues, for ever boding ill!
> Still must that tongue some wounding message bring,
> And still thy priestly pride provoke thy King?
>
> POPE'S HOMER. IL. I. L. 127.

It is thus that not only the "*Genus Irritabile Vatum,*" but controversial authors of all descriptions, have been so prone, in defence of their particular sentiments against their opponents, to descend to personalities. Theologians in particular have been accustomed to evince their zeal for sacred truths, by the most unchristian hatred against the imagined supporters of error; and they have not failed to ascribe unworthy motives, or depravity of heart, to those who remain unconvinced by the force of their arguments. This is the latent cause of all religious persecutions, which have deluged the world with blood, and disgraced humanity.

As in the transports of Gratitude we are disposed to imagine virtues, where they do not exist, thus in the transports of Resentment we are prone to the contrary extreme. A single cause of enmity blackens the whole character of our antagonist; and the man who has been guilty of one fault that touches us to the quick, becomes to an heated imagination the vilest of miscreants. The friends and connections of the aggressor are also considered as participants in his crimes: nay, the adherents and dependants upon the grand offender are contaminated by his guilt. Thus have towns and countries been laid waste without remorse, murder and rapine have been deemed laudable, and the sacrifice of thousands, in resentment of the vices and disorders of a few, has been frequently celebrated, as an heroic display of vindictive justice! Hence it is that disgrace of character is unjustly spread over a whole family, on account of the ill conduct or ignominious punishment of one of its members. Even the unconscious instruments of mischief, according to this propensity of our nature, are frequently treated as guilty, or as participants in the crime. Imprudent parents have thus nourished a spirit of revenge in their children, by encouraging them to beat the play-things which have accidentally given them pain, or the ground against which they have fallen.

It is recorded of the celebrated Cranmer, who flourished in the reign of Queen Mary, that having repented of his impiety, in yielding to the solicitations of the priesthood, and seductive promises of the Court, and signed an acknowledgment of the Pope's supremacy; when he was brought to the infernal stake, he resolutely held the offending hand in the flames, till it was consumed, from a spirit of resentment at its having been the instrument of his apostacy. In this singular instance of imputed guilt, our sympathy with the sufferings of the unfortunate man,

man, our admiration of his magnanimity, and our surprise at the strange manner in which he indicated a pious indignation of his former conduct, furnishes an apology for an act, which, under other circumstances, must have been contemplated as the excess of childish cruelty. (See Hume's History of England, Vol. IV. P. 431.)—For the same reason we admire the undaunted courage of Mucius Sævola, who, as we are informed by *Florus*, thrust his hand into the fire, because it had not succeeded in its attempt to strike the King of *Etruria*. But had he caused a dependant to be punished in this manner for a similar failure, he would have been held forth to execration.

It is upon the same principles that the strong impressions of fear or of sorrow change the appearance of every thing around us. Every trifle becomes the cause of terror; and every object loses its power to charm, unless it should administer to our melancholy. Sorrow naturally disposes to impatience, discontent, and fearful apprehension, in cases which have no connection with the primitive cause. Heavy disappointment, where expectation was ill-founded, forbids us to indulge hope where the encouragement is the greatest. Fear and dread dispose to cruelty, to treachery, and sometimes to acts of desperation which resemble courage.

As the passions and affections which are most analogous to each other, so readily blend together, or succeed in an easy currency, it is natural to suppose that those which are of an opposite nature and tendency must be repulsive; as joy and sorrow, hope and fear, love and hatred. For although complicated circumstances may place the mind under their influence, at the same period, yet the one is calculated to oppose and check the other; each exerting its characteristic influence. Thus when the success of any desired event is partial, sorrow may accompany joy. The effects of glad tidings are rendered incomplete, by the addition of some mournful catastrophe; when victory, for example, is purchased by the death of a friend, or of a favourite general. In such chequered incidents, the mind passes over from one event to the other, and feels the influence of each separately and alternately. In cases of a dubious nature, the mind is sometimes stagnated, or suspended between hope and fear; and sometimes agitated by each passion by turns. In this manner may love have some intercourse with anger; as in parents, whose resentment, at the improper conduct of their children, may even be inspired by the warmest affection; and the lover may be tormented by the caprices of his mistress, whom he cannot resolve to hate. The opposite passions and

and affections are, in instances of the like nature, excited by different and opposite circumstances, residing in the same exciting cause; each producing its own characteristic effect.

Fearful anxiety and joy in the extreme, are so diametrically opposite, and their pathological effects upon the system so contrary, that an immediate transition from the one to the other is extremely difficult, if not impossible; and by the violence committed upon our natures, it might be productive of fatal consequences. It is observable that in such cases, the salutary transition is made through the medium of the pathological effects, which are the usual indications of Sorrow. Tears and joyful lamentations are the first tokens of the removal of excessive fear. A sudden relaxation, as it were, succeeds to the agonizing constriction which accompanies that passion, and this prepares the mind for the pleasing vivacity which is the natural character of joy. Every medical practitioner, as often as he has assisted at any painful and dangerous operation, which has proved successful, must have observed these effects produced upon the sympathizing attendants; and every affectionate Female will recollect these singular emotions upon the happy delivery of her friend, whom she has supposed to have been in imminent danger. This singularity may perhaps be explained in the following manner. Previous to the happy issue, sorrow for the sufferings of the distressed object, and anxious fears respecting their issue, were intimately blended together; while the pathological tokens of the latter, suppressed those of the former. Upon the sudden removal of fear, its characteristic restrictions are removed, the residue of sorrow becomes permanent, and the agitated spirits are tranquillized by the effusion of tears.

A Melancholy state of mind is most soothed at the commencement, by what seems to feed its melancholy. The excess of grief will listen to nothing that is not somewhat in unison with it. It may afterwards be alleviated by a degree of cheerfulness in a friend who has wept for the distress, and whose sympathy has thus inspired a confidence. But no greater violence can be committed upon persons in the anguish of sorrow, than an attempt at gaiety, or the proposition of frivolous amusements.

Nothing so effectually subdues the violence of Anger, as the fortunate suggestion of ludicrous ideas. Whatever excites a smile or a laugh, excites a sensation totally incompatible with rage, or with deep resentment. It has often happened that a something ridiculous, in the ideas or conduct of the offender, has averted the punishment due to his carelessness and inadvertency; or that some gay and cheerful

ful thought, has at once obliterated resentment, against a conduct not entirely trivial. We are told by ancient fabulists, that when Apollo was about to shoot Mercury, disguised as an herdsman, incensed at this thievish deity for having stolen some cattle which Apollo was destined to watch, he applied to his quiver for an arrow, that he might revenge the offence; but discovering that the arch thief had prevented the effects of his anger, by previously stealing all the arrows, he was so diverted at the jest that his anger immediately subsided. *Iracundiam voluptate superante.*

In the quarrel between Jupiter and Juno, Homer represents the Queen of Heaven terrified into silence, and merely attempting to suppress the signs of a resentment which she could not subdue. But he informs us, that it was the jest of Vulcan, in taking upon him an office, for which he was so ill qualified, and becoming cup-bearer, which effectually restored mirth and good-humour among the Celestials.

Vulcan with aukward grace, his office plies;
And unextinguished laughter shakes the skies.

POPE.

OBSERVATION IV.

On the Seat of the Passions.

IT is usual for Writers on the Passions to speculate concerning their *Seat*, whether it be in the *spiritual*, or in the animated *material part* of Man. Some philosophers place the passions solely in the corporeal system. Among these was the celebrated *Des Cartes*. Mr. *Grove*, on the contrary, defines the passions to be " the affections attended with pe-
" culiar and extraordinary motions of the animal
" spirits;" and in opposition to the sentiments of *Des Cartes*, he says, " I am inclined to think that a
" sensation of the soul generally precedes a change
" in the spirits; external objects not being able to
" raise a ferment in the spirits till they have first
" struck the mind with an idea of something noble,
" frightful, amiable, &c."

Others again ascribe some of the affections to the *animal* principle, and some to the *rational*. Dr. Reid

Reid is in doubt whether " the principle of *esteem*, " as well as *gratitude* ought to be reckoned in the " order of animal principles, or if they ought not " rather to be placed in a higher order." He has finally, however, placed the esteem of the wise and good in the order of *animal* principles; not from any persuasion that it is to be found in brute animals, but because it appears in the most unimproved, and the most degenerate part of our species, even in those in whom we hardly perceive any exertion either of reason or of virtue.

But what is still more singular, the *same* affection is sometimes placed by this philosopher under the *animal*, and sometimes under the *rational* principle. Speaking of resentment he observes, " that " *sudden* or *instinctive* resentment is an *animal* prin-" ciple, common to us with brute animals; but " that resentment, which some authors call *delibe-*" *rate*, must fall under the class of *rational* princi-" ples." He also excludes " the *parental affection* " from the rational principle, because it is not " grounded on an opinion of merit in the object." (See Reid's Essays on the active powers of Man. Es. III. Ch. 4.)

This contrariety of opinions among philosophers themselves; the vague conjectures and arbitrary positions they have advanced, too plainly evince that we are not prepared for disquisitions of this kind.

kind. They prove that it will be impossible to arrange the passions and affections, with any precision, under these two heads, until we shall have obtained more accurate ideas of the nature of the rational and spiritual part of man, on the one hand, and of the vivified matter which is supposed to constitute his animal nature, on the other.

Those who place the passions, or any of the affections, in the body, confess that it must be an *animated* body: but they do not explain to us the *cause* of this animation; or what is that vivifying principle which so wonderfully changes the properties of dead, insensible, inactive matter. When we shall know the cause of sensation or of perception in its lowest stage; and when we shall have discovered *what that is* which thinks, reasons, and wills, we may be better qualified to decide concerning the seat of the passions and emotions.

The reason which induced Des Cartes and others, to make all the affections *sensual*, is obvious. It is easy to perceive that we cannot ascribe *affections* to the spiritual part of man, without admitting the *passions* also; nor these, without being perplexed with the *appetites*; which although confessedly sensual, frequently excite those emotions and passions, which must be ascribed to the Spirit, if it be susceptible of emotions. But this combination, or reciprocal influence, they deem to be totally inconsistent with those

those intellectual honours they are solicitous of ascribing exclusively, to our spiritual natures.

Dr. Reid's embarrassment seems to arise from the expectation that the rational principle must always act rationally; which leads him to infer that whenever the passions and affections do not receive the sanction of reason, they are to be assigned over to the animal principle. But this hypothesis will tempt us to doubt of the very existence of the rational principle, in numbers of our species;—it leads us to conclude that the two natures, deemed so diametrically opposite to each other, possess powers so perfectly similar, that it is difficult for the keenest discernment to distinguish between their operations;—and it compels us to infer, that whenever some of our affections become conformable to reason, they have changed their seat from the animal to the rational principle.

Philosophers and Divines, who distinguish Man into the three separate parts of Body, Soul, and Spirit, which notwithstanding the intimacy of their union, they suppose to be different in their natures; ascribe the appetites to the body, the passions and affections to the soul, and to the spirit, those intellectual powers which seem remote from passions or emotions of any kind. By such an arrangement they mean to compliment the spirit with the most exalted station; but the honour, like many other projects

projects of ambition, is entirely at the expence of its happiness. If the affections pertain to the soul exclusively, that alone is capable of *enjoying;* the spirit is deprived of every motive for speculation: and since it sometimes happens that speculations of the most abstruse kind excite pleasing sensations, the spirit must certainly *perceive*, though it has no faculties to *lament* its hard lot, as often as it is conscious that these delightful sensations, which are its own work, are transferred to the soul.

Without entering therefore into inquiries of this nature, which for want of *data* must be conjectural and unsatisfactory, it will be more correspondent with my plan, simply to state interesting facts, and leave it to the metaphysician to draw such consequences as he may deem most legitimate.

It must be admitted that every passion, emotion, and affection proceeds from certain impressions or ideas excited concerning the nature, or state, or quality, or agency of the exciting cause. These ideas have undoubtedly their seat in that part of man we distinguish by the appellation of *mind*. The exciting cause therefore changes the state of the mind, respecting the particular object. From total indifference it becomes some way or other *interested*. This new impression, if it be possessed of a certain degree of strength, produces a correspondent change

change upon the body. Universal observation and universal phraseology, which is doubtless founded upon this observation, unite to evince that a very perceptible influence of every strong emotion is directed towards the *heart*. The heart experiences various kinds of sensation, pleasant or unpleasant, over which it has no controul; and from thence the influence of agitated spirits seems to be diffused over the body. Their more gentle effects are not visible to the spectator; nay, the subject himself is not conscious perhaps of any thing more than either a change of sentiment, or the perception of the stronger influence of a former sentiment, connected with something agreeable or disagreeable in this perception; a something which attaches more strongly to the object, or creates some degree of repugnance. This state of mind is styled an *affection*, and it appears to be totally mental; but stronger influences produce such changes, that the inward disposition becomes obvious to the spectators, through the medium of the corporeal frame. It is now called an *emotion*, and this may increase in strength until the whole system becomes agitated and convulsed.

From this statement it appears incontestible, that the Affections and Passions have their origin in the mind, while Emotions are corporeal indications of what paſſes within; according to the conjecture expreſſed by Mr. Grove.

It alſo proves, that to confine the affections to the mind, and refer the paſſions to the animal principle, is to theorize in oppoſition to facts. For numerous inſtances have preſented themſelves in the courſe of our Analyſis, which indicate that the difference between the gentleſt affection, and the moſt turbulent paſſions conſiſts in *degree*, not in *nature*. Whatever produces ſilent ſatisfaction, in its mildeſt influence, will produce the extravagance of joy in its ſtrongeſt. Fearful apprehenſion, in its exceſs, is *terror*; and diſpleaſure, in its moſt inordinate exertions, is *rage*. When the gentleſt affections are rendered conſpicuous, their exiſtence is known by ſome viſible change produced in the countenance, through the medium of the nervous ſyſtem; while the moſt violent agitations of the mind, operating upon the ſame nervous ſyſtem, produce ungovernable tranſports. Hence it is rational to infer, that the fineſt affections and the ſtrongeſt paſſions are equally ſenſitive, or equally ſpiritual in their natures.

It is natural for thoſe who favour the hypotheſis, that man conſiſts of "different natures marvellouſly mixt," to aſcribe the *appetites* ſolely to the corporeal ſyſtem, or to the animal nature of man, and to call them *carnal*, becauſe the immediate objects

jects of the appetites relate to the wants and gratifications of the body. But do they recollect that these appetites are frequently awakened by the attention paid by the mind to their particular objects, exciting Concupiscence, which is always attributed to the mind? When the desires considered as carnal are excited by a particular state of the body, that is by certain changes made in the corporeal system, which generate particular wants, as in the sensations of hunger and thirst; the mental part of our natures is immediately conscious of these uneasy sensations, wills to remove them, and expects gratification in attending to the demands of appetite. Thus the whole man becomes interested, without the possibility of placing a barrier, to arrest the operations of the mind, and render the appetite purely corporeal.

When the power of immediate gratification is possessed, none of the accessary passions and emotions are called forth, and, in some cases, we are not conscious of mental exertions. But if the gratification cannot be immediate; if it be uncertain; if any formidable impediments present themselves; then the whole soul is powerfully aroused: hopes and fears are excited concerning the event; anger and jealousies are indulged against rivals and causes of impediments; sorrows and vexations are inspired by our disappointment. These betray the interest

which

which the mind has taken in pleasures which are termed sensual. Where the indulgence has been illicit, repentance also and remorse confess that the soul feels itself responsible for gratifications which are deemed merely carnal.

On the other hand, the finer affections of love, such as the filial, the parental, the social; and benevolence in its more tranquil exertions, being so much exalted above the appearance of every thing *selfish*, and having no immediate personal gratification for their object, are generally attributed to the higher principle in our natures. But the love of beauty and of attractive qualifications between the sexes, becoming sexual, may create desires denominated carnal; and benevolence becoming sympathy and compassion with deep distress, produces the corporeal effects of agonizing grief or fear, and is virtually as sensual or carnal as any of the appetites; though usage is offended at such an application of the terms.

Thus it appears that the grand principles of love and hatred, desire and aversion, produce their effects upon the whole system, when they operate with a certain degree of force: though for the sake of discrimination we give different names to these effects; and to manifest our sense of the superiority of one class of our desires and affections, when compared

pared with another, we annex various degrees of respectability to those which are most remote from the gratification of corporeal wants.

When the affections of love and desire are placed upon objects deemed the most sensual, they are called *appetites;* and they are stigmatized with the epithet of *carnal* appetites, because they are merely corporeal in their object, and are peculiarly liable to the most shameful abuse. They begin and terminate in gratifications which do not call forth one amiable quality or respectable exertion of the mind. When indulged within the limits permitted, they are void of merit; if illegitimate, or indulged to excess, they are accounted ignominious. In this singular predicament are those gratifications, which have for their final cause, the support or produce of life, exclusively placed.

The finer species of *corporeal* enjoyments reject the degrading epithets of sensual and carnal with disdain. No one is said to be carnally disposed, when his ears are gratified with the charms of music; when his eye surveys the beauties of nature. He is not charged with having an insatiable appetite for paintings, or condemned for inordinate concupiscence, though he should expend his fortune in making purchases, or exhaust his health by incessant application to the art. For though his senses are equally gratified, as in the other instances, yet the enjoyment is furnished by objects which are more dignified in their nature, and have been the result of skill and ingenuity. It is here that *merit* commences, both in the power of enjoyment, and in the power of execution; and language distinguishes gratifications from these sources by the more elevated appellation of *taste*. This very term, by the way, is an indication of the power of the object of our pursuit to elevate our ideas respecting the expressions employed. The word *taste*, although it is a metaphor borrowed from one of the carnal sensations, loses the grossness of its original meaning in the new mode of its application. It is ennobled by its object, till we forget that it is of a plebeian origin.

The pleasure derived from agreeable odours being, as it were, the medium between the grosser appetites, and the pleasure inspired by harmonious sounds or the objects of vision, neither exposed to the disgrace of the former, nor possessing the merit of the latter, has no epithet either of contempt or respectability.

When love and desire are placed upon nobler objects than any of the preceding; such as knowledge, virtue, or any other mental qualification, the superior dignity of these pursuits, and their elevation above every thing deemed sensual, and above the gratification of a refined taste, confers a dignity upon the affections themselves until they seem to be

of

of an higher origin, and emulate every thing we can conceive of the most exalted spirits. For we cannot entertain more elevated sentiments of immaterial created intelligences, than that they possess an ardent love of knowledge, wisdom, and moral obligation.

Nor have we any reason to ascribe those powers of the mind, which by way of pre-eminence we denominate *intellectual*, to any other principle than that which is the source of the affections, and is interested in the cravings of the appetites. The state of mind, and its conscious perceptions, must vary according to the kind of employment in which it is engaged. When its occupation is simply to investigate truths of any kind, to examine, deliberate, judge, and resolve, it is in a very different state, than when it is forcibly struck with the *beneficial* or *pernicious* nature and tendency of these truths, or of any influential quality with which it is become acquainted. It contemplates abstract ideas which may have a distant reference to utility, in a mood very different from that it experiences when very *attractive* or very *alarming* properties present themselves to the imagination, whose influence upon our *well-being* seems to be direct and immediate.

Yet in the calmer exercise of the mind, in its most abstruse speculations, there is a species of permanent pleasure of which it is conscious, and which is preferred, by the philosopher, to the strongest emotions which are as transient as they are violent; until by some new and interesting discovery he is surprised into joy, or intricacies occur which disturb and irritate. He then experiences, that passions and emotions will sometimes intrude themselves into the apartment, where the door seems to be most obstinately shut against them. Nor can his more tranquil pleasures be ascribed to any other cause than to a strong *predilection* for the study which most occupies his attention, to his *love* of knowledge, to the *gratification* of his curiosity, to the *satisfaction* derived from the enlargement of his ideas and improvement of his understanding, to his ardent *desire* of discovering something which may extend his fame or prove beneficial to humanity; that is, to honourable, noble, and useful affections.

The Reader will perceive that these remarks have not the most distant reference to the grand question concerning the materiality or immateriality of the Soul. They are simply opposed to those unfounded hypotheses, and vague conjectures which instead of explaining any one phenomenon, render our ideas more embarrassed. They indicate that we ought not to multiply principles, until we are qualified to assign to them their distinct offices, without encroachments or confusion. What can be more

more unsatisfactory than to suppose the existence of principles totally opposite in their natures, in order to explain the contrarieties observable in human character and conduct; and yet to allow that, in some instances, the operations of these principles are so similar, that philosophers themselves cannot ascertain the distinct province of each ? Or what can be more superfluous than to imagine the existence of these distinct principles, merely to confer honour upon the one, and load the other with disgrace, when the nature of the object pursued, and the dispositions towards it, will solve every difficulty; will indicate an exalted or a depraved state of the *mind*, without suggesting a single doubt whether the spiritual man ought in any respect, to become responsible for the disgraceful propensities of the carnal man, with whom he is compelled to inhabit?

It has been alleged that during the impetus of passion, the soul is in a state of much greater activity than at any other period. In most instances this is probably the case. Yet we should recollect that during the excitements of passion, the soul must necessarily *manifest* the greatest activity to the spectator, from its peculiar exertions upon the corporeal system. Whereas in the exercise of deep thought, the activity of the soul is concentrated within. Of consequence, when the mind is absorbed in profound

found meditation, instead of indicating more activity than usual, the external appearance will indicate less. Hence it is that deep thinkers are so frequently confounded by those who are not deep thinkers, with the stupid. In such cases, the activity of the soul can only discover itself by the result of its labours; or by the injuries which intense application may have committed upon the constitution. Instances have existed in which mental occupation has produced an insensibility to every foreign impression. The subject has remained unmoved, in the midst of scenes calculated to excite the most horrid tumults of soul. When the Philosopher of Syracuse was so wrapped in contemplation as to be insensible to all the horrors of a siege, his mind could not be less active than theirs who were the most agitated by the scenes of complicated distress which surrounded them.

CHAP. II.

Causes which create a Diversity in our Affections enumerated.

IT may seem natural to expect that men, formed with similar, and often with equal powers of discriminating the nature of objects;—in whom the sensations of pleasure and pain, happiness or misery are also similar;—and who are exposed to similar causes of excitement, should indicate a correspondent similarity in their affections, instead of such a diversity which is so conspicuous, not only in different persons, but frequently in themselves. It is well known that the predilections of individuals for the supposed means of happiness are extremely various; that one man will pursue with ardour, what another will contemplate with indifference, or with disapprobation and disgust. Nor is there any person who entertains invariably the same disposition towards the same object. At one instant he will

not

not only feel a much stronger affection for it than he did at the preceding, but he may to-day contemplate with contempt and abhorrence that which yesterday may have excited raptures.

It is of considerable moment to trace the principal causes of this diversity, or point out some of those circumstances which have a very powerful influence over our minds. The number and extent of these will permit little more than an enumeration.

§ 1. *The Influence of Experience.*

These diversities and changes may in many cases be ascribed to the difference observable between the suggestions of a lively imagination, and the more faithful reports of experience. Our pre-conceptions are seldom accurate. If they be not entirely false, or totally opposite to the nature of the subject, they are almost sure to err on the side of excess, or of defect. Experience, in numberless instances, corrects these errors, and teaches us to estimate the qualities of objects as they really exist, and not according to a prejudiced conception or an heated imagination. This will of consequence teach us highly to prize many things which we had before

neglected

neglected or defpifed, and to difmifs with indifference and contempt, many things on which a deluded imagination had placed our fupreme happinefs. Such changes will take place in every individual in his paffage through life. Their nature, and the ufes made of them conftitute the difference between the wife man and the fool.

But there are many other caufes which act more uniformly upon whole claffes and bodies of people, and give to each clafs a certain caft of character. Some of thefe are very fimilar in their effects; others diffimilar, irregular, and capricious.

Among thofe which are more uniform in their influence, may be placed the diftinctions in character and difpofitions obfervable in the

§ 2. *Difference of Sex.*

In moft animals of the inferior order, there is a manifeft difference between the male and female, both in external appearance, and in inftinctive properties. The former being in general of a ftronger make than the latter, and excepting at the moments when the powers of the female are called forth to the protection of their young, more courageous in difpofition.

Similar laws manifeftly prevail in the human fpecies.

cies. The very form and constitution of the man indicate that he is rendered capable of more robust employments; and his stronger contexture is, generally speaking, connected with a disposition to greater exertions: whereas the superior delicacy of contexture which distinguishes the female, is mostly accompanied with a much greater delicacy of character. Her dispositions to strong and vigorous exertions, either of body or of mind, are not so universal, and she generally places her affections upon objects and duties which are more confined and domesticated.

Nor do the customs prevalent in savage, or less polished nations, invalidate the above remarks. In those countries where bodily labour, or the fatigues of husbandry, are wholly consigned to the females, while their husbands appear indolent and inactive, this indolence is merely the repose enjoyed in the intervals of still greater exertions. War, or the chace, are exclusively their province, and when engaged in these, the men endure much greater fatigues and hardships than those allotted to their partners.

It is readily acknowledged that these peculiarities of make and of character, are not so uniform as to resist the influence of causes which have a tendency to counteract them. Singularity of temperament, the force of custom and education, particular situations

ations in life, may place individuals of each sex out of their proper sphere, and induce a peculiarity of individual character. But this change seldom meets with the approbation of either sex. An effeminate man is despised, and a masculine female has little power to charm.

An essential difference is also observable in sexual predilections. The female prefers the strong, the bold and courageous, the spirited and enterprising. Her ideas of beauty and comeliness are instinctively such as correspond the least with the delicacy of her own person. Men in general are most enamoured of those qualities and dispositions which indicate a contrary character. They talk of the delicacy of form, and amiable softness of the sex. They think that the milder virtues fit with peculiar grace upon the female; such as gentleness, patience, compassion, and tenderness. It is expected that she should excel in piety, in faith, hope, resignation. Men contemplate a female atheist with more disgust and horror, than if she possessed the hardest features embossed with carbuncles. They excuse, and many are disposed to be pleased with, such foibles as proceed from delicacy of frame, or greater sensibility of mind; while they express their disapprobation of a bold forward temper, though it should be accompanied with a great superiority of talents. Although moral obligation, as referring to

the

the grand ftandard of virtuous conduct, may be the fame; yet the rougher vices of oaths and intoxication are appropriated by men; while the fly, evafive ones of artifice, &c. are deemed lefs opprobrious in the female.

It is maintained that men are moft impetuous, but that females are moft deeply affected with the tender paffion: that if the man have not a fpeedy recourfe to the piftol or the rope, he will probably furvive the agonies of difappointment, under which the fofter fex will gradually pine and die. Thefe facts have induced a French author to remark, that women confider love as the ferious bufinefs of life, and men render it fubordinate to many others. It is however univerfally deemed to be the province of man firft to declare his paffion; and it is univerfally expected that the female fhould receive the declaration with a modeft coynefs, and experience fome degree of ftruggle with her delicacy, before fhe acknowledges the paffion to be reciprocal. The female has in general a ftronger affection for every thing fhe purfues than men, who are more frequently impelled to act from neceffity. She always follows her inclination in the difcharge of her focial and domeftic duties, as well as in the purfuits of pleafure, elegant accomplifhments, or of literature; Thofe who are of a fcientific turn compenfate for any defect in extent of erudition, or depth of inveftigation, vestigation, with which they are sometimes charged, by brilliancy of language and beauty of sentiment, which so frequently pervade and embellish their writings. Females are supposed to be much fonder of ornaments than those of the other sex who are not reputed fops; and it is said that they more deeply resent any neglect or slight of their persons. They are warmer in their friendships, and their strong attachments can scarcely be weakened by any thing but rivalships. If slighter incidents more easily discompose their tempers, this is abundantly recompensed by their superior patience under severer trials. In cases of extreme danger and difficulty, they have not only been equal to the support of their own spirits, but they have set an example of heroic courage to their desponding lords. But it is also allowed, that when the female mind becomes thoroughly depraved, they greatly surpass the other sex in cruelty, revenge, and every enormity; which is justly supposed to elucidate the common proverb, " *Corruptio optimi, est pessima.*"

In giving the above epitome, either of facts or opinions, the author has purposely avoided entering into the controversy relative to *rights* and *powers*, or to equality or superiority of capacities. He does not wish to draw a comparison between the lustre of the respective virtues, or nicely to balance the respective vices of each sex. His concern is with *differences alone*. If these exist; if characteristic differences commencing with early childhood,—when the little Miss delights in her doll, and arranges her domestic play-things, while her more hardy brother is driving a hoop or whipping a top,—run through every period of life, it is of no moment to the subject under consideration, whether they are to be ascribed to natural and physical, or to artificial or incidental causes; or *which* characteristics have a preponderancy of excellence. (See Note *S*.)

This manifest diversity, and in some respects total contrariety, in disposition and character, is necessarily connected with an equal diversity and contrariety of tastes and affections: since the former derive their origin from the latter; the character being itself both formed and indicated by a series of predilections and aversions. If therefore each sex has its distinguishing characteristics, if their tastes and inclinations be not precisely similar, sexual difference must be productive of different ideas respecting the qualities of objects, and create the most opposite affections respecting them: so that objects and circumstances perfectly the same, shall to each sex appear in different points of view. That which makes little or no impression on the one, being calculated to produce strong emotions in the other; becoming the source of pleasure or displeasure, of enjoyment or of infelicity. Another

Another cause which operates in a similar manner is

§ 3. *Diversity of Temperament.*

Without entering into the physiological characteristic of each temperament, concerning which physiologists themselves are not agreed, it has never been disputed, that there is such a diversity in the original constitution of individuals of each sex, as may not only influence the mental powers, but also the affections of the mind; which may pre-dispose one person to be affected by scenes and circumstances, in a manner very different from another.

Some are naturally more irritable in their tempers, others more placid: that is, one will perceive and feel causes of provocation in situations or conduct, which excite no emotions in the mind of another. Some are naturally of a melancholy cast; which spreads a gloom over every object, and prevents them from observing and enjoying those qualities which excite cheerful ideas, and communicate pleasurable sensations to another. This man is naturally sanguine in his disposition: he forms a thousand projects, and is full of hopes respecting each.

He is highly delighted with such prospects as are invisible to others; and is charmed with ideal properties, which never entered into the imagination of those who are not under the agreeable delusion. The disappointments to which such a temper is inevitably exposed, become plentiful sources of vexation, which the less sanguine fortunately escape. The timid, on the contrary, ruminate over every possibility of evil. They dare not to indulge hope through fear of disappointment. They see and magnify pernicious tendencies, which were totally overlooked by persons of the contrary disposition. Some are naturally indolent; and this indolence of temper prevents them from perceiving those qualities in objects which arouse the attention of the more active; and it induces them to give the preference to their beloved ease. Some are of a social cast; and they discover a thousand joys in societies, which appear indifferent or insipid to the lover of retirement.

Thus is there a natural and habitual disposition to be differently affected by the same objects; to each of which the imagination gives a colouring corresponding with the permanent and characteristic state of mind.

Another cause invariably produces a change in our ideas and dispositions towards particular objects, in a manner equally uniform and characteristic; and that is

§ 4. *The Regular Progress of our Natures from Infancy to advanced Age.*

The changes which take place in our affections and pursuits from this cause, are incontestibly marked by the hand of Nature herself; and they maintain a degree of uniformity in every person, of every nation and age, whose longevity carries him through each period.

The strong desires of the infant are at first confined to its corporeal wants. No part of nature is known to him, excepting that which serves to satisfy the cravings of appetite, and the nurse who administers it. During this state, agonies of grief and ecstasies of joy are instantaneously excited, and as instantaneously subside. In advancing childhood curiosity begins to awake, and increased attention is paid to every thing around us. Our pursuits, our pleasures, our pains become daily more numerous and complicated. With growing powers the love of action accompanies this inquisitive disposition. The healthy and vigorous chiefly delight in those amusements which occupy the attention, increase corporeal strength and address, and imperceptibly enlarge the stock of ideas. At this period, varied affections, and a thousand gushes of passion, engage and agitate the breast by turns. Hopes and fears, quarrels and reconciliations, eager pursuits and quick satiety occupy every hour.

Upon advancing towards manhood, new passions and desires are implanted. Social connections acquire strength and permanency. Sexual affections arise, and the multitudinous passions which surround them. Ambition is roused, and means are pursued productive of important ends. Interesting objects crowd upon the attention, increasing the ardour of the mind, and calling forth the most vigorous exertions. Gay and lively imagination gilds every scene with delight, and to enjoy seems to be the whole object of our existence.

Parental affections, cares, solicitudes, hopes and disappointments, joys and griefs of a more durable and serious nature, succeed to the thoughtlessness of younger years. The social affections, which seemed at an early period to be instinctive, ripen into a lasting and benevolent concern for the good of others. These manifest themselves, in some characters, by directing the attention to plans and projects of public utility; while in others, inordinate self-love and insatiable ambition become the first springs of action.

A

A placid state of mind and love of ease, naturally form the habitual disposition of the aged. Their other affections mostly derive their complexion from the scenes of their preceding years. Repeated injuries, confidence abused, and various disappointments, united with their growing infirmities, are apt to inspire a peevish humour, and render suspicion and the excess of caution the prevailing disposition. Long habits of frugal industry, joined with repeated observations, or with personal experience of the dependent and neglected state of the needy, will often create an inordinate love of wealth, which, a conviction that it cannot be long enjoyed, is not able to subdue. A desire of ease and tranquillity, which now constitute their principal enjoyment, is apt to render the aged vexed and irritated at the smallest interruptions. Some aged persons, on the other hand, acquire a placid cheerfulness, by the recollection both of difficulties surmounted, and of arduous duties performed, which are never to recur. Conscious of having filled the various connections and relations of life with propriety and usefulness, they have treasured up a fund of complacency and lively hope to console the decline of life. Even the difficulties with which they struggled, and the dangers they have escaped, now become the sources of satisfaction.

Thus has every period of life its characteristic

influence upon our ideas and our affections; placing new objects before the mind, and representing the former ones in very different shapes and colours, from those which first occupied the imagination.

§ 5. *National Customs.*

National customs, however widely they may differ from each other, have also a very powerful and permanent hold on the affections. For these the inhabitants of every country imbibe a pre-possession from the earliest infancy. Early habits seem to be propagated with the species; so intimately are they formed and moulded into the growing frame! and these early propensities are every day strengthened and confirmed by universal example. Custom and habits reconcile whole nations to climates the most unfriendly, and to occupations the most arduous and servile.

> What softer natures start at with affright,
> The hard inhabitant contends is right.

The history of the manners and customs of different nations, fully demonstrates that they are divided into large masses of predilections and prejudices, strong attachments and strong aversions! It evinces
the

the feeble influence of the rational faculties, either in forming or correcting customs, the most beneficial, or the most pernicious. Nay, should experience itself begin to suggest better principles, to some superior and reflecting minds, ages may roll before any one will venture out of the common course, and attempt to reduce them to action; and his best endeavours will probably be rewarded with ridicule, contempt, and general detestation. Though causes merely incidental may have conspired to introduce a peculiarity of manners and to form national characters, yet being once formed, they become the sovereign rule of thought and action. They are diffused over the most extensive communities; and unless freedom of intercourse be held with neighbouring nations, not an individual can escape the impression. Thus it is that the inhabitants of one district, contemplate those things as essential to well-being, which others hold in abhorrence;— that one class of people reveres as incumbent duties, observances which others contemplate as the greatest absurdities;—that some are inspired with invincible attachments to rites, which those who are not under the influence of the same pre-possessions, justly consider as a disgrace to humanity.

Whether custom should influence opinion, or opinion introduce custom, they both operate upon the affections, and generally manifest the plenitude

of

of their power, by the number and magnitude of the absurdities they render familiar and acceptable to the mind. These have for successive generations established the empire of imaginary beings; and the affections of reverence, love, and gratitude have been thrown away upon ideal objects! These have sanctioned the most inveterate hatreds; they have consecrated immoralities, and dignified theft, prostitution, and murder! They have rendered the austerities of Brachmen and Monks venerable to the multitude; have laden the Gentoo Female with insufferable disgrace who refuses to expire in torments, from affection to her deceased husband! These, in the most enlightened countries, enjoin it upon the Man of Honour to murder his best friend for a hasty expression, or some other indiscretion of a momentary transport! Opinion has clothed a frail mortal with infallibility; has communicated that exclusive attribute of Deity to councils and synods, and bowed the neck of myriads to the empire of their decrees. It has elevated the worthless into the character of saints, and those who have most deserved the Divine indignation have been invoked as the most prevalent intercessors! It has represented the Universal Parent as the tyrant, instead of the benevolent friend of mankind; conducted to the torture those who presumed to think more worthy of him,

him, and it now threatens a total abnegation of his existence!

But the diversities of opinions and manners, with their correspondent predilections and aversions, exceed enumeration. It is these diversities which furnish the amusement derived from the perusal of travels; and as no two nations on the globe correspond in every instance, the peculiarities of each illustrate in a striking manner the truth of our observation. They indicate the inconceivable variety of sentiments and affections, which incidentally take place among beings of the same species, inhabitants of the same sublunary system, conversant with similar objects, and possessing similar powers of mind.

§ 6. *The Force of Habit.*

Similar to the customs which pervade large bodies of men, is the force of habit over individuals. The mind frequently acquires a strong and invincible attachment to whatever has been familiar to it, for any length of time. Habits primarily introduced by accident or by necessity, will inspire an affection for peculiarities which have the reverse of intrinsic merit to recommend them. These become, as it were, affimilated to our natures. We contemplate them as belonging to ourfelves fo intimately, that we feel an irkfome vacuity in their abfence, and enjoy a great degree of fatisfaction in their being re-placed; merely becaufe we have been habituated to them. How frequently does it happen that the moft trifling circumftances, in early life, will decide the lot of our future years; creating affections and averfions, which have the moft lafting influence! To this caufe we may frequently afcribe, a preference for one trade, purfuit, or profeffion, rather than for another. Thus we perceive that children fometimes make choice of the employments of their parents or their neighbours, becaufe it had agreeably engaged the attention of their juvenile hours. They love to imitate and play the man, till an affection is acquired for the occupation itfelf. This is generally the cafe where the occupation is of an active nature, and moft adapted to the vivacity of youth. If, on the other hand, their minds are ftrongly impreffed with the confinement, flavery, or any other difagreeable circumftance attending the employment to which they are daily witneffes, they are inclined to the contrary extreme, contract an averfion, and give the preference to any other purfuit, the inconveniences of which are unknown to them.

It is needlefs to enlarge farther upon thefe particulars;

culars; as every individual muft be confcious of their truth. There is no one who does not feel the power of habit, both as the fource of pleafure and of difpleafure. It is experienced in every ftation and connection in life; it is experienced in what we eat, or drink, in particular modes of drefs, in our habitations and their furniture, and in our own characteriftic peculiarities.

§ 7. *Principle of Self-love.*

The influence of this principle has frequently fhewn itfelf in the courfe of our Analyfis. Its tendency to magnify the good or evil which relates to ourfelves is perpetually felt. But we fhall now confine our attention to the effects of *appropriation;* or the attachment generated, and the affections indulged, refpecting every thing we call *our own.*

Mr. Hume has collected together many ftriking inftances of the effect of this principle. (See Differtation on the Paffions.) He attributes it to *pride;* but then he defines pride to be a *certain fatisfaction in ourfelves on account of some accomplishment or poffeffion which we enjoy.* Without examining the propriety of this definition at prefent,

(See

(See Note *I.*) the influence of *Self*, respecting appropriation must be universally admitted. "It is "always," says he, "*our* knowledge, *our* sense, "beauty, possessions, family, on which we value "ourselves.—We found vanity upon houses, gar- "dens, equipage, and other external objects; as "well as upon personal merit and accomplishments. "—Men are vain of the beauty either of *their* "country, or *their* county, or even of *their* pa- "rish; of the happy temperature of the climate, in "which they are born; of the fertility of their na- "tive soil; of the goodness of the wines, fruits, or "victuals produced by it; &c." "Every thing "belonging to a vain man, is the best that is any "where to be found. His houses, equipage, fur- "niture, clothes, horses, hounds, excel all others "in his conceit, &c."

These, and many other facts, which might be enumerated, indicate an innate propensity to value whatever we possess, merely from the incidental circumstance of its being *our own*. That this disposition frequently gives rise to the excess of vanity, is not to be disputed: but the disposition itself is so important that it cannot be dispensed with. The strong attachment to whatever is our own, *because* it is our own, is one of the happiest propensities of our natures. It is the recompence of all our desires, pursuits, and exertions. Without this principel, ciple, every object in life would appear uninteresting and infipid; and the majority of our habitual affections would be annihilated. It is this which forms that intimate and pleafing connection with every thing around us; and enables trifles themfelves greatly to adminifter to our comfort and fatisfaction.

But the diverfity which it creates in our individual affections is no lefs obvious. Every man has a diftinct atmofphere of good. A circle which is his own. Every particle compofing it, is viewed by another with eyes of indifference; but by himfelf with complacency and delight.

§ 8. *The Influence of Education.*

By education in this place is underftood, any attempt to enlarge the ideas and improve the mind by the acquifition of general knowledge, or proficiency in any particular branch. Education introduces to an intimate acquaintance with numberlefs objects which are totally unknown to the ignorant; and every object poffeffes fome quality of a pleafant or unpleafant nature, proportionably multiplying or diverfifying our agreeable or difagreeable fenfations.

With

With the ignorant, objects are comparatively few. Scenes before them are of no great extent; and even these are overlooked by the majority, whose years pass away in a kind of sensitive indolence, without their testifying the marks either of apathy or affection.

Sometimes however a natural acuteness of understanding is observable among the most illiterate, accompanied with lively sensations and very strong affections; and when they are once aroused by objects that appear interesting, their passions are most violent. What they know can alone appear important to them, and the very little they possess is their *all*. Their whole souls are concentrated in that which gives pleasure, and all the powers of body and mind are exerted to repel whatever gives pain. This will indicate the cause of that remarkable strength of passions and affections, both of the benevolent and malevolent kind, so observable in savage nations; and the impetuosity of character so often to be met with among the active and uninformed in every nation.

The cultivated mind, by increasing its acquaintance with innumerable subjects, will inevitably discover some pleasing quality in every object of its pursuit; of consequence, both attention and affections are divided and subdivided into innumerable ramifications; and thus, although enjoyment may upon

upon the whole be augmented by aggregate numbers, yet each individual quality possesses but a moderate share of influence.

The young and inexperienced are generally affected by simple objects. The causes of their joy or anger, sorrow or fear, are seldom complex. As the powers of the mind are more enlarged, the affections are more diversified and rendered more complicated! Thus upon the perception of favours and obligations, the joy from good becomes united with *gratitude* to the author of that good; with *love, veneration, respect,* for his character; with *admiration* at the extent of the good, or at some peculiarity in the delicacy and liberality with which it was conferred. Experience introduces the passions of hope and fear, by teaching us the knowledge of good worth possessing, on the one hand, and the accidents to which it is liable on the other.

It is observable further, that the young and inexperienced, whose habits are not yet formed, and to whom every thing is new, are most apt to be influenced by the introductory emotions of *surprise* and *wonder*. Their inexperience renders things and events, which are familiar to others, new and strange to them. They are prone to be in ecstasies for acquisitions and advantages comparatively trifling, and to be agitated by small or imaginary evils,

because

because their imaginations have not been corrected by experience. But, if these *passions* from more simple causes, are frequently stronger in *them* than in others, it is equally true that their *affections* are less permanent. A rapid succession of novelties, and the immense variety which increased knowledge introduces, quickly efface the preceding impression.

But this subject is inexhaustible. A whole *Encyclopedia* could not do it justice. The infinite diversity of pursuits, which in this age engage the attention of an awakened world, exceeds enumeration; and each pursuit is accompanied with its peculiar predilection, and presents an infinite variety of qualities to the inquisitive mind, which excite their correspondent emotions and affections.

Other causes which influence our ideas of qualities have a very powerful, though very transient effect. They are merely the ephemerons of the mind; nor have they that immediate relation to the supposed merit or demerit of the object, which exerts its influence in all the preceding cases. These are the influence of *Novelty* and of *Fashion*.

§ 9. *Influence of Novelty.*

As by the power of habit we are reconciled to circumstances, and even enjoy complacency in situations,

tuations, merely because we are accustomed to them; thus will the *novelty* of an object frequently render it interesting for the moment, and give it a temporary pre-eminence to many things which we know to possess intrinsic merit. Novelty is in itself the most transient of all qualities, being solely adapted to that instinctive curiosity, which may be considered as an appetite for knowledge. Novel objects will at first excite a degree of wonder and admiration, from their being supposed to possess something strange, rare, or peculiar: but as these are relative qualities alone, and as this relation refers solely to our ignorance and inexperience, their effects are evanescent; for when the subject is no longer novel to us, it does not seem any longer to possess them: when novelty is no more, we shall either reject them with indifference or displeasure; or they may continue to attract our attention by our perception of other and more permanent qualities.

The love of novelty may, in some minds, be considered as a disease; as a false appetite which craves more than it can digest, and seeks a variety of viands, from whence it derives but very little nourishment. This passion, though it renders us perpetually inquisitive, perpetually impels us to see objects through a false medium. At first, they are rendered peculiarly attractive, through the adventitious colouring which the imagination has given them.

them. They appear infipid when their novelty is gone, or become depreciated beyond their deferts, from the difappointment of our expectations concerning them. Fondnefs for novelty, when carried to an excefs, renders a perfon whimfical in his choice, and unfteady in his purfuits. Momentary pleafures terminate in fatiety and difappointment, which are infuperable impediments to that deliberate inveftigation and habitual experience, which alone can enable us to judge of the real nature and intrinfic qualities of the objects around us.

But no caufe whatever is fo whimfically verfatile and tyrannical, in exciting attachments and averfions, as the

§ 10. *Power of Fashion.*

This power is an ideal influenza that fpreads with the utmoft rapidity, infecting a whole community where it commenced; fometimes extending to diftant nations, and acquiring fuch ftrength in its progrefs that nothing can refift its force! It does not poffefs the degree of merit attendant upon the excefsive love of novelty, which always imagines the object to poffefs fome degree of worth; a circumftance this, by no means effential to the influence of fafhion;

fashion; whose authority is in general derived from things known to be idle and insignificant. Fashion gives absolute sway to modes, forms, colours, &c. wantonly introduced by the whim of an individual, with whom the majority have not the most distant connection, concerning whom they are totally ignorant, unless circumstances and situations of notoriety should render their characters either *equivocal*, or *unequivocal*. It is capable of instantaneously altering our opinion of the nature and qualities of things, without demanding any painful exertions of the understanding, or requiring the slow process of investigation. With the quickness of a magic wand, it in a moment subverts all those ideas of beauty, elegance, and propriety, we had before cherished. It makes us reject as odious what we had lately contemplated as most desirable; and raptures are inspired by qualities, we had just considered as pernicious and deformed. Unwilling to renounce our title to rationality, unable to resist the power of fashion, we make every attempt to reconcile reason with absurdity; thus in numberless instances we attempt to vindicate to ourselves and others the novel affection. We are assiduous to find out some peculiar excellence or advantage, in whatever becomes the idol of the day; and to discover some insufferable defect in the divinity we have discarded. That which was once deemed grand and majestic, in size or form, will now strike the eye as insupportably clumsy; and the regularity we once admired, now renders an object stiff, precise, and formal. Colours, which were yesterday so delicately elegant, will appear to-day faint, faded, and lifeless; and those which were lately much too strong and glaring for our weak optics, become in an instant bright, glowing, and majestic. Fashion will render that particular garb which we once thought so warm and comfortable, hot and insupportable as the sultry *dog-days;* and it makes the slightest covering, contrary to its pristine nature, remarkably pleasant in the depth of winter. The flowing hair, or adjusted ringlets, shall at one period be considered as becoming and elegant; at another, be rejected as an insufferable mark of effeminacy, and reprobated as demanding a culpable waste of our most precious time; while their close amputation is deemed both manly and commodious. Fashion has power to influence our ideas of graceful proportions; it elongates or contracts the form of the leg in one sex, and of the waist in the other. At one period it imperiously orders the tightest ligatures to encircle the neck; as if the separation of some excrescence were intended: at another it recommends the large and swoln cravat, as if it thought a poultice were necessary to assuage the irritation occasioned by the preceding mode; and it benevolently permits the chin to partake of the soothing warmth. It directs decency to *excite* a blush, at being detected without any other head-dress than that ordained by nature; and it is also able to *suppress* the blush of female delicacy at exposures, which scarcely leave any room for the exercise of the most licentious imagination!

§ 11. *Love of Singularity.*

This is the direct opposite of the former; and though the love of singularity cannot in its own nature be so extensive as the power of fashion, yet it is very operative, where it does exist. It constitutes the motive and the pleasure of those, who are bold enough to deviate from the accustomed modes of thinking and acting, in order to attract the public attention. As the servile imitators of fashion are *ashamed* of being singular, these on the other hand, *glory* in singularity. They disdain to be placed in the line with common men, and think that they shall be respected as *commanding officers*, by starting out of the ranks. This disposition indicates itself in those who are the first introducers of fashions, which the multitude so eagerly follow. But it has its influence in more important cases. It has eventually a powerful sway over the public at large, who seem ready to enlist themselves under some chief, without being choice about either the nature of the service, or of the recompence. Speculative philosophy, politics, and religion are the three provinces, in which the influence of this disposition is remarkably conspicuous. It is often the source of new theories, which sometimes instruct, sometimes astonish, and sometimes infatuate the world. It is always discontented with whatever *is*, and is always stimulated to seek something different. In *politics*, it is inimical to monarchy, aristocracy, or democracy, according as either of them is the established form of government. In *religion*, it deviates from the popular creed, whatever that may be. The creed being popular, is deemed a sufficient indication of its being erroneous. This disposition has a much closer affinity with *free thinking* than *free inquiry*, for it proposes *private* opinion as the only counterpoise to the *public* opinion, without paying any respect to the *weight of evidence*, on either side. The love of singularity has too often a pernicious effect in disputing societies, and sometimes in seminaries of learning; and it is highly prejudicial to that investigation of truth, which is the professed object of these institutions. The disputant opposes opinions generally received, from the love of disputation, or from the desire of exercising and displaying his talents. He directs all his attention to the arguments which appear to be the most novel,

specious,

specious, and embarrassing. Thus he not only excites doubts in the minds of others, and triumphs in his success, but being habituated to search arguments of *opposition*, without attending impartially to the force of evidence, he is finally caught in the web of his own sophistry. He seriously imagines that truth is on the side he at first supported from vanity; and he rejects as errors, sentiments he secretly revered, when he wantonly began to combat them. Thus does he experience a total revolution in his manner of thinking and acting. He considers those things as indifferent, absurd, and pernicious, which he once thought of the highest importance; and this state of mind is necessarily productive of a change in his affections and dispositions towards them.

§ 12. *Popular Prejudices.*

As whole communities sometimes entertain an uniformity in sentiments, with correspondent predilections and aversions; thus are they not unfrequently divided and subdivided into sects and parties, each of which is rigidly tenacious of a particular class of ideas, contracts very strong attachments to the espousors of the same cause, and thinks itself fully authorized to treat those of opposite sentiments with contempt and hatred. Philosophy, religion, and politics manifest also in a thousand instances the influence

influence of this principle. The two former are distinguished into a diversity of *schools* and *sects*, which cherish the flattering idea that they are the sole supporters of truth. Thus it is that a zealous attachment to particular sentiments is not always the result of an impartial examination; it is sometimes the consequence of an early education, and sometimes it proceeds from an implicit confidence in the virtues, talents, and superior judgment of their chief, or some other incidental circumstance, which has cast the mind in the mould of particular opinions, and made an impression upon it too deep ever to be obliterated.

Nor does this principle cease to operate in countries which deem themselves the most remote from servile attachments, or unfounded prejudices. The rancorous spirit that too frequently prevails in every contested election, will avouch the truth of this assertion. Candidates for some particular office, professedly of high importance to the interests of the community, at once start forth from obscurity. They are immediately idolized by one party as the mirrors of every excellence, and stigmatized by the other, as totally devoid of merit, and unworthy the name of man. Social intercourse is interrupted;—intimate friends become implacable enemies;—and during this wretched ferment a total suspension takes place of all the principles of honour

and

and integrity; while every sluice of scandal and defamation is thrown open without reserve and without remorse. Partiality and prejudice act and react like the waves of the troubled sea, until they are worked up into a tremendous storm. At these periods such phrensies have been known to disturb the brain, that the wanton shouts of a mob have been productive of outrage and murder, and the colour of a ribband has excited convulsions, as violent as those produced by the sight of water in the canine madness!

To this principle also may we not ascribe a phenomenon, which appears otherwise inexplicable. Persons, who in their individual characters are highly respectable, both for sense and integrity, will frequently in their *political* capacities, pursue a conduct the most inconsistent with either;—uniformly act on the extravagant idea, that the existent Minister, whoever he may be, is uniformly right in his principles, perfectly disinterested in all his actions, and infallible in his plans: or, on the contrary, will regularly and incessantly oppose him as a compound of depravity and ignorance; whose every plan is big with mischief, and every exertion of power the application of the strength of a Sampson, to the overthrow of the pillars of the constitution!

§ 13.

§ 13. *Associated Affections.*

The influence of association in suggesting of thoughts has frequently engaged the attention of philosophers; and the power of trivial incidents to recall former ideas is universally confessed. But their power is perhaps equally extensive over the *affections.*

As one passion or affection pre-disposes the mind to the indulgence of that which most nearly resembles it, thus every passion or affection which has been indulged to a considerable degree, seems to change the complexion of every surrounding object. Places in which we have been happy, strike us as if they had been both witnesses and participants of our bliss; and distress invariably diffuses a gloom over locality itself, and every circumstance that reminds us of what we have felt. Nor can we call to our recollection any place in which we have enjoyed peculiar satisfaction, without feeling an affection for that spot; or recollect scenes of unhappiness, without feeling something like resentment against the theatre of our sufferings. The traveller, who has been made happy in a foreign country, contracts a partiality for every thing belonging to it;

it; both in consequence of that quick transition which so frequently accompanies our affections, and its being calculated to recall seasons of pleasure. If he has been ill received and ill treated, the gayest scenes and most advantageous circumstances belonging to that country, will, upon recollection, inspire him with disgust and horror.

This principle is very extensive in its influence. It is this which renders the spot where the lover enjoys the company of his mistress, a paradise in *his* sight, however different its aspect may be to another. The slightest present, as a token of affection, inspires exquisite delight: a trinket, or a lock of hair are to him of more worth than a kingdom. It is this principle which enstamps an inestimable value upon the relicts of saints and martyrs, and empowers fragments of their garments, their very teeth and nails, to work miracles, in the opinion of the devotee. In its more moderate exertions, it inspires a strong attachment to every thing which was once our friend's. It is this principle of association, which so easily implants in the religious and devout mind a veneration for the place destined to the offices of religion; and inscribes holiness upon the edifice devoted to sacred purposes.

The same principle renders innumerable circumstances in common life of considerable importance; and in conjunction with habit, enables us to derive

comfort

comfort from peculiarities of state and situation, which do not possess any intrinsic advantage. Every thing around us becomes, as it were, congenial to our natures; and the pleasures of yesterday are revived in the objects of to-day.

This associating principle extends its influence to the article of dress, and inspires a degree of respectability, or the contrary, according to the shape of a coat, or the cock of a hat. In the days of our ancestors it was reduced to a regular system, and occasioned that classification in dress which distinguished individuals in the three professions, and in the departments of justice, from the vulgar herd. In those days the venerable wig, the robe, and the band, invariably excited the ideas of superior skill, gravity, piety, and equity. These were venerated as *emblems*, until they were so frequently employed as *substitutes*, that the charm was finally dispelled.

But although this kind of association has not, in the present day, so extensive an effect as at former periods, yet it is not entirely destroyed. It is felt in our navies and armies, where the raw recruit is despised, and often very roughly treated by his more veteran associates, until they have lost sight of his ignorance and inexperience in the uniformity of garb. It is felt by every actor, who cannot fully enter into the spirit of his part, until he has assumed

the

the character in his external appearance. It is invariably felt by those distinguished for their attachment to ornaments; who so frequently mistake the elegance of their dress, and the value of their jewels, for their own personal accomplishments. It is at times felt by every one in a greater or less degree; for his mind experiences something of a conformity with the state of his dress; and the remark of *Sterne*, that a propensity to meanness is increased by the want of clean linen, possesses a portion of philosophy as well as of humour.

This principle of association exerts an illicit influence in more important matters. It inspires a disposition to substitute one thing for another, because of some points of similarity; however they may differ in more essential articles. Thus it frequently substitutes the means for the end. In *religion*, it confounds the observance of rites and ceremonies with the spirit of true devotion; and a punctual attendance upon the means of improvement, is deemed equivalent to *progress* in improvement. In *morals*, it sometimes respects a vice that is contiguous to a virtue; and it degrades a virtue, that is contiguous to a vice. Thus because a generous man is liberal in his donations, the *Prodigal*, who squanders in thoughtless profusion his own property and that of others, boasts of his *liberality*. Because *œconomy* is a virtue, *avarice* assumes the title.

title. The *rash* and *impetuous* give the character of cowardice to *caution;* and the *coward* confounds genuine courage with unpardonable *rashness.*

In like manner are degrees of atrocity calculated, not by the innate baseness of an act, or by the quantity of misery it diffuses, but according to the nature of the punishment inflicted by human laws; or to the quantity of reputation that is in danger by the commission. Thus some have imagined that they respect virtue, because they abhor ignominy. These pay peculiar attention to mere *appellations*, and *modes of expression*, which are designedly adopted to conceal the enormities of guilt. The man, who in his social habits apparently scorns to be unjust, will not scruple to ruin his best friends by rash and adventurous projects; and he simply calls the issue, an unfortunate *speculation.* The ruin of female honour, to the destruction of the peace and happiness of respectable relatives, being termed an *act of gallantry*, is scarcely deemed inconsistent with the character of a man of honour.

These few specimens shew the nature and extent of the associating principle. They indicate that it sometimes operates as a *remembrancer*, sometimes as an *emblem* or *representative*, and sometimes as a *substitute;*—that it may be the handmaid of innocent and virtuous affections; the source of bigotry and superstition,

superstition; and an apology for the deepest depravity.

When our ideas of the qualities of objects, and dispositions towards them, are not under the influence of these adventitious circumstances, when they are the most correspondent with their real natures, yet the impressions they make upon our feelings are extremely different at different seasons. Sometimes we perceive that they exist, but we contemplate them without either emotion or affection; at other times they acquire such an irresistible influence, that they will not suffer a competitor. We have already observed that the novelty of an object, and the sudden manner in which it is presented to our notice, have a very powerful influence over our affections; but there are many other adventitious circumstances, which from their striking effects upon the mind, deserve to be enumerated. For example:

§ 14.

§ 14. *The Manner in which Information is conveyed to us.*

It is natural to expect that a full conviction of the truth of interesting particulars, would at all times be attended with an impression proportionate to their importance. But this is not the case; much depends upon the *manner* in which such interesting subjects are presented to the mind. The information obtained by *reading* a plain and simple statement of events, for example, is the weakest in its influence. A *narrative* of the same events from an *eye-witness*, whose credit may not be superior to that of the historian, brings us, as it were, nearer to the object, and makes a much deeper impression. Both of these are feeble compared with the influence of *sight*. It is through the organs of sight alone, that the most vivid and most permanent effects are produced. Every minute circumstance is now placed before us, and each exerts its own impressive influence at the same instant. The information is now complete and indubitable, without any mixture of obscurity in the mode of representation, or remains of incredulity on our parts,—which seems to weaken the evidence of what is considered to be authentic history, more than is generally suspected. We are *our own evidence*, and we must give credit to ourselves. Hence we speak of *ocular demonstration*, and agree that *seeing is believing*.

It is a singular fact, that in reading the most terrible events with which the pages of history are filled, we not only *bear to read*, but *take delight* in the perusal of those incidents which would be too affecting, were they immediately described to us by an eye-witness; and which would excite insufferable anguish were we ourselves spectators of the scenes. The cool narration of those vices, follies, intrigues, cruelties, oppressions, of which the history of states and kingdoms is chiefly composed, is just sufficient to awaken within us that degree of horror, indignation, and sympathy, which is not inconsistent with the pleasure we take in the gratification of curiosity. We feel also self-approbation, which is far from being unpleasant, in the perception that we are always interested in the cause of the innocent, the weak, and the oppressed; that we can detest vice, and rejoice in the triumphs of virtue.

Nor does the professed historian descend to those *minutiæ*, which in scenes of this kind have the strongest hold upon the mind. His narrative consists in a general representation of facts. He tells us of thousands and tens of thousands that were destroyed,

troyed, or led into captivity, or reduced to extreme diſtreſs by peſtilence and famine, without expatiating upon minuter circumſtances, which are abſolutely neceſſary to compoſe an intereſting picture. Thus are we much more affected with the parting of *Hector* from *Andromache*, than with the conflagration of Troy; and we ſympathize more deeply with the fate of this hero, when his lifeleſs body was dragged at the chariot-wheels of his proud conqueror, than with all the real diſtreſſes of the Trojan war. We ſuffer more from the ſimple ſtory of *Le Fevre*, than from the reports of an hoſpital; and the countryman's pathetic lamentations over his dead aſs, have called forth tears of commiſeration, which much more extenſive diſtreſs will not always produce.

This leads us to other cauſes which have alſo a powerful influence in exciting or directing our affections; and have ſome relation both with the ſympathy of our natures, and with the aſſociation of ideas and affections already noticed: and theſe are

§ 15.

§ 15. *Imitative Tones and Representations.*

We are so constituted as to be strongly affected by the *representation* of particular states and situations, notwithstanding we may be convinced that they are imaginary or artificial. Mere tones, attitudes, gestures, imitating or resembling any of those produced by one or other of the passions and affections, are calculated to excite correspondent feelings and emotions in susceptible minds. Like musical instruments attuned to the same key, our feelings are made to vibrate with the vibrations of surrounding objects. Even the voice and accents of inferior animals, expressive either of fear, or pain, or lamentation, or joy, or affection, have a tendency to render us apprehensive, cheerful, melancholy, or sympathizing. Rude and harsh sounds not only create unpleasant sensations, but suggest unpleasant and foreboding ideas, in all those who have not corrected their sensations by their reason. It is from this kind of association probably, that the croaking of the raven, and the scream of a night-owl, are so universally deemed *ominous of mischief* by the ignorant. The sprightly music of the feathered songsters inspires an exhilarating vivacity. The solitary and melodious notes of the nightingale, the cooing of the turtle-dove, &c. have always furnished imagery for Poets in their description of the tender passion of love, or sympathetic sorrow. The bleating of the sheep, and lowing of the kine, &c. although they possess no real melody in themselves, yet as they denote the affection of the dam for its offspring, they universally inspire a pleasing sympathetic tenderness.

The principal charms of the music which aims at a higher character, than that of difficult or rapid execution, consist in the imitation of those tones and movements which are most intimately connected with the passions and affections of the soul; which exhilarate the spirits, and excite to the sprightly or graceful dance, arouse and animate, induce a bewitching melancholy, or diffuse a pleasing serenity over the mind;—which charm by displaying something like the power of persuasive eloquence without words,—by holding a kind of conversation without ideas,—and by exciting whatever disposition the artist pleases, without suggesting a motive.

It has been occasionally remarked in our Analysis, that the powerful influence of any exciting cause, manifests itself by emotions correspondent to the nature of the passions; to seize these external appearances, or to imitate the expressive looks, attitudes, and gestures peculiar to each, is the professed

fessed object of the statuary and historic painter: and to do justice to these characteristic emotions, constitutes the difficulty and excellence of their art. It is the professed design of the Artist to excite some emotion, or call forth some particular affection correspondent to the nature of his object. Although the power of the sculptor is confined to forms and attitudes principally, yet how interesting may these be rendered to the spectator! Who can contemplate the *Apollo Belvedere*, the *Venus de Medicis*, without admiring the human shape in its characteristic beauties? or the *dancing Fawns*, without partaking of their vivacity? Or the *Farnese Hercules*, without a degree of awe? or the *Laocoon* and his sons, without a mixture of compassion and horror? Or any of these, without being astonished at the skill, ingenuity, or sublimity of the artist? The enthusiastic encomiums bestowed upon the paintings of celebrated masters; the eagerness with which their labours are purchased; the wealth and renown which the most distinguished of them enjoy; and the respect paid to their memories, demonstrate the amazing effect of their performances upon the mind; —the strength of our sympathy with every representation of passion;—and the surprise we experience that these powerful effects are produced by the mere distribution of colours, or of lights and shades upon board or canvass!

§ 16. *Rhetoric, Oratory, Eloquence.*

If mere tones and representations so warmly interest the affections, though they are not able to convey information, or suggest any ideas to the mind, perfectly novel; much deeper impressions are to be expected from means, whose professed object it is, to increase our knowledge of particular subjects, extend our views, enlarge our conceptions, and to employ all the force of language and all the power of sympathy, to give them weight and energy; which is the province of *Rhetoric* and *Oratory*.

Rhetoric is generally considered as the art of persuasion. It attempts to inspire conviction concerning some particular object, that it may influence the will to determine in a manner correspondent. It seeks either to arouse the mind to action, or to dissuade it from acting upon the resolutions already taken, or that are in contemplation. Its immediate employment is not to search after truth, but to render acknowledged or supposed truths influential. It leaves to logic the province of cool investigation, and of drawing legitimate conclusions from admitted premises, without any regard

regard to *motives*. The rhetorician is solicitous to effect some particular purpose, and calls in the aid of reason merely as an auxiliary. He attempts to influence the will by reasoning with the *affections*; knowing that if they be gained over to the party espoused, the *will* is ready to follow. He therefore artfully conceals, or slightly passes over every circumstance which is not favourable to his views, brings forward and largely expatiates upon those which are. He suggests motives of pleasure, utility, safety, honour, pity, &c. as the subject admits. He not only pre-supposes the object in view, of the first importance, but he employs every method to implant this conviction in the minds of those whom he endeavours to persuade.

These attempts become most successful, by a close imitation of that train of ideas, and those modes of expression which any particular passion or affection is prone to suggest. If the design be to excite anger and resentment, rhetoric imitates the language of anger. It places the supposed offence in the strongest point of view, and describes it in the most vivid colours. It assiduously collects and expatiates upon every circumstance which contributes to the aggravation of the crime. It is indignant against that spiritless tranquillity which can patiently endure such insults, and attributes reluctance to revenge to mean and cowardly motives. If its object be to excite

terror,

terror, it assembles together every circumstance which has a tendency to alarm with a sense of danger. It stigmatizes courage with the epithet of rashness, and flight is dignified with the title of prudence, &c. If *compassion* be the object, it expatiates upon the wretched state of the sufferer; his fears, his apprehensions, his penitence. It palliates his faults, extols his good qualities; and thus collects in one point of view all his claims to commiseration.

The species of argument, which persons under the influence of passions and strong affections perpetually adopt, is rendered more efficacious by appropriate language. The rhetorician therefore studies and imitates the particular language of each passion, either in its energy, vivacity, or diffuseness. Hence he liberally employs all those tropes and figures of speech, which nature suggests, and art has classified.

Oratory adds to rhetorical compositions the advantages of *elocution*. It adapts the manner of delivery to the nature of the subject and the appropriate language. It takes the characteristic signs of each emotion for its model, as far as it dares to imitate without the imputation of mimickry; it enters into the attitudes, gestures, tones of voice, accents, emphasis, expressions of countenance, inspired by the particular emotion, in such a manner, that not an idea is suffered to lose its proper effect, by any

deficiency

deficiency in kind or degree of energy communicated to it; and thus it enjoys every advantage to be derived from the power of sympathy.

Eloquence, according to the modern ideas of it, appears to be the medium between the impetuosity which oratory admits, and which was highly characteristic of ancient oratory, and the studied artifice of the professed rhetorician. The term is sometimes applied to *composition*, sometimes to *delivery*. When applied to both it comprehends a certain degree of elegance, both of diction and of manner. The want of that energy which approaches to violence, is compensated by pertinency of language, fluency of utterance, and guarded chastity of address. In a word, its excellency consists in a pleasing adaption of language to the subject, and of manner to both. It refuses too close an imitation of the turbid emotions, but it delights in animated description. It seems rather partial to the pathetic. The elegance and graces which it loves, harmonizing most easily and successfully, with the softest and finest feelings of our natures.

The power of oratorial eloquence is almost irresistible. It penetrates into the inmost recesses of the soul. It is able to excite or to calm the passions of men at will; to drive the multitude forwards to acts of madness, or to say to the contending passions,
" Peace,

" Peace, be still." It changes the whole current of our ideas concerning the nature and importance of objects, and of our obligations and advantages respecting them: it rouses from pernicious indolence, and it renders the sentiments and dispositions already formed most influential. In a word, it has made of the human species both angels and monsters. It has animated to the most noble and generous exertions, and it has impelled to deeds of horror!

§ 17. *The Drama.*

The successful dramatic Writer catches the ideas and imitates the language of every passion, emotion, and affection, in their different stages and degrees. His professed object is to suppose a diversity of characters, and to support them with a correspondent train of ideas; to inspire them with predilections and aversions, or call forth particular passions and affections, according to the situations in which he has placed them. His hopes of success depend upon the closeness of the imitation; and success itself consists in being able to interest the heart, by exciting affections and emotions similar to those which would be felt by the reader or spectator, were he

an

an immediate witneſs to ſimilar ſcenes in real life.

The complete *Actor* poſſeſſes the happy talent of expreſſing, by manner, the ſtate of mind repreſented by his author. He adopts what modern orators reject; he attempts to give force to pertinent ideas and language by imitative tones, geſtures, and countenance. Theſe he varies according to the verſatile ſtate of thoſe who are toſſed upon the billows of paſſion, agitated by ſome contending emotions, or under the more permanent influence of particular affections.

In theatrical exhibitions there is a conſpiracy to delude the imagination; and all the powers of ſympathy are called forth to produce the effect. By appropriate dreſſes the perſons of the actors are loſt in the characters they aſſume; and correſpondent ſcenery points out the very ſpot of action. The ſpectator leaves every idea of real life at the door of entrance, and voluntarily yields himſelf up to the pleaſing deluſion. He finds himſelf in a new world. He is tranſported in an inſtant into diſtant regions and remote ages, and feels in fiction all the force of truth. He laughs at mimic folly, ſincerely weeps at artificial miſery, is inſpired with horror and indignation at imaginary baſeneſs, and is in an ecſtaſy of joy at counterfeit happineſs!

§ 18.

§ 18. *Pre-disposing Causes.*

All the above causes which operate so powerfully upon the mind, and impress it with such a diversity or contrariety of sensations, have still a degree of uniformity in their mode of action. We may still suppose that the same individual, placed under their immediate influence, would always entertain similar ideas, and receive similar impressions. But this is not always the case. Certain circumstances create such a *pre-disposition* within us, that we shall at different seasons be very differently affected by the same object, both respecting the *kind* of passion or affection excited, and the degree of power it may exercise over us: and they constitute that state of mind, which we frequently describe by being *in the humour*, or *not in the humour*. The circumstances to which we now refer, exert their primary effect upon the corporeal or nervous system, render that more susceptible of impressions at one time than another, dispose it to be very differently affected by the same objects; and through its channel, to affect the state of our minds concerning them.

These observations relate to the power of what the medical world has termed the *non-naturals*, which

which exert as great an influence over the difpofitions of the mind, as they are productive of falutary or morbid pre-difpofitions refpecting the body. All thofe circumftances, for example, which are calculated to invigorate the frame, and roufe it from a ftate of indolence and inactivity, neceffarily communicate a correfpondent vigour to the mind, by which it becomes more adapted to receive impreffions of a certain clafs, and to be more powerfully influenced by particular circumftances and qualities in objects, than at the preceding period. Such are the manifeft effects of refrefhing fleep to fatigued and exhaufted natures,—of invigorating viands,— of cheerful weather, &c. Whatever produces an uneafy fenfation in the corporeal fyftem, is apt to render the mind peevifh and fretful, and difpofe it to be more powerfully affected than ufual, by incidents of a difagreeable nature; fuch as loffes, difappointments, the improper conduct of others, &c. It has been frequently noticed by practitioners, that patients are much more fretful and *impatient* in a ftate of convalefcence, than they were during the feverer periods of their difeafe. Their returning powers of fenfation, make them feel the ftate of the difordered frame more minutely than during the oppreffive ftate of the difeafe; and their comfortlefs fenfation communicates an unufual fretfulnefs to the temper. Again, thofe things which heat
and

and irritate to a considerable degree, foster all turbulent and irritable passions; while those which diffuse a pleasing sensation over the system, dispose to benevolence and good-will. It is a maxim with some, in modern days, never to ask a favour of an epicure, till after his meals; and the Ancients were not unacquainted with the *mollia tempora fandi.* Whatever chills and debilitates, disposes to timidity; and local situations which are retired and gloomy, are most conducive to melancholy impressions. Indeed so dependent is the state of the mind upon that of the body, that nothing can produce a considerable change in the latter, without exciting pre-dispositions somewhat analogous in the former. The food which recruits the exhausted powers of animal nature, exhilarates and invigorates the *mind*: the excess which burdens the body, *benumbs* the powers of the *soul*. The painful and comfortless sensations produced by flatulencies and indigestions in hypocondriac temperaments, have sometimes produced, and sometimes been mistaken for an anxious state of mind; and the medicines which relieve the one, will administer comfort to the other. The sensations of hunger, cold, fatigue, &c. being disagreeable in themselves, induce a painful restlessness in the disposition, and great petulance of temper. The state of the atmosphere, peculiarities of climate, seasons of the year have their mental influence; they dispose to a cheerful vivacity or gloominess of difposition, induce a languor or invigorate the mental powers. The influence of narcotics upon the mind is univerfally noticed. The exhilarating effects of opiates, the extravagant wildnefs, the pleafing delirium with which they affect the brain, the Elyfian pleafures they fometimes communicate to the imagination, and the confequent torpor and debility diffufed over the whole fyftem, have been frequently noticed. Under their ftimulating influence, man has fhewn himfelf equal to undertakings which it was apparent madnefs to attempt; and the fubfequent depreffion has marked him for a coward. The effects of fpirituous and fermented liquors are no lefs obvious, as every one has too frequent an occafion to remark. Thefe effects are obferved to vary according to the quality of the liquor, the previous ftate of the fubject's mind, or the temperament of his body. Some kinds of potations have a tendency to induce a kind of pleafing ftupefaction; fo that if they do not infpire new ideas, they feem to render the Sot perfectly contented with the few he poffeffes. Thefe are the frequent effects of malt liquors, and the ingredients mixed with them. While other liquors, as the fparkling champaine, exhilarate the fpirits to an unufual degree, and promote a flow of lively and witty ideas. Tempers naturally warm and impetuous are generally very litigious and

quarrelfome

quarrelsome in their cups. Others are rendered quarrelsome in a state of intoxication, contrary to their usual dispositions, through the disagreeable irritation diffused over the system, by the unusual stimulus. Some persons, on the other hand, who are surrounded with distracting cares, or oppressed with extreme poverty, having, for the instant, drowned thought and reflection in the bewitching draught, which operates like the waters of *Lethe*, they obtain a temporary release from their mental sufferings, and enjoy an extraordinary and frantic flow of spirits in the oblivion of their misery.

Instances similar to the above are infinitely numerous; but these are sufficient to illustrate the fact, that many circumstances, by primarily affecting the body, produce a correspondent change upon the mind; strengthen many of its affections, and predispose to passions and emotions, by which it would not otherwise have been affected. It may be remarked, in general, that the sensibility of the system, or susceptibility of impression, when greatly increased by intoxication or any other cause, will render the same individual, amorous, or generous, or courageous, or passionate and quarrelsome, according as occasions and incidents, favourable to one or other of these affections and emotions, may present themselves.

Thus

Thus have we enumerated the principal caufes, exerting a powerful influence over the affections; which occafion that great diverfity obfervable in the human fpecies, endowed with fimilar capacities, and apparently placed in fimilar fituations: caufes, by the influence of which, one clafs of rational beings differs fo effentially from another equally rational; individuals from individuals in each clafs, and individuals fo frequently from themfelves.

Our remarks have been extended far beyond the limits propofed: but we have been imperceptibly carried forwards both by the fingularity and importance of the fubject; which would require volumes to do it juftice, and which volumes could fcarcely exhauft.

CHAP. III.

Particular Effects resulting from the Operation of the Passions and Affections, considered.

IN every part of our Analytical Inquiries, the powerful influence of the passions and stronger affections upon the whole system has been manifested. The sudden changes made in the state of the mind respecting particular objects, and the effects as instantaneously communicated to the corporeal frame, according to the nature and force of the impression, have been repeatedly considered. We have also remarked, that as the exciting causes are of very different and opposite natures, they possess various degrees of merit and demerit; and that some of them being of a pleasant, others of an unpleasant nature, they excite correspondent sensations within us, as long as we remain under their immediate influence. These peculiarities are productive of certain effects and characteristic states, different from the primary object of the paffion, although they are fo intimately connected with it. Such effects may be placed under the following heads. The *phyfical*, or medical influence of the paffions; their *metaphyfical*, or influence upon the train of our ideas, correfpondent language, &c.; their *moral*, or influence upon character and happinefs. Thefe remain to be briefly confidered.

SECTION I.

Medical Influence of the Paffions.

IF we advert to the ftrong impreffion made by every violent emotion upon the corporeal fyftem, we fhall not be furprifed that the fudden and powerful changes produced fhould, under certain circumftances, exert a medical influence, in common with many other caufes that act powerfully upon the body. Accordingly have the paffions and affections of the mind uniformly had a place given them among the *non-naturals*, as they are termed,

or

or those incidental causes, which may occasionally induce either a salutary or morbid effect upon the body; such as air, exercise, rest, watchings, medicaments, food, heat, cold, &c.

To enter minutely into this subject, to enumerate the various facts, upon which our observations and assertions are founded, to advance and defend any particular theory, would be totally foreign from the nature and design of this treatise, and become tedious to the class of Readers, for whom it is principally designed. Yet some observations upon the influence of the passions in the medical department, necessarily belong to a general history of the passions.

In what manner salutary or pernicious effects are produced by the instrumentality of the passions, it is not agreed. Without adopting any particular hypothesis, it will be sufficient for our purpose to remark, that the physicians of the present day generally ascribe the primary changes produced, to their influence upon the nervous power or grand principle of vitality, by which animated bodies are rendered susceptible of an infinite variety of impressions. In consequence of this influence, either the system in general, or some particular organ, is made to deviate from the exercise of those functions, on which health depends; or is restored to its pristine office, after such deviations have taken place.

Not to inquire farther into the laws of phyfiology and pathology, I fhall only add, that fuch bodies, or fuch circumftances as are able to effectuate any important changes, produce thefe effects,—either by temperating every inordinate and irregular action,—by infufing a falutary vigour in oppofition to languor and inactivity,—by exciting to fome excefs through the power of their ftimulus,—by inducing a temporary torpor,—or permanently debilitating the frame. Properties thefe, which perfectly correfpond with effects produced by the different paffions and affections of the mind: fome of which manifeftly elevate and invigorate the fyftem,—others greatly deprefs,—fome of them violently irritate,— others induce a torpid languor,—and others an incurable *atonia*. A few inftances will illuftrate thefe remarks.

But as both deviation and reftoration refer to fome ftandard, we muft firft fuggeft that the lively, yet temperate action of the vital influence through every part of the fyftem, conftitutes the perfection of health. The Mind, undifturbed by any violent emotions, agitations, or depreffions of a corporeal nature, is able to exercife its nobleft powers with a tranquil vigour. The Body continues in the regular difcharge of its proper functions, without the leaft fenfation of difficulty and embarraffment. Refpiration is free and eafy, neither requiring confcious

ous exertion, nor even a thought. The action of the heart and arteries, with the confequent circulation of the blood, are regular and placid, neither too rapid nor too indolent, neither laboured nor oppreffed. Perfpiration is neither checked nor exceffive. Aliments are fought with appetite, enjoyed with a relifh, and digefted with facility. Every fecretion and excretion is duly performed. The body is perfectly free from pain, oppreffion, hebetude, and every fpecies of uneafinefs; and a certain vivacity and vigour, not to be defcribed, reign through the fyftem.

Hope.

The effects of that cordial, *Hope*, are peculiarly favourable to this envied ftate. In its more temperate exercife, it communicates a mild, but delectable fenfation to the heart. It elevates and invigorates both mind and body. Its grateful ftimulus produces a pleafing and falutary flow of the animal fpirits, and diffufes a temperate vivacity over the fyftem, directing a due degree of energy to every part. In fhort, it is the only paffion or affection, which unites moderation with vigour, checks every violent

violent impetus, and removes every species of morbid languor.

By comparing the effects peculiar to the passion of hope, with the above description of perfect health, the closest analogy will immediately become obvious. Its characteristic is to produce a salutary medium, between every excess and defect of operation, in every function. Consequently it has a tendency to calm the troubled action of the vessels, to check and soothe the violent and irregular impetus of the nervous system, and to administer a beneficial stimulus to the oppressed and debilitated powers of nature. Hence it has been the constant practice of physicians, to support the hopes of their patients in the most alarming diseases, of almost every description. But it is peculiarly beneficial in those disorders which proceed from fear, sorrow, and every species of anxiety, or which occasion a great prostration of strength, and dejection of spirits. In intermittent and pestilential fevers, various chronic complaints, the most efficacious remedies have proved inert, if administered to persons destitute of hope; while an unmeaning farrago which could scarcely be deemed innocent, taken with a confidence of success, have exceeded in their efficacy the utmost efforts of the most skilful practitioner.

Hope therefore demands a place among the medicaments

dicaments that are the mildeſt and moſt grateful in their operation, and exhilarating in their effects.

Joy.

The medicinal influence of *Joy* is very ſimilar to that of hope. But in its general effect, it is a more powerful ſtimulant. Joy diffuſes a much greater vivacity over the whole ſyſtem. It quickens the circulation of the blood, and, in its firſt impulſe, it frequently excites violent palpitations of the heart. It renders the eyes peculiarly lively and animated, and ſometimes, when the mind has been previouſly in a ſtate of anxious fear, it ſtimulates the lachrymal gland to the ſecretion of tears, accompanied with redneſs, and a ſenſation of warmth in the countenance. Both mind and body become ſo alert, that they cannot refrain from ſome lively manifeſtation of feeling, either by loud acclamations, or extravagant geſtures.

All that has been ſaid of hope is applicable to this paſſion, under its more moderate influence. But as it is in general a much more powerful ſtimulus, in many caſes it is ſtill more efficacious. In all thoſe diſeaſes where the powers of nature are particularly oppreſſed and impeded, it is a potent remedy.

dy. In lenchophlegmatic habits, where languid circulation, hebetude, chilness, &c. are prevalent, the grateful cordial of joy, acts like a charm. Pervading the whole system, it instantaneously produces universal vigour, imparts vivacity to the most indolent, and paints the most pallid cheek with the glow of health. We are also assured that by its penetrating, exciting, and exhilarating power, it has cured paralytics, and restored to their senses those who had been rendered insane, through the excess of melancholy.

But as every thing possessing great energy may in some circumstances prove injurious, either by its own excess, or by co-operating with other causes, thus have the transports of joy, though in their nature so salutary, sometimes induced diseases, and sometimes rendered them more severe. They have increased the paroxysms of acute fevers, aggravated inflammatory symptoms, and in plethoric habits, have been productive of apoplexies. Immoderate and ungovernable transports of joy, have sometimes induced *epilepsies, catalepsies, paralysis*, and that class of maladies which arise from too great agitation of mind in delicate and susceptible frames.

There are many instances upon record, of sudden death having been occasioned by the hasty communication of very joyful tidings. Like a stroke of electricity, indiscreetly directed, the violent percussion cuffion has probably produced a paralyfis of the heart, by the excefs of its ftimulus. Thefe incidents are moft likely to take place in fubjects who were, at the inftant, deeply oppreffed with the oppofite paffions of fear and anxiety; by which the natural and falutary action of the heart and arteries was greatly impeded. This, of confequence, will create a refiftance to the impulfe, and render it more liable to deftroy the tone of that fenfible organ. In moft of the inftances recorded, the perfons who have fallen a facrifice to the excefs of joy were in this particular fituation; nor was there an opportunity given to foften the agony of fear by a cautious manner of communicating the tidings. (See Note *T*.)

Cheerfulnefs, hilarity, and *focial mirth,* are in their effects fo fimilar to hope and moderate joy, that their medical powers may be collected from what has been obferved concerning thefe. Operating alfo by the laws of focial fympathy, they promote a delectable flow of fpirits, which affords a temporary relief from the oppreffive and pernicious influence of cares and folicitudes, refrefhes and exhilarates after the fatigues of labour either corporeal or mental; and thus by renovating the man, infpires him with frefh vigour, to difcharge the arduous duties which his ftation in life may require.

Love.

Love.

Love has been confidered in the former part of this Treatife, both as an affection and a paffion. As an affection, in which complacency and good-will are the principal ingredients, it places the corporeal frame in a ftate of pleafing tranquillity; in the falutary medium between languor and inertnefs on the one fide, or of violent incitement on the other. Its influence therefore is too mild to be at any time prejudicial; and it is calculated to moderate the effects that each extreme is capable of producing. General benevolence has alfo a fimilar tendency. It efcapes the rude effects of all the irritating paffions, and diffufes a falutary placidnefs over the whole fyftem.

Love between the fexes, commencing with predilection and ftealing into warm perfonal attachment, when reciprocal and unalloyed by adventitious caufes, infpires the mind with delight, connected with a fatisfaction unknown to other delights. It is the reward of perfevering hope, and correfponds with that pleafing paffion in its beneficent effects on the corporeal fyftem. It is fo inimical to the rougher paffions and emotions, that they cannot poffibly

fubfift

subsist together. The blandishments of love have tamed the most ferocious natures, and calmed the most turbulent spirits. The passion rising to desire acts as a powerful stimulant; gives fresh energy to the system, diffusing a general warmth, and increasing the sensibility of the frame.

As sexual attachment is one of the strongest propensities of animal nature, and peculiarly exposed, in civil society, to numberless contrarieties, it frequently becomes the source of many other affections and emotions, such as hope, fear, joy, sorrow, anger, envy, jealousy, &c.

Such various effects of love according to their complexities and degrees, must, it is self-apparent, vary their pathological and therapeutic influence on the animal œconomy; and medical writers have accordingly given us numerous instances both of its salutary and pernicious powers. Its brisk incitements, in cold and torpid temperaments, have removed the various indispositions to which such temperaments are exposed. It has fortified the body against dangers, difficulties, and hardships, that appeared superior to human force. It has cured intermittents; acting, it is probable, like invigorating cordials administered before the access of the cold fit, by which its return is prevented, and the habit destroyed, by which this disease is particularly governed. In its violent and impetuous energies,

it

it has excited inflammatory fevers, and the whole train of evils proceeding from the excefs of ftimulus, which it will be needlefs to enumerate. It has alfo, in confequence of that contrariety of paffions to which it is fubject, occafioned the moft dangerous and obftinate maladies, hyfterics, epilepfies, hectic fevers, the rage of madnefs, or the ftill more pitiable ftate of confirmed and wafting melancholy.

Anger.

The fymptoms indicating a violent paroxyfm of *Anger*, as ftrongly indicate the exceffive perturbation it occafions throughout the fyftem. The fire flafhing in the eyes, the rednefs of countenance, the ftrong and agitated pulfe, the wonderful increafe of mufcular ftrength for the inftant, manifeft that all the powers of nature are roufed to the moft violent exertions. Anger acts as a ftimulus of the moft potent kind, upon the mufcular, vafcular, and nervous fyftems. It is not furprifing therefore that its pathological effects fhould be numerous and alarming. Inflammatory and bilious fevers, hæmorrhages, apoplexies, inflammation of the brain, mania, have arifen from the increafed impetuofity it has given to the vafcular fyftem; as alfo fudden death,

death, either from ruptured veffels, or the excefs of its ftimulating power upon the vital organs; particularly in plethoric and fanguineous temperaments. Palfies, epilepfies, aphonia, or lofs of voice, diarrhœas, involution of the inteftines, and thofe difeafes which may be attributed to the exceffive perturbation of the nervous fyftem, and alfo to exhaufted ftrength, have too frequently fucceeded to its tremendous exertions. In fhort, as there is no paffion fo turbulent, fo is there none fo immediately dangerous as exceffive anger.

Yet even this paffion has been occafionally beneficial. As there are cafes in which arfenic itfelf exerts a medicinal virtue, thus are we affured by writers of veracity, that there are inftances in which the paffion of anger, by giving unufual energy to the fyftem, has cured difeafes which demanded a potent ftimulus. We are told that it has cured agues, reftored fpeech to the dumb, and for feveral days arrefted the cold hand of death; that its ftimulating power has, like the electric fhock, proved a remedy in rheumatic affections, palfies, and various chronic complaints.

Fortitude.

The medical virtues of *Fortitude* are univerfally admitted. The determined refolution of the mind, communicates a correspondent energy to the body. Cheery hope is, in these cases, a powerful auxiliary. Fortitude is not only a preservative against the pathological effects of fear and grief, but it renders the body less subject to the morbid influence of putrid and contagious diseases. It enables the warrior to support hardships and fatigues which would otherwise prove fatal to him. In the hour of conflict, the hopes of conquest, the power of social sympathy, a spirit of emulation, and enkindled anger against the foe, impel to achievements, to which the powers of nature would be unequal, at any other period.

Sorrow.

Whoever attends to the pathological effects of *Sorrow*, and marks its different stages;—the stupefaction and horror with which the sufferer is sometimes seized, upon the sudden communication of evil tidings;—the agitations that immediately succeed, introducing subsequent languor and debility;—and the deep melancholy into which the mind subsides, after the first conflicts are passed, will be prepared to credit the narrations, that excessive sorrow has been the cause of sudden deaths, of confirmed melancholy, loss of memory, imbecility of mind, of nervous fevers, of hypochondriac complaints;—that it renders the body peculiarly susceptible

tible of contagious diforders;—and that the lofs of appetite, perpetual watchfulnefs, confirmed apathy to every thing focial and exhilarating, the attention immutably fixed upon the caufe of its diftrefs, &c. have rapidly introduced the moft terrible difeafes, and haftened the diffolution of the fufferer.

Nor does any cafe prefent itfelf, in which the paffion of forrow, or the affection of grief, have produced falutary effects, unlefs by their being calculated to moderate the tranfports of anger; and thus they may have prevented or removed the pathological fymptoms, of which fuch tranfports are productive.

Fear.

The changes inftantly induced upon the body by abject *Fear*; the univerfal rigour, the contracted and pallid countenance, the deep funk eye, the quivering lip, the chilnefs, torpor, proftration of ftrength, infufferable anxiety about the region of the heart, &c. are fo perfectly analogous to the morbid influence of exceffive cold, to the fymptoms of typhus fevers, and the firft ftage of intermittents, that no one can doubt of the pernicious influence of this paffion, in pre-difpofing the body to the like difeafes, and in aggravating their fymptoms. It is peculiarly dangerous in every species of contagion. It has instantaneously changed the complexion of wounds, and rendered them fatal. It has occasioned gangrenes, indurations of the glands, epilepsies, the suppression of natural or beneficial secretions. It has induced a permanent stupor on the brain; and the first horrors of the imagination have, in some cases, made too deep an impression to be effaced, by the most favourable change of circumstances. We have seen that joy itself, though in its nature so pleasing, and in its general effect so salutary, has proved the cause of sudden death; it is therefore not difficult to admit that the agonizing effects of *this* dreadful passion, may be able to paralyze the grand organ of circulation, and like some pestilential diseases, instantaneously induce the torpor of death.

So pernicious are the natural and characteristic effects of fear! Yet in that state of body where a sedative power is requisite, and where a considerable degree of torpor has a tendency to check too great incitement, even this passion may become beneficial. Thus it has been known to relieve excruciating fits of the gout, to have rendered maniacs calm and composed, and in some cases it has restored them to the regular use of their faculties. The effects of fear, in affording temporary relief in the tooth-ach are universally known; acting as

some

some systematics express themselves, by its sedative power, by which an inflammatory tension is appeased; or as others, by inducing a torpor on the nerves, and thus rendering them insensible to pain.

Terror, which is the agitation of fear, sometimes produces effects upon the body common to agitation, simply. In somes cases it rouses the energy of the system to an unusual degree, and in others, it produces the irregular and convulsive action of the muscular system. Hence it is said to have *caused*, in some instances, and in others, to have *cured* the attacks of capalepsies, epilepsies, and other spasmodic disorders. We read of its having cured tertian fevers induced by fear;—restored speech to the dumb, and motion to paralytic limbs;—that by agitating the vascular system, it has been productive of hæmorrhages;—and also that it has been successful in dropsical habits. Perhaps the contractile power of fear, united with the agitations of terror, have both constricted and stimulated the relaxed and indolent absorbents, and enabled them to renew their office. The passion of terror has frequently excited languid hypochondriacs, to exertions they had deemed impossible; and all their former maladies have been obliterated by their apprehensions of impending danger.

Shame.

Shame is sometimes connected with fear, sometimes with terror; and consequently it will, in particular instances, manifest symptoms belonging to these emotions. But young persons of great sensibility, who are delicately susceptible of honour or disgrace, are apt to blush at every trifle, without violent paroxysms either of fear or of terror. In these cases, where the effects of shame are the least complicated, though they be strong, they are momentary. The heart is certainly agitated, sometimes with pleasure, sometimes with pain; but as the suffusion chiefly manifests itself in the face, and in the smaller vessels spread over the neck and breast, the singular effects of shame cannot be attributed solely to the sudden impetus given to the heart. The passion itself seems to have an influence principally local; which we know to be the case with some other stimulants. The modest blush, unmixed with guilt or fear, seems to be inert, respecting medical effects. Nor are there any instances of its having been decidedly beneficial or injurious. It seems most calculated to increase cutaneous inflammations; but facts are wanting to confirm this idea.

Attention of Mind.

Habitual attention of mind to any particular object, should it be of a pleasing nature and proceed from a passionate fondness for that object, has proved pernicious to the constitution. The fatigue of the brain has indicated itself by *cephalalgias*, giddiness, &c.—the animal spirits have been exhausted;—the body has been rendered insensible to its accustomed stimuli;—weariness, and universal lassitude, prostration of strength, loss of appetite, indigestions, flatulencies, &c. have ensued;—and the corporeal system has been rendered very susceptible of various morbid impressions. Yet salutary effects have issued from an eager attention to things novel, interesting, and mysterious. It has thus proved efficacious in diseases subjected to periodical returns. It has prevented hysteric and epileptic fits, and charmed away agues. By connecting the pernicious effects of habitual attention to the same object, with those accompanying fear, anxiety, sorrow, it is easy to perceive that the union of both must be peculiarly pernicious;—that when the whole attention is employed upon things mournful, irritating, or calculated to inspire painful apprehenfions,—when it is abforbed by corroding cares and anxious fears,—when it is the prey of chagrin and difappointment, the body may be expected to fall a fpeedy victim to the combined influence of fuch deadly poifons.

Imagination.

The power of *Imagination* in inducing and removing difeafes, has been generally acknowledged. But this imagination could only produce its effects by the ftrong affections which accompany it; otherwife it would be as inert as the moft abftract idea. Thefe affections are indicated in the various paffions and emotions we have been contemplating. It is moreover worthy of notice, that in every powerful exertion of the imagination, fome change takes place in the body correfpondent with its nature. In a keen appetite, upon the thoughts of fome favourite viand, the falivary glands are ftimulated to a fecretion of faliva, as preparatory to deglutition. We feel ourfelves collected, firm, elevated, upon the lively reprefentation of the firm, heroic, dignified conduct of another. The blood thrills in our veins, and the fkin corrugates at the defcription of any

any thing peculiarly horrible: and under the strong impression of fictitious danger, the attitude of our bodies attempts to evade it! Full confidence in the mystic power of another, places the whole system in a situation most favourable to the effects, which the object of his confidence undertakes to produce. This will explain much of what is genuine in the pretensions of magnetizers; and the exaggerating dispositions of both operator and patient, will contribute to explain the rest. (See Note *U*.)

The above sketch, concise and imperfect as it is, will be sufficient to evince, that the passions and emotions have a medical influence upon the body: and that each of them has its own characteristic influence in its general mode of acting, although various and opposite effects may sometimes be produced by incidental circumstances. This however is precisely the case with the most esteemed medicaments; with every thing that is deemed noxious or beneficial in the mineral, vegetable, and animal kingdoms; and with every part of nature that possesses the power of acting upon the human frame.

In this investigation the Author has simply endeavoured to be the historian of facts, without intending to pay any deference to theory. But as medical language has chiefly been formed by different theories, which have most rapidly succeeded to each other, it is difficult to use terms that do not acknowledge some system or other for their parent; or to express ideas, without seeming to have a predilection for one hypothesis in preference to others, where the sole object is to establish indisputable facts. (See Note *W*.)

SECTION II.

Influence of the Passions on Thoughts and Language.

IT has been remarked in our Analysis, that whenever any subject presents itself to the mind, with sufficient force to excite a passion, or very strong affection, all the powers of the imagination become immediately active. The whole soul is engaged upon its object, and the whole train of ideas is turned into a channel correspondent with the view we entertain of that. The mind, with wonderful facility, collects together whatever has been laid up in the storehouse of the memory, or can be combined by the force of the imagination. Every thing alien is totally excluded; and it is in vain that others who are free from the impulse, attempt to suggest ideas of a contrary tendency. Reason becomes impotent, nor can the attention be directed from such circumstances as are intimately connected with the exciting cause; and these are magnified and aggravated to the utmost extent. Subjects of joy appear at the instant to be the harbingers of essential and permanent bliss: the evils we fear, the injuries we suffer, the losses we sustain, seem to be the greatest that could possibly have been endured.

This state of mind not only manifests itself by gestures, looks, and tones correspondent with the nature of the passion; but it has a characteristic influence upon the language and expressions employed to *give vent* to the passion, as it is emphatically termed.

Upon the first impulse, the thoughts are tumultuous and confused. A thousand half formed suggestions and apprehensions crowd in upon us in rapid or disorderly succession!

Whoever contemplates the effects of the passions

at this moment, will difcover their perfect correfpondence with the nature of thofe introductory emotions of *furprife, wonder,* and *aftonifhment,* defcribed in the analytical part of this Treatife. It is manifeftly through their influence that the mind is thus confufed, and that every idea is embarraffment and conjecture. The wonder and amazement, fo precipitately excited, are accompanied by ftrong, abrupt, and indefinite language. The firft impulfe of furprife deprives the fubject of the power of utterance; and the firft exertions of this returning power confift in loud exclamations, adapted both to the nature of the emotion itfelf, and to its confufion and wonder relative to the object.

As all thefe introductory emotions are obvioufly founded on the weaknefs, ignorance, and confcious inferiority of our natures, thus do they prompt to language which confeffes an humiliated ftate. Powers above us are, as it were, inftinctively addreffed, either with exclamations of gratitude, of appeal, imprecation, or invocation of aid! Incredulity itfelf becomes moft credulous; will thank the heavens for caufes of exceffive joy,—call aloud upon higher Beings for help in the moment of danger,—mourn its *deftiny*,—or curfe its *ftars* in the hour of vexation and difappointment! Thofe who in a tranquil ftate of mind, ridicule the idea of future retribution, often become the moft extravagant in their

benedictions

benedictions or imprecations at the instant of tumultuous passion.

After the first impulse of passion, we begin to advert to the particular state in which the exciting cause has placed us. As a lively imagination is always disposed to magnify; we deem ourselves for the instant, the most *happy* or the most *wretched* of mortals; and a new train of thoughts is suggested to prove or illustrate the supposition.

Thus as the *passion* approaches somewhat nearer to an *affection*, the mind recovers in some degree its power over itself; yet it is still carried forwards by the torrent of ideas, which this novel situation has inspired, and which never would have been suggested, with such copiousness and energy, in a more tranquil state. As it still continues to feel strongly, so is it eager to do justice to its feelings, by the strength, pertinency, and impetuosity of its language. Common terms are too cold, or too limitted to do justice to the energy of thought; and it perceives no exaggeration in expressions the most exaggerated! All nature is ransacked for points of resemblance, to set forth the novel situation in the strongest colours. Impetuosity equally despises precision or detail. It eagerly seizes upon tropes and figures the most concise, and the most suited to its new conceptions!

All nature is full of analogy! Every thing that exists

exists possesses certain qualities or properties, which are not so peculiar to the individual, as to be destitute of some resemblance to other things that may be, in various respects, essentially different: and many of these properties are possessed in an extraordinary degree, by particular objects. To these the mind rapidly adverts as descriptive of the peculiarities of its own situation; and as in the warmth of our sensations we are disposed to exaggerate every thing, thus are we disposed to make quick transitions from one property to another, seated in the object referred to, by which a peculiar colouring or cast of character, is given to the subject which interests us, and the desired energy is imparted to our feelings concerning it: to this, associated ideas and affections lend a very considerable aid. Thus it is that we not only catch the precise point of resemblance, but we instantaneously elevate or debase a subject, hold it forth to admiration or contempt, render it respectable or ridiculous, according to the sources from whence our allusions are borrowed.

When passions and emotions give place to more permanent affections, language becomes less vehement and more diffuse. Under the influence of a particular affection, the mind loves to expand itself upon the circumstances which gave it existence, and

and to dwell upon such minutiæ as have a tendency to feed its flame. Thus, under the influence of resentment, every species of aggravation is deliberately dwelt upon; every thing in the conduct of the aggressor that may augment his culpability, and every part of our own demeanour, are brought forwards to manifest the greatness of the offence, and how little we deserved it. In a state of fearful apprehension, every possibility of danger is placed before us with all its horrors;—every difficulty is magnified;—and in every remedy or plan of security proposed, busy apprehension suggests reasons to evince that it will be ineffectual. In sorrow we delight to expatiate upon the excellent qualities of the particular object, the pleasures and advantages of which we are now deprived; and the imagination enumerates all the evils that will probably ensue. Under the influence of love, the mind dwells upon the accomplishments which have inspired the affection, recalls the scenes of pleasure past, anticipates those which are to come; and in the expression of these feelings, or in the acknowledgment of this influence, it purposely prolongs the phraseology, which best prolongs the fascinating idea.

The address of Eve to her consort, in a state where the best affections alone could be indulged, is so beautiful an illustration of this subject, that a

transcript

transcript of the whole paffage cannot appear tedious.

> With thee converfing I forget all time;
> All feafons and their change, all pleafe alike.
> Sweet is the breath of morn, her rifing fweet,
> With charm of earlieft birds; pleafant the fun,
> When firft on this delightful land he fpreads
> His orient beams, on herb, tree, fruit, and flower,
> Glift'ring with dew: fragrant the fertile earth
> After foft fhowers; and fweet the coming on
> Of grateful evening mild; then filent night,
> With this her folemn bird, and this fair moon,
> And thefe the gems of heav'n her ftarry train:
> But neither breath of morn, when fhe afcends
> With charms of earlieft birds; nor rifing fun
> On this delightful land; nor herb, fruit, flower,
> Glift'ring with dew; nor fragrance after fhowers;
> Nor grateful evening mild; nor filent night,
> With this her folemn bird, nor walk by noon,
> Or glittering ftar-light, without thee is fweet.
>
> PARADISE LOST. B. IV. L. 639.

It is obfervable, that when a paffion or ftrong affection is not fuddenly raifed, but is produced by deliberate meditation upon the fubject, the procefs is oppofite to the preceding. From indifference, the mind begins to conceive an affection of one kind or other; and according to the difcovered nature, magnitude, or importance of the object, it may gradually *work itfelf up*, as the phrafe is, into paffion passion and ecstasy. In such cases, the train of thoughts will flow with increased velocity and force, according to the increased interest taken in the subject. Sterility of sentiment and of language is succeeded by a rapid flow of each. Pertinent thoughts and copious expression immediately present themselves, which the deepest study, and all the powers of recollection would not have been able to produce: they are only to be inspired by the affections. In this state of mind, the language gradually changes its tone; from the cool didactic style, it rises into the animated and energetic; though it seldom, if ever indicates the embarrassment and confusion of thought, which are the offspring of wonder and surprise. Excess of animation will indeed sometimes check utterance, and the orator will feel a deficiency of language to do justice to the numerous ideas which crowd in upon the mind. See many excellent observations on this subject in Elements of Criticism, Vol. II. *Comparisons: Figures.*

If the above remarks be admitted as pertinent, they will point out the difference betwixt the language of the passions and affections, and that of cool dispassionate reason. The one is the language of *feeling*, which attempts to enforce some interesting idea; the other, that of *discrimination*, which carefully

carefully marks the diſtinctions and differences which ſubſiſt in things apparently analogous. The one ſubſtitutes ſtrong impreſſions for realities, and miſtakes exaggerations for accurate ſtatements: the other analyzes and ſeparates truth from error, facts from miſrepreſentations. The language of paſſion and of ſtrong affections is always employed in pleading ſome cauſe. Aiming to give to that, the aſcendency over every other conſideration, it rapidly collects and ſets forth in glowing colours every circumſtance favourable to its object, regardleſs of whatever may be advanced in oppoſition: while the language of reaſon is that of a Judge, who compares, balances, and decides according to the force of *evidence*, without being deceived by the force of expreſſion, or ſeduced by the ſympathy of the paſſions.

In theſe characters it is that the diſtinction between rhetoric and logic indicates itſelf. The former attempts to perſuade; it is the province of the latter to convince. This employs itſelf in demonſtrations reſpecting the truth and nature of things; the other excites to feel and act according to the opinion entertained of the good or bad properties which they poſſeſs, and are capable of exerting.

In our deſcription of the different Paſſions and Affections, it was requiſite to point out thoſe external

ternal signs which were the characteristic marks of each; and to note the attitudes, gestures, and expressions of countenance which are most correspondent to the nature of the emotion. We have only to subjoin upon the subject, that when utterance is given to thought, the tone of voice becomes a powerful auxiliary to the train of ideas suggested. Nature has accommodated the mode of utterance to the character of the passion. Thus it has rendered

Joy loud and vociferous, producing strong exclamations mixed with triumphant *Laughter*.

Sorrow communicates a plaintiveness to the voice, best adapted to wailings and lamentations.

Anger is loud and turbulent. The voice rises with the passion, in order to strike terror and silence opposition.

Fear is oppressed and breathless, or screams aloud for help.

Love is soft, soothing, insinuating, and gentle; sometimes assuming the plaintiveness of sorrow, sometimes the vivacity of hope, and the transports of joy.

The other compounds partake of mixed effects. (See Note *X*.)

The minute investigation of the passions in which we have been engaged, presents us with numerous observations

observations of a moral and practical nature. But as the present Treatise is purposely confined to philosophical researches, we shall not enter upon so copious a subject. There are two inquiries, however, which although they have an intimate relation to morals, cannot be refused a place in the philosophical department. They refer to the influence of the passions upon *character*, and upon *happiness*; and with these we shall close the subject.

SECTION III.

Influence of the Passions and Affections on Character.

THE Nature of the Passions and Affections indulged, and of the objects by which they are excited, and the degrees of influence and permanency which they are suffered to exert upon us, constitute the moral characters of men; pointing out either their innocence, their excellencies, or defects.

By Character is generally understood the kind of reputation acquired by the prevalent disposition or temper, which suggests almost every motive, and takes the lead in almost every action: and *moral* character refers to that prevalent temper which relates

lates to moral obligation, respecting either ourselves or others. This disposition consists in the prevalence of *affection*, that is, in the habitual pleasure or displeasure we take in certain modes of thinking and acting; and our *opinion* of the disposition, is regulated by the different degrees of merit or demerit, which in our judgment is annexed to it. Mankind are so far uniform in their opinions, that they universally acknowledge some actions and the affections that produce them, either to be innocent, or to be deserving of various degrees of approbation or censure. They pay due honours to characters, which appear to be formed upon the best of principles, and load the opposite with proportionate disgrace.

The grand distinctions in moral conduct are indicated by the terms *virtue* and *vice*: and the subordinate ones under each, are either not marked, or they are discriminated by appropriate appellations.

The cardinal affections of Love and Hatred, in themselves possess neither merit nor demerit. Founded upon the ideas of good and evil, which may render our existence a blessing or a curse, they are as it were, moulded in the very frame and constitution of all percipient beings. It is therefore neither a duty, nor a possibility to divest ourselves of them. The passions, emotions, and affections which are immediately consequent upon these, or may be deemed simple modifications of them, are also inseparable from our natures, and are both unavoidable and innocent: such as joy, satisfaction, contentment, hope, desire, fear, sorrow, anger, resentment, &c. These being derived from situations and circumstances to which we are perpetually and necessarily exposed, are the natural result of impressions made upon susceptible beings. A virtuous or vicious character therefore depends upon the nature of our choice, and the manner and extent to which those passions and emotions indulged, are in their nature permitted. Thus virtue requires that the affections of love and hatred be properly placed; that real, not imaginary good; real, not imaginary evil be the objects of them. It requires that we proportion the degrees of our affection to the value and importance of objects; that we be neither indifferent to essential worth, nor suffer things trifling and insignificant to engross the best of our affections. Virtue allows the first impulse of anger, where the provocation is great; as insensibility would invite injuries, and give to unreasonable and wicked men a decided superiority over the moderate and just. But virtue forbids anger to exceed the magnitude of the offence: being in every case a species of punishment, if it be excessive, the surplus becomes an injustice. Virtue requires anger to be of short duration, where offences

ces are not permanent; strictly prohibits it from seeking revenge, unconnected with private or public security, and it abhors habitual hatred and malignity. It allows and requires us to cherish the feelings of contempt and indignation, as long as mean and atrocious vices continue; but it absolutely commands us to pardon, where the character and conduct of the offender are changed by repentance and reformation. Virtue stigmatizes with peculiar disgrace the want of those affections which benefits received, and a great superiority of character ought to call forth; such as ingratitude to benefactors, and want of respect for superiors in wisdom and goodness. As we experience that the possession of the good things of life contribute to our happiness, we cannot be insensible to the privation of them: virtue accordingly permits a degree of sorrow and grief correspondent to the nature of our loss; but it forbids the obstinate indulgence of melancholy, as this forgets or destroys the benignant effects of every remaining blessing; and it is of consequence chargeable with both folly and ingratitude. Virtue requires repentance as the medium of restoration to order and to duty; for this purpose it permits remorse, but it never enjoins despair. It allows of fear as far as this excites to caution; and even of terror, when the mind has been surprised by something tremendous; but habitual fear it terms cowardice,

wardice, and to terror perpetually excited by small causes, it gives the appellation of pusillanimity. It approves of the emulation which animates to worthy deeds, or to advancement in every species of excellence; nor does it forbid the ambition which is productive of general good; but it execrates the wretch that wades through seas of blood, and tramples upon the slain, to rise above all those whom its baneful sword has spared. Envy, which is the antipode to benevolence, virtue knows not: and though it admits of jealous alarms upon great occasions, and prompted by strong presumptive evidence, yet it is a stranger to unauthorized suspicions. It permits the moderate desire of wealth, as the means both of comfort and usefulness; but it lays rapaciousness and avarice under the severest interdict. It allows of self-defence, and nature itself inspires with strength and courage for the purpose; but it disdains the use of treacherous means of security, and the acts of cruelty which characterize the barbarian and the coward.

These remarks point out another distinction of the passions and affections, as they relate to the moral character, indicating a scale of comparative merit and demerit. Some are innocent simply, as hope, joy, moderate grief. Some are laudable, as contentment, satisfaction, complacency. Others are

are deemed peculiarly noble. Thus the virtue of benevolence is much more dignified than any of the affections that originate and terminate in *Self*. In the different branches of this virtue there are also degrees of excellence. Warm sympathetic emotions, when they prompt to peculiar exertions, are in higher estimation than the calmer feelings and offices of charity; and Mercy by subduing resentment is justly deemed more transcendent than either. Some feelings are so essential, that to be destitute of them is highly disgraceful; as the want of gratitude. The angry passions, though they may be innocent, yet they stand upon the very brink of demerit, being so proximate to injustice and cruelty. Some affections and dispositions are contemptible, as sordid avarice, envy, malice: these are despised by all who are not under their influence. Ingenuous shame is viewed with approbation, as it indicates a consciousness of defect, united with reverence for opinion. Guilty shame, though not criminal in itself, yet being the detection of criminality, it sometimes exposes the offender to the severest contempt; as when it marks the countenance of a detected hypocrite: sometimes it will excite compassion, and prompt to forgiveness; when, for example, an offence highly disreputable is proved to be a total deviation from the general tenour of conduct. The blush indicates a mind not inured to vice. It sues for compassion, and proves that it is not totally unworthy of it.

Again, in our search after happiness, each particular desire and pursuit is either deemed innocent, or assumes an honourable or ignominious character, according to the nature of the object, the eagerness with which it is followed, and the means employed for its attainment. Some desires are discriminated by particular appellations, that serve to stigmatize, or do honour to the affections; while others, not marking either excellence or culpability, have no terms of discrimination.

Several instances of this nature have been given under the article of Desire, by which it appears that a prevalent love of virtue and detestation of vice have, in every case where personal interest has not perverted the judgment and alienated the affections, taught all mankind, without previous consultation or conspiracy, to invent the concisest mode of testifying approbation or disapprobation, according to the apparent degrees of merit or demerit. Similar to the plan of an universal language, which some have deemed practicable; or to pre-concerted signals, and telegraphic signs, very complex ideas are conveyed by simple terms, which immediately express satire or applause, crown with honour or call forth abhorrence. The numerous occasions which incessantly

cessantly present themselves, of expressing our opinions of human actions, and our eagerness to approve or censure, render us impatient of paraphrase, or circumlocution.

It is also observable that our ideas of character, are invariably formed, according to the habitual tendency of disposition and conduct to become beneficial or pernicious, to promote or to destroy good! Where conduct has no immediate relation to these, it does not call forth animadversion. In proportion as it produces and disseminates good, makes exertions and consents to liberal sacrifices for this purpose, does it meet with our applause and admiration. In proportion as vice diffuses misery, as it is the result of mean and selfish principles, indicated by pre-concerted plans and propensities to sacrifice the felicity of others to our own narrow personal gratifications, it becomes detestable and abhorrent. Hence compassion meets with warmer applause than the simple love of justice, because compassion is an actual participation in the sufferings of another; while justice is only a due solicitude that they shall not suffer any unmerited injury from us. A merciful and forgiving disposition is still more noble, because it generously removes a very powerful impediment, which the offending party himself has raised, against the exercise of our compassion for the distress

distress to which his injustice towards us has exposed him. On the other side, treachery and cruelty are more detestable than common acts of injustice, because the one is a grosser abuse of that confidence without which society cannot subsist; and the other manifests not only inordinate self-love, but the want of that natural affection which is due to every being, substituting the affection of hatred in its place.

It is further manifest from the above remarks, that both virtue and vice are the offspring of passions and affections in themselves innocent. The natural desires and affections implanted in our very make are void of guilt. Respecting these, virtue simply requires a proper choice, innocent pursuits, and moderation in our enjoyments. Vice consists in an improper, or forbidden choice, in the excess or perversion of the natural propensity of our natures. Lawless ambition is the excess of a desire to distinguish ourselves, which, under certain restrictions, is a blameless incentive to useful actions. As every species of debauchery consists in the irregular indulgence of the appetites, in themselves natural and innocent, thus are the most disorderly and malevolent affections the abuse of some affections, which in certain circumstances may be allowable and beneficial. Envy is anger, unjust and pettish, at the good fortune of another, mixed with a very false
idea

idea of our superior deserts. Cruelty is the excess of a severity which in itself may be justifiable; and malice the most inveterate is the cruelty of envy, attempting by words and actions to destroy or diminish the good we cannot participate.

Thus then it appears that character depends upon the prevalent use or abuse of certain propensities or affections of our natures. Those who select and cultivate the most beneficial are the *best* of characters; those, who are habituated to the most injurious, are the *worst*.

SECTION IV.

Influence of the Passions and Affections on Happiness.

THOUGH the desire of good is in reality the efficient cause of every passion, emotion, and affection, yet the immediate effects of each on our sensations are correspondent to its own specific nature. To be under the influence of some, is productive

ductive of temporary well-being; while others are comfortless, irksome, or productive of a great degree of wretchedness.

Love, considered as an affection placed upon a deserving object and recompensed with reciprocal affection, joy, ecstasy, complacency, satisfaction, contentment, lively hope, these are decidedly the sources of present enjoyment. The social affections of benevolence, sympathy, compassion, and mercy, are also other ingredients of happiness from a less selfish and more refined source than the preceding. A steady, uniform disposition manifested by incessant endeavours to promote happiness, is invariably rewarded with a large portion of it. Benevolence places the mind at a remote distance from little jealousies and envyings: it tempers the irritative nature of anger, and teaches compassion to subdue it. Through benevolence, the good enjoyed by another becomes our own, without a robbery or privation. This divine principle harmonizes the mind with every thing around, and feels itself pleasingly connected with every living being. In a word, it generates, communicates, and enjoys happiness. When benevolence manifests itself by sympathy, compassion, and mercy, some portion of uneasiness, it is acknowledged, accompanies the sensation congenial to its nature; but the exercise of of these affections communicates a *pleasing* pain. The degree of uneasiness is more than recompensed by the satisfaction enjoyed from the relief of distress; and even from the consciousness of a disposition to relieve. There is often a luxury in sympathetic sorrow; and every tear shed over distress becomes a pearl of inestimable price. Every species of benevolence possesses the quality which our great dramatic Poet has ascribed to a *merciful* disposition.

> The quality of Mercy's not restrain'd:
> It droppeth as the gentle rain from heaven,
> Upon the land beneath. It is twice blessed;
> It blesses him that *gives*, and him that *takes*.
>
> SHAKESPEAR.

The mildest of the affections that belong to the family of love, diffuse a pleasurable tranquillity over the mind. They constitute the healthy state of the soul, united with a consciousness of this health. The more lively affections invigorate and excite a delectable vivacity; and the impetuous emotions, termed ecstasies and transports, infuse a wild tumultuous pleasure. Moderation leaves the helm; the animal spirits uncontrouled violently agitate the corporeal frame, and confound the mental faculties in a pleasing delirium.

In some of these kindly emotions, circumstances and situations in themselves displeasing are rendered capable of communicating pleasure. Thus in the sudden possession of good conferred by a superior, Gratitude, though it is so closely connected with the idea of our own wants, and the dependency of our state, rises above these natural causes of depressed spirits. The attention is arrested by the good received, and the heart glows with affection towards the benefactor; which is a more pleasing sensation than independency itself could ensure. Thus in the contemplation of the unrivalled excellencies possessed by another, lively enjoyment becomes intimately connected with the deepest sense of inferiority: as in the emotions of admiration, reverence, and awe. Nor is *Humility*, notwithstanding its abject appearance, devoid of dignity. It is accompanied with a strong affection for the excellencies which it laments that it cannot attain: and a conscious wish, to subdue remaining defects, inspires more satisfaction than the self-sufficiency of *arrogance* can boast. Even desire itself, which is an eager longing for gratification,—if it be not intemperate,—if it be united with hope,—if it be not prolonged to the weariness of patience; is cherished with a great degree of pleasure. The expectancy of enjoyment more than counterpoises the pain created by suspense.

Another

Another set of emotions and affections are of the unquiet and irritating class; as the whole family of anger. The exciting objects are unwelcome to the mind which contemplates them, and the sensations they produce are turbulent and painful. It is true, some degree of satisfaction may be inspired by the vivid idea entertained, at the instant, of the justice of our cause, as also by the gratification, or even the resolution to gratify the newly created desire of revenge, or by the conscious superiority that accompanies contempt and disdain; but these are purchased at the expence of the infinitely superior pleasures infused by the opposite spirit of love, complacency, and benevolence. The mind finds itself in bondage to its emotions, and feels that it is driven by their impetuosity, not only to the greatest distance from the nobler sources of enjoyment, but to the verge of misery itself. Danger is apprehended from the excess of passion while it is indulged; and the subject himself trembles lest it should be productive of irreparable evil, repentance, and remorse.

Sorrow and grief, though they are certainly in the class of the most unpleasant affections, yet they have something so fascinating in them, that the mind under their influence is arrested, and absorbed, as it were, in the contemplation of their cause.

The good of which we are deprived is now appretiated, perhaps for the firſt time, according to its value; perhaps beyond its value. This contemplation of qualities, which once gave delight, or which were fondly expected to give delight, mingles a pleaſure with the ſevere pain, that privation or diſappointment has occaſioned.

Even penitence and contrition, when they are inſpired by ingenuous motives,—when a deteſtation of former conduct proceeds from a conviction of its baſeneſs, and ſorrow for the injury it has done, and not from the apprehenſion of puniſhment or the ſhame of detection, even penitence and contrition are not devoid of pleaſure! The penitent, in the midſt of his painful ſelf-condemnation, feels a latent ſatisfaction in the diſpoſition and reſolution to return to the paths of virtue.

The emotions and affections of fear, dread, horror, deſpair, are of the moſt horrid and tremendous claſs. They vary in degrees of wretchedneſs, according to the degrees of their intenſeneſs, whether this be increaſed by temperament, by the extreme importance, or by the complicated nature of the exciting cauſe. Exceſſive jealouſy, envy, remorſe, deſpair, ſhame ariſing from the detection of guilt, are miſery unmixed. They render life inſufferable, and tempt the deſpondent and diſtracted mind to

venture

venture upon all the horrors of an unknown state, rather than support the pangs of his present feelings.

Surprise, wonder, astonishment, principally receive their complexion from the subjects that inspire them; and they are introductory to happiness or misery according to the nature of the cause exciting them. In surprise particularly, the sudden and unexpected arrival of an interesting event, correspondent with the nature of the affection already indulged, will turn hope and joy into ecstasy, displeasure into anger, and fear into terror and dismay.

Thus in the pleasing emotions, the idea of good necessarily predominates; and in the painful ones, the idea of evil. Accordingly those emotions which are produced by complicated good, or by the union of such causes as separately possess the power of calling forth pleasing emotions and affections, contribute most to happiness. In the emotions of hope, satisfaction, and joy, when personal concerns are intimately connected with some common interest, and the blessings received have an extensive influence, these pleasing emotions receive additional vigour, and are enjoyed with peculiar suavity. Social affections are now blended with self-love. The two torrents which so frequently oppose each other, fortunately unite and enlarge the stream of enjoyment: and the most desirable branch of benevolence,

lence, rejoicing with those that rejoice, is superadded to the natural pleasure we take in our own good.

Again: Gratitude unites to the joy inspired by a benefit received, the pleasure derived from an affectionate sense of the obligation, and of love to the benefactor: and if the magnitude of the benefit, or the mode of conferring it be productive of surprise, wonder, admiration, the delectable affections of joy, gratitude, and love, will, by the operation of these vivid passions, be proportionably augmented.

Were the imagination commanded to paint the highest felicity to be enjoyed by created beings, it would surely point out the union of the following emotions and affections. Ardent *love* for an object decidedly worthy of our love, chastened with high *veneration*;—*astonishment* inspired by the contemplation of the number and extent of its excellencies, and at the unremitted exertion of these excellencies in the diffusion of good;—*admiration* at the wise means adapted to the accomplishment of the interesting purpose;—*joy* and *gratitude* for benefits already received;—lively *hope* of good incalculable in reserve for ourselves, conjointly with others whose welfare we ardently desire, accompanied with a *consciousness* that we also have contributed a something to the general mass of felicity, according to the

extent

extent of our ability! These are ingredients to constitute the perfection of bliss! Love, joy, gratitude, surprise, admiration, complacency, hope, and benevolence unbounded, may thus occupy the mind in a transporting variety, or by exerting their united powers at the same instant occasion inconceivable raptures!!!

END OF PART THE SECOND.

NOTES

TO THE

PRECEDING TREATISE.

NOTES

TO THE

PRECEDING TREATISE.

NOTE *A*.

After, " Whether its influence be of a pleasant, or unpleasant nature." Page 6.

THIS opinion has the support of respectable authorities. Dr. Watts remarks that "the word properly signifies receiving the action of some agent." (See Watts on the Passions.) Mr. Grove observes that "the mind in certain circumstances, and within certain degrees has no dominion over itself, or the body. It is in a manner *passive*, can neither help the agitation of the blood and spirits, nor help being itself affected by them." (See Syst. of Moral Phil. Vol. 1. Ch. VII.)

Seneca

Seneca alfo thus expreffes himfelf: " Omnes motus
" qui non voluntate noftra fiunt, invicti, et inevitabiles
" funt: ut horror frigidâ afperfis; ad quofdam ictus, af-
" pernatio; ad pejores nuntios fubriguntur pili; et ruber
" ad improba verba fuffunditur; fequitur vertigo prærup-
" ta Cernantes. Ifta ut ita dicam, *patitur* magis animus
" quam *facit*." (De Ira. L. 2. C. 2.)

Note *B*.

After " are the moft appropriate." Page 13.

It is acknowledged that thefe words are frequently ufed indifcriminately, and fometimes without manifeft impropriety; but if they cannot be ufed at *all times*, with *equal propriety*, there muft be a fpecific difference between them. Now it is obfervable that the word Emotion is not frequently applied to thofe paffions in which the external figns are the leaft violent. We feldom fay that any one is under the emotion of fear; becaufe abject fear has fomething oppreffive in its nature, and is frequently filent and motionlefs. When fear is indicated by violent agitations, it acquires the character of *terror;* and we feel that the phrafe *emotions* of terror is ftrictly proper. We never apply the epithet to *hope*, diftinctly confidered, becaufe though it be lively and animating, it is not accompanied by external figns of tranfport. When thefe appear they are always afcribed to the *joy*, which is frequently connected with hope; and we perceive a peculiar propriety in the term *joyful emotions*, because joy is so frequently indicated by some eccentric tokens.

Whoever attends to these circumstances, in addition to the principles already advanced, will be surprised at the assertion of Lord Kaims, that " an emotion is in its na-" ture quiescent, and merely a passive feeling." (Elements of Criticism, 5th Edit. Vol. 1. Page 44.) Both the etymology of the word, and almost every connection in which it is used with decided propriety, confute this strange position. The Author was probably led into the idea by the very confined view he has taken of the passions, in his elegant Essay. He chiefly considers them as connected with the fine Arts, and subjects of taste; and as expressive of those agreeable or disagreeable effects which they produce, when first presented to our notice. These effects, it is allowed, are seldom so violent in cultivated minds, as to occasion emotions which indicate themselves by strong and characteristic marks.

His Lordship having denied external signs to *emotions*, has transferred them to the *passions*. But in order to establish his hypothesis, he is obliged to give a very different definition of the passions from any that his predecessors have adopted, or that either etymology or usage will justify. According to his system, a passion is compounded of this quiescent emotion, and a desire to obtain the object which occasioned it. " An internal motion or agita-" tion of the mind," says he, " when it passeth away with-" out desire, is denominated *an emotion;* when desire " follows, the motion or agitation is denominated *a pas-" sion.*" Numerous objections might be opposed to the position. I shall only observe that according to this hypothesis,

pothesis, the external signs of the passions would be the strongest where *desires* are the strongest; which is directly opposite to what we perceive in the *avaritious* man:—that joy can neither be considered as a passion nor an emotion; because its visible transports would destroy its title to the latter, and its being excited, not by desire itself but by the accomplishment of a desire, will exclude it from the former.—Nor can we discover what should at any time excite those transports which are sometimes both visible and tremendous; for emotions being quiescent, and desires not being of themselves turbulent, their union, could they possibly exist together, is not likely to produce those corporeal agitations so frequently observable, unless we were to admit a process similar to a chemical fermentation. But they cannot exist together, and consequently an emotion can receive no assistance from desire, by which it may be transformed into a passion; for according to his own system, desire *succeeds* to emotion.

His Lordship's embarrassment on this subject, which he ingenuously acknowledges, manifestly proceeds from his not having made a fortunate selection of terms to discriminate existent differences. To every simple *impression* he has given the name of an *emotion;* and he has applied the term *passion* exclusively, to what is in its own nature an *affection;* and whenever it is considered as a passion, it is merely in its secondary sense, expressing the captivating influence of any particular object of desire, or of an irresistible attachment to it. By admitting these few alterations, what he has written on the subject may be read with much edification and pleasure.

Note C.

After " It would be to annihilate misery."
Page 21.

Dr. Hartley, in establishing the doctrine of vibrations, and the hypothesis of associated ideas founded upon it, asserts that " the desire of happiness and aversion to " misery, are *not inseparable* from and essential to all in- " telligent natures."

Without venturing to oppose unnecessarily so cautious and conclusive a reasoner, I shall just observe, that the above assertion is expressed in much stronger language than the principles he attempts to enforce absolutely require. It is acknowledged that his theory opposes the existence of innate ideas; and whoever admits the theory must allow, that there can be no desire after happiness or fear of misery, before we have, some way or other, been made acquainted with their natures. Therefore, when he asserts that the desire of happiness, and aversion to misery are not inseparable from and essential to all intelligent natures, he can only mean, that they are not co-existent with the power of intelligence, and that they are desires and aversions acquired by experience; not, that the *reflective* mind can at any time be totally indifferent about happiness and misery. For by whatever method we may have obtained a knowledge of either, the position remains indubitable, that no one ever tasted of happiness, or possessed the smallest degree of ease or pleasure, without contracting

an

an affection for them; or experienced misery and uneasiness, without contracting an hatred towards them.

Note D.

After " The individual stock of each would render happiness universal." Page 26.

It would not only be a severe but an absurd requisition, to expect that mankind should universally be more attentive to the welfare of others than to their own. This mode of exercising benevolence could not be productive of so much good, as the present constitution of our natures; nor would it be so favourable to the cause of benevolence as has been imagined. No mind truly generous or deserving of attention, could possibly receive the gift of well-being entirely at the expence of the donor. Thus, were the selfish principle totally extinguished, the reciprocal communication of Good would be little more than a complimentary exchange.

Note E.

After " not always in our recollection." Page 29.

Some Authors, of great respectability, have expressed themselves in a manner which conveys ideas very different from those we have attempted to establish. Dr. Reid
speaks

speaks of loving things for their own fakes, and confiders the clafs of philofophers who fuppofe that the love of every object may be refolved into its utility, to be in an error. Lord Kaims maintains that fome affections are neither felfifh nor focial.

These opinions feem to receive fupport from the fentiment of *Cicero*, who obferves " Eft quiddam quod fua vi " nos illiciat ad fe; non emolumento captans aliquo, fed " trahens fua dignitate: quod genus, *virtus, fcientia, ve-* " *ritas.*"

It is fo prefumptuous to differ from fuch authorities, that I am reluctant to expofe myfelf to the fufpicion. Their doctrine is expreffed in very ambiguous language. It is poffible that a proper inveftigation of the fubject will indicate that it does not, in its tenour, oppofe the fentiments advanced in the text. If I fail in this attempt, it may ftill appear that it has not confuted them.

When it is faid that we love things for their own fakes, let us examine what fignification can be attached to the expreffion. We could not poffibly love any thing totally void of qualities, were it poffible for fuch a thing to exift; becaufe there would be nothing to love. But the things fpecified by thefe authors, as being attractive by their dignity alone, manifeftly poffefs qualities of the higheft utility: for their dignity itfelf confifts in the fuperiority of their ufefulnefs. When therefore it is alleged that fuch things are loved for their own fakes, the only confiftent ideas we can annex to the phrafe muft be, that we love them from their capacity of producing, in certain circumftances, fome great and extenfive good; though we fhould not experience the good, or obferve the application of this power, in particular inftances, either in ourfelves or others.

others. For example, it is as certain that *virtue, science, truth*, are of infinite importance to the welfare of the whole intelligent creation, as that they possess the powerful attractions ascribed to them by *Cicero*. A society of *Liars* would create greater confusion than that of Babel; nor could it exist for a day. *Science* dispels pernicious ignorance; it makes us acquainted with the choicest qualities existent; and universal *Virtue* would be productive of universal happiness. Every man therefore, whose mind is not upon a level with the brute creation, and who has perceived, in a single instance, the beneficial effects flowing from these excellencies, or the baneful consequences engendered by their contraries, must respect them. This respect however will be founded either upon his own experience, or his observation of their influence upon others. In the first case they are the result of personal love of good; and in the second, of the benevolent principle. For it is very obvious that the class of objects of which it is asserted that they are loved for their own sakes, alone attract the attention of the cultivated mind, or of such as possess a considerable share of natural benevolence.

Innumerable are the proofs that the very *capacity* of being useful, will inspire an affection for many things which are permitted to remain in a dormant state. The miser loves his gold so intensely, that he will not part with it, in exchange for the choicest blessing it is able to purchase. The man of science loves his library, though it may contain many hundred volumes which he has never consulted. The good housewife delights in the plate or porcelain, which is perpetually locked up in her cabinet; and the eastern Monarch is watchful over a seraglio infinitely too extensive for his enjoyment. These

The above instances point out the sense in which we may be said to love any thing for its own sake. These different objects are loved as powers of utility or gratification in reserve; that is, we are so constituted that we cannot avoid approving, admiring, or loving whatever possesses in a great degree either the capacity or disposition to promote, what we deem to be good for us, or what is pleasing to us.

NOTE *F*.

After " threaten to endanger our well-being."
Page 38.

MR. HUME commences his *Dissertation on the Passions* in the following manner: " Some objects produce " an agreeable sensation, by the original structure of our " organs; and are thence denominated GOOD; as others, " from immediate disagreeable sensation, acquire the ap- " pellation of EVIL. Thus *moderate warmth* is agree- " able and good; excessive heat painful and evil.

" Some objects again, by being naturally conformable " or contrary to passion, excite an agreeable or painful " sensation, and are thence called *good* or *evil*. The pu- nishment of an adversary by *gratifying revenge* is GOOD; " the sickness of a companion, by affecting friendship, is " *evil*."

Will it be necessary to point out to any of my Readers the pernicious sophistry of this statement? Is it not a wanton introduction of a chaos, I will not say in morals, but in the nature and character of human motives and human conduct? It gives the important appellation of *Good* to the greatest opposites, without discriminating the specific natures of each; merely because in some circumstances, and in some characters, they may produce pleasing or painful sensations. Thus is *moderate warmth* placed upon a level with sentiments and dispositions calculated to produce the most exalted felicity; and to the gratification of revenge, is given the same colouring as to the pardon of an injury or alleviating distress!

This studied confusion of ideas may in some connections be productive of wit; it is always " *such stuff as* " Conundrums *are made of*," but it is directly opposite to the genius of true philosophy!

If my ideas of a conundrum be accurate, it consists in an attempt to make two things appear closely to resemble each other, which are the most opposite in their natures. This is done by directing the attention to some middle term, which may, in one sense or other, be applicable to each. For example, if it be asked why is a person in the upper part of a house committing theft, *like a man of the strictest virtue?* The answer is, because he is *above*, doing a bad action. The word *above* being in certain senses applicable to each subject, we are surprised and amused at the unexpected points of resemblance. Thus again if it be asked, In what does a person, who attempts to kill another in a fit of anger, resemble the *man who protects his life?* The answer will be, both actions are *conformable to passion*, excite *agreeable sensations*, and are therefore GOOD! The first conundrum is allowed to be better than the second; but this will only prove that

there

there are degrees of excellence in this kind of writing, as well as in every other; and that it is much better adapted to subjects of amusement, than to philosophy.

Note G.

After "the passions and affections could not have been excited." Page 40.

PERHAPS there is no branch of philosophy more difficult than that of distinguishing between real and apparent qualities in objects. Since all that we know of qualities is derived from the impression made upon us, a previous question presents itself, whether our susceptibility of impressions be always accurate, or perfectly correspondent with the real nature of the object? Until this point be settled, our ideas of qualities must be vague and indeterminate. Lord Kaims has in one instance made the attempt; but his observations are so unsatisfactory, and his mode of reasoning so inconclusive, that I feel myself much relieved in not being obliged to imitate his example.

In a Chapter where he treats of *Emotions and Passions as pleasant and painful, agreeable and disagreeable*, he attempts to prove that *agreeable* and *disagreeable* are qualities in the object perceived, *pleasant* and *unpleasant* are descriptive of the emotions we feel; the former are perceived as adhering to the *object*, the latter are felt as existing in *us*.—At first view these distinctions appear specious,

but upon critical examination apprehensions may be justly entertained, whether they be not instances of that inaccuracy which he considers " not at all venial in the sci-
" ence of Ethics."

" Viewing a garden," says he, " I perceive it to be
" beautiful or agreeable; and I consider the beauty or
" agreeableness as belonging to the object, or as one of
" its qualities. When I turn my attention from the gar-
" den to what passes in my mind, I am conscious of a
" pleasant emotion, of which the garden is the cause; the
" pleasure here is felt as a quality, not of the garden, but
" of the emotion produced by it. I give another example.
" A rotten carcase is disagreeable, and raises in the spec-
" tator a painful emotion: the disagreeableness is a quality
" of the object; the pain is a quality of the emotion pro-
" duced by it." (Elements of Criticism. Vol. I. Chap.
II. Part II.)

With deference to so respectable an authority, this distinction does not appear to be just. *Agreeable*, according to its etymology, manifestly relates to the effects produced upon us, as much as the word *pleasant*. The difference is in *degree*, not in *nature*. *Agreeable* expresses something that appears suitable or correspondent with our natures, dispositions, and tastes: something that perfectly *agrees* with us; exciting the idea of comfort, and inspiring *contentment* and *satisfaction*. What is *pleasant* goes farther. It excites a sensation within us, more nearly approaching to an *emotion*. That agreeableness cannot be allowed to exist in the subject itself, is plain from the diversity of opinions concerning it, without the possibility of discovering a standard by which to mark a deviation

from

from the law of nature. Were it refident in objects, the effects muft be uniform and abfolute, in every one whofe powers of perception are not difordered. But this is not the cafe. Numberlefs caufes confpire to change our ideas of the qualities of objects, and may render fome objects agreeable or difagreeable, pleafant or unpleafant to the fame perfon at different times. To give a familiar inftance. Sweet things are moft agreeable to children; but when they become adults the tafte is changed. It is poffible that the fmoke of tobacco, and the tafte of porter may become agreeable to the *man*, who detefted them when a *child*. Can we fay therefore, that there is an inherent agreeablenefs in tobacco that pleafes the adult, and an inherent difagreeablenefs that difgufts the infant? Or to admit his Lordfhip's example of a *garden*. It is acknowledged that the idea of a garden excites pleafant fenfations in moft perfons. Plenty of the delicate luxuries of nature, beauty, verdure, variegated flowers, &c. elegant retirement from the noife and buftle of the world, crowd in upon the imagination. But are we agreed in every circumftance refpecting a garden? Was not the ftiffeft formality once deemed an effential beauty? Has not this tafte given way to irregular clumps and clufters? Are not thefe of late become the fubject of ridicule, and a ftyle more correfpondent with the wild beauties of nature preferred? And when thefe have been enjoyed for fome time, a future race may poffibly obferve that the diftinction between a *garden* and a *field* is not fufficiently marked, and may again place their ideas of beauty in that formal regularity, which is at prefent fo much defpifed.

Note *H.*

After " Either taste or address, &c." Page 68.

Dr. Watts does not seem to have expressed himself with sufficient accuracy, when he observes, that " If any " object appear pleasing and fit to do us good, it raises " the love of complacency." These two expressions are not synonymous. Many things may be pleasing to us, from which we apprehend mischief; and in these we cannot take complacency.

Again he says, " Complacency dwells upon its object " with delight: We gaze upon a figure, we listen to mu- " sic, we dwell long in a fine garden, we dwell in the " company of our friends." All these instances contain attributes calculated to inspire complacency, as *ingenuity* and *taste* may be manifested in the three first, and *worth* moral or mental, may be possessed by the last. Yet it may be justly doubted whether precision of language will permit us to apply the word Complacency to these cases, unless there be some kind or degree of *appropriation*. We may approve, we may enjoy great pleasure and delight in inanimate objects, when we view them as belonging to strangers. But it has never been said of a connoisseur, that he took *complacency* in the *Apollo de Belvedere*, or in the *Venus de Medicis*, in *Stowe Gardens*, or the *Leasowes of Shenstone*, however he may have been *delighted* by these objects. Some circumstances of approximation, however slight, appear necessary, to enable even such objects to inspire complacency. If we take

complacency

complacency in garments, or flowers, or gardens, it is when they belong either to ourselves or to our friend; or when they manifest our own taste or skill, or that of another for whom we are interested. Nor will the most perfect concert excite complacency in the audience at large, though it may in the composers, performers, directors, or any of their particular acquaintances.

Note *I.*

After " Pride." Page 71.

THE above definition and descriptions of Pride, are founded upon the various acceptations of that word in common language, and supported by the authority of our best Writers. But Mr. Hume, in defiance of both, has given a very different definition of pride, which I believe to be totally his own, and ought of consequence to possess great internal merit to justify its boldness, in opposing those ideas which have hitherto been received *universally*. Let us examine it.

He defines pride to be a " certain satisfaction in our-
" selves on account of some accomplishment or possession
" which we enjoy." Again. " The object of pride is
" *self*, the cause, *some excellence*." Again. " Our *me-*
" *rit* raises pride, and it is essential to pride to turn our
" view on ourselves with complacency and satisfaction."
(See Dissertation on the Passions, *passim*.)

As Mr. Hume has made no distinction between real

and supposed merit, he necessarily directs our thoughts to absolute merit; nor can there, according to this statement, be any place for a *vitious* pride, or an *ill-founded* confidence in our own superiority. This is excluded by his definition from the character of pride.

Our Philosopher has also advanced in another place, that " Self-satisfaction, in some degree at least, is an ad-
" vantage which equally attends the FOOL and the
" WISE." (On Qualities necessary to ourselves. § 6.)
Now what is the *cause* of this self-satisfaction in the *fool*? According to the above position it must be *Merit*. And in the *wise man*? *Merit*. Thus the wise man and the fool are made to resemble each other so closely in the most interesting of all desirable qualities, *merit*, and *self-satisfaction*, that there is no material difference between them. What there is will probably be to the advantage of the *fool*. As he will be much more liable to be *pleased with himself*, our Author's hypothesis leads us to suspect that he may possess the most *merit*.

Should it be alleged that the above statement is a misrepresentation; I would answer, that such an allegation can alone be supported by explanations which will militate against the sentiments so repeatedly and assiduously advanced. Recourse must be had to a distinction between *real* and *supposed* merit. This will demonstrate that there are two *species* of pride included in the definition; and that these are as opposite to each other as light and darkness, knowledge and ignorance; and consequently that it is not only very *unphilosophical* to comprise the most opposite qualities under the same genus; but very *ungenerous* to confound the good principle with the evil one, by giving indiscriminately the same appellations to both.

NOTE

Note K.

After " the ambitious passions is a familiar expression." Page 78.

Dr. Reid places desires among the *animal* principles; but he distinguishes them " from the appetites by this, " that there is not a sensation proper to each, and always " accompanying it; and that they are not periodical but " constant, not being satiated with their object for a time " as the appetites are." He adds, " the desires I have in " view are chiefly these three, the desire of power, the " desire of esteem, and the desire of knowledge."

This is not the place to inquire whether the desires here specified deserve to be ranked among the animal principles; but as the above description of a particular class of desires appears to oppose the sentiments we have advanced, it demands a few observations.

We may first remark that the distinction made between appetites and desires is inaccurate, as the appetites are doubtless one class of desires; nor is there a sensual appetite totally separate from the mental affections and desires; if there were, the grossest appetites might be indulged without culpability.

2dly. The doctrine itself is very obscurely expressed. It may import, that desires have no uneasy sensation attending them; or that one sensation is common to them all. But neither of these positions can be admitted. If the Doctor means that desires are not uneasy sensations,

and

and adduces thofe fpecified as proofs, we may obferve that they are here confidered in their mildeft ftate, and we are taught to imagine from the defcription given of them, that this was their permanent character: whereas it is well known that the defire of power is frequently as rampant as the ftrongeft appetites, degenerating into infatiable ambition; that the defire of efteem may become fo exceffive as to ftir up painful emulation, and ftill more painful envy; and that the defire of knowledge is frequently fo reftlefs as to induce the poffeffor to forego his eafe, and encounter dangers and difficulties innumerable in order to gratify it.

But although in their mildeft ftate they may not equal the appetites, they are attended with a degree of uneafinefs which impels to active endeavours after the defired objects. If no uneafy fenfation accompanied either, there could be no motive to counteract the love of eafe and indolence, fo natural to man. The profpect of fuccefs may indeed infpire the pleafure of hope, and the benefits promifed by each purfuit may be fo powerfully anticipated by the imagination, that the pleafing fenfations from thefe adventitious caufes fhall greatly preponderate; but if no uneafy fenfation were excited by the comparifon of our actual fituation with that we may poffibly attain, our endeavours after the attainment could never have been excited.

The Profeffor's fubfequent obfervations perfectly correfpond with thefe remarks. He fays that " the purfuits " of power, of fame, and of knowledge, require a felf- " command no lefs than virtue does:" which is an acknowledgment that they are not always fo pacific as was reprefented.

represented.* And when he observes that "the desire of "esteem and of knowledge are highly useful to society as "well as power, and at the same time are *less dangerous* "in *their excesses*," he tacitly allows that they are not totally exempt.

In support of another argument he asserts, that "innu-"merable instances occur in life, of men who sacrifice "ease, pleasure, and every thing else to the lust of pow-"er, of fame, or even of knowledge." A demonstration this that the sensations they sometimes excite, are not only uneasy but ungovernable.

If by the expression, "there is not a sensation proper to "each," we are to understand that one particular sensation is common to them all, the proposition is still more extravagant. Our sensations, in every species of desire, are as different as the objects desired. Nor is there a greater difference between hunger and thirst, than there is between the desire of wealth and the desire of power. The desire of knowledge is also distinct from, and superior to both.

Note L.

After "feelings of humanity." Page 84.

Dr. Reid remarks, that "it seems to be false religion "alone, that is able to check the tear of compassion."
"We

---

* This expression is also inaccurate, since it is the province of virtue to correct these as well as every other desire, when they are in danger of becoming inordinate.

"We are told," he adds, " that in Portugal and Spain, " a man condemned to be burned as an obstinate heretic, " meets with no compassion even from the multitude;" observing that " they are taught to look upon him as the " enemy of God, and doomed to hell-fire. But should " not this very circumstance move compassion? Surely " it would if they were not taught that in this case, it is a " crime to shew compassion, or even to feel it." (See Essay on Active Powers, Page 156.)

In addition to the motive assigned, we may mention the influence of custom in rendering the heart insensible to the sufferings of these devoted objects. I was once passing through *Moorfields* with a young Lady aged about nine or ten years, born and educated in Portugal, but in the *Protestant* Faith, and observing a large concourse of people assembled around a pile of faggots on fire, I expressed a curiosity to know the cause. She very composedly answered, I suppose that it is nothing more than *that they are going to burn a Jew.* Fortunately it was no other than roasting an ox, upon some joyful occasion. What rendered this singularity the more striking, were the natural mildness and compassion of the young person's disposition.

Another instance of the influence of perverted principles, occurs to my remembrance in the conduct of a pious Mother, towards a most excellent and dutiful Son; who from a principle of conscience, in opposition to his interest, renounced the religious system in which he had been educated, for another, which he deemed more consonant to truth. She told him that " she found it her duty, how-
" ever severe the struggle, to alienate her affections from
" him, now he had rendered himself an enemy to God, by
" embracing

"embracing such erroneous sentiments." My Friend added, that she was completely successful in these pious endeavours; and that the duty she enjoined upon herself, was scrupulously performed during the remainder of her days.

Note *M*.

After "past, present, and future." Page 86.

It is singular, with what precision common language marks the difference between to *wish* and to *desire*, according to our power to obtain the object of our wishes, or influence over the means. Thus we never say to any one, I *desire* you to be well; but I *wish* you well, because generally speaking we have no influence over another's health; but a sick man not only *wishes* but *desires* to be well, because he possesses the power of applying the means; and if he rejects the means, we conclude that he does *not desire* to be well. If we are solicitous that some kind office should be performed by any one, we may either *wish* or *desire*, according to our claims upon his aid. As we may sometimes *desire* where we cannot *command*, thus we may *wish*, where it would be presumptuous to *desire:* and sometimes we manifest our desires by expressing our wishes, from a principle of delicacy, leaving it to the party, from whom we expect the kind office, to increase the obligation by conforming to our wish, rather than

than complying with our desires. These distinctions being founded in nature are common to every language.

Note N.

After "to impede our progress." Page 96.

THIS seems to be the genuine sense of the substantive *Humility*. But its verb, and participles are not equally confined in their signification. They express states of debasement, in which the spirits are peculiarly depressed, and the mind deeply chagrined and mortified, but to which the term *humility* has never yet been applied. There are situations, in which persons may feel themselves very much *humbled*, and they may be exposed to many *humiliating* circumstances, without their being possessed of the disposition denoted by *humility*. Such expressions never relate to the prevailing habit of the mind, but to certain incidents which check pride, vanity, ambition, emulation; or deprive us of the reputation we had enjoyed. They all relate to some degree of elevation to which the mind had in vain aspired, and felt mortified at the disappointment; or to some particular state from which the subject has fallen, and in consequence of which he suffers a *degradation*. He may thus be in a state of *humiliation*, without being in a state of *humility*. This word refers alone to mental excellence, either intellectual or moral; concerning which the subject himself entertains painful apprehensions

apprehensions that he is or shall remain deficient. The adjective *humble* has the same signification. When we say of a person that he has an *humble* mind, we mean that he is modest, unassuming, diffident of himself. These distinctions are very obvious, and though they may indicate the caprices of language, they are nevertheless highly important; for they serve to discriminate things which differ very essentially in their natures. The *humble* mind is neither mean nor abject, which may be the case with the *proud*, who by being detected in his baseness, or disappointed in his vain presumptuous hopes, may be *humbled to the dust*. To the man who is clothed with humility, may possibly belong all those excellencies which Mr. Hume has ascribed to *pride*. He may in reality possess more merit than he dares to imagine. The disposition is inspired by the contemplation of excellencies which he loves, and which he almost despairs to obtain. How different is this from the *humiliation* any one may suffer from disappointed ambition, from a perception of involuntary blemishes and accidental defects, from the mortification that self-love may experience, by being defective in beauty, elegance, or wealth, or laden with corporeal infirmities! all of which Mr. Hume has arbitrarily chosen to comprehend under *Humility*. For example. " If beauty or deformity belong to our own face, shape, " or person, this pleasure or uneasiness is converted into " *pride* or *humility*.—*Pride* and *humility* have the quali- " ties of our mind and *body*, that is, of self, for their na- " tural and more immediate causes.—*Bodily* pain and *sick- " ness* are in themselves proper causes of *humility*. Con- " cerning all other bodily accomplishments, we may ob- " serve

" serve in general, that whatever in ourselves is either use-
" ful, beautiful, or surprising, is an object of pride, and
" the contrary of *humility*."

Mr. Hume must have known that whimsical deviations from etymology, constitute an essential part of the idioms of a language; which render it not only so difficult to be acquired, but occasion ludicrous effects in the attempt. Would he not have been the first to smile at the mistakes of a foreigner, who should suppose that all persons labouring every day at their particular occupations, were equally *Day-labourers?*—that to possess an elegant or lively fancy, was to be *very fanciful?*—that a man was *insane*, because he had *ill health?*—and that every *child of nature*, was a *natural child?*—But are these blunders more inconsistent with the idioms of our language, which custom has universally established, than the assertion that bodily pain or sickness are in themselves proper causes of humility? or placing " the *Epilepsy*," " the *Itch*," " the " *King's-Evil*," in the catalogue? (See *Dissertation on the Passions*, passim.)

It is easy to collect from the above passages, and from the amiable character he has given of pride, as remarked in a preceding note, that Mr. Hume, " delighted to *exalt* " the *proud*, and give *disgrace* to the *humble*." Had it been his province to translate the Bible, how would he have rendered the following passages?

Every one proud in heart, is an abomination to the Lord. An high look and a proud heart is sin. He that is of a proud heart stirreth up strife. Pride was not made for man, &c. &c. &c.

Before

Before honour is humility. By humility and the fear of the Lord, are riches, honour, and life. God giveth grace to the humble, &c. &c. &c.

It is not intended by these quotations, to confute his notions *by divine authority;* but by that of *common phraseology.* They indicate what were the ideas universally annexed to the terms Pride and Humility, at the period when this book was translated; and these continue precisely the same every time such passages are read either in public or private. To the universal usage of expressions every author must conform, who means to be intelligible. Nor is the misrepresentation of facts more injurious to the credit of an historian, than the perversion of language to that of a philosopher.

The singularity of Mr. Hume in his definitions of both these words, will appear still more assuming, when we consider that it opposes the phraseology not only of the *English* language, but of most, perhaps *all,* the *European* languages, which employ an appropriate word to distinguish that amiable consciousness or apprehension of inferiority in mental excellence, from other painful imperfections; and that word is perfectly synonymous to the explanation we have given of *humility.*

Note *O.*

After " dread of their arrival." Page 102.

The Author once attended a prisoner of some distinction in one of the prisons of the metropolis, ill of a typhus fever;

fever; whose apartments were gloomy in the extreme, and surrounded with horrors: yet this prisoner assured him afterwards, that upon his release, he quitted them with a degree of reluctance. Custom had reconciled him to the twilight admitted through the thick barred grate, to the filthy spots and patches of his plastered walls, to the hardness of his bed, and even to confinement. He had his books, was visited by his friends, and was greatly amused and interested in the anecdotes of the place.

An Officer of the municipality at Leyden also informed the Author of an instance, which marks yet more strongly the force of habit. A poor woman, who had for some misdemeanour been sentenced to confinement for a certain number of years, upon the expiration of the term, immediately applied to him for re-admission. She urged that all her worldly comforts were fled; and her only wish was to be indulged in those imparted by habit. She moreover threatened, that, if this could not be granted as a *favour*, she would commit some offence that should give her a *title* to be re-instated in the accustomed lodgings.

Note *P*.

After " may possibly follow." Page 103:

As these distinctions may appear too refined to some of my Readers, it will be proper to shew that they actually exist; and that there are situations, in which a discrimination

tion is both obvious and necessary. Take the following instances.

When a young and inexperienced soldier is first ordered to march to battle, his legs will tremble under him, and the presaging colour of death will be in his face, notwithstanding his strongest resolutions, aided by the power of drums and trumpets and the apparent gaiety of his associates. These mark his *fear*. Should he during the engagement meet with a single foe, and be provoked to single combat, from which he cannot possibly or honourably escape, the emotion of *terror* will subdue the listlessness of fear, and arouse every power of action. If the army to which he belongs should experience a total defeat, the province whose safety depended upon its success will be thrown into the utmost *Consternation;* because this commencement of evil may be productive of horrors, which the liveliest imagination cannot fully represent: and it was the apprehension of a possible defeat with its consequences that had inspired their minds with *Dread*, long before the engagement took place.

These ideas are in themselves very distinct, and although some of the terms used to express them may be used indiscriminately, where nice precision is not so requisite, yet the arrangement given them evidently shews the place destined for each. Thus we may say that the young soldier dreads to go into battle as he is marching forwards; but strictly speaking, this dread may have been indulged immediately after he had enlisted, when the object of *Fear* was remote; it will be increased into that passion as he approaches the enemy.

Note Q.

After " though a degree of hope is still indulged."
Page 105.

The embarrassed and fluctuating state of the mind under the influence of doubt, has seduced Mr. Hume into a singular hypothesis, which not only opposes the universal opinion of mankind, but confounds the future with the present and the past. Could he establish his hypothesis, it would follow that the mind is first oppressed with *grief* concerning a particular object, and then torn with *fear* and anxiety concerning its arrival: for he makes grief to be the parent of fear, instead of considering the accomplishment of fearful apprehensions as a cause of grief.

" Suppose," says he, " that the object concerning
" which we are doubtful, produces either desire or aver-
" sion; it is evident, that according as the mind turns it-
" self to one side or the other, it must feel a momentary
" impression of joy or sorrow. An object, whose exis-
" tence we desire, gives satisfaction, when we think of
" those causes which produce it; and for the same reason,
" excites grief or uneasiness from the opposite considera-
" tion. So that as the understanding, in probable ques-
" tions, is divided between the contrary points of view,
" the heart must in the same manner be divided between
" opposite emotions.—According as the probability inclines

" clines to good or evil, the paffion of grief or joy predo-
" minates in the compofition; and thefe paffions being in-
" termingled by means of the contrary views of the ima-
" gination, produce by the union, the paffions of hope
" and fear. Again:

" The paffions of fear and hope may arife, when the
" chances are equal on both fides, and no fuperiority can
" be difcovered in one above the other. Nay, in this fitu-
" ation the paffions are rather the ftrongeft; as the mind
" has then the leaft foundation to reft upon, and is toft
" with the greateft uncertainty. *Throw in a fuperior de-*
" *gree of probability to the fide of grief, you immediately*
" *fee that paffion diffufe itfelf over the compofition and*
" *tincture it into fear.* Increafe the probability, by that
" means the grief, the fear prevails ftill more and more;
" till at laft it runs infenfibly, as the joy continually dimi-
" nifhes into pure grief. After you have brought it to this
" fituation, diminifh the grief, by a contrary operation to
" that which increafed it, to wit, by diminifhing the pro-
" bability on the melancholy fide; and you will fee the
" paffion cheer every moment, till it changes infenfibly
" into hope; which again runs by flow degrees into joy,
" as you increafe the part of the compofition by the in-
" creafe of the probability." He adds, " Are not thefe as
" plain proofs that the paffions of fear and hope are mix-
" tures of grief and joy, as in optics it is a proof, that a
" coloured ray of the fun, paffing through a prifm, is a
" compofition of two others, when, as you diminifh or
" increafe the quantity of either, you find it prevail pro-
" portionably more or lefs in the compofition." (See
Differtation on the Paffions, Sect. I.)

The miftake which runs through the whole of this laboured argument, manifeftly arifes from Mr. Hume's not having fufficiently attended to the complication which exifts in an uncertain and embarraffed ftate of mind. The object both of hope and fear muft, according to his own hypothefis, be future, or problematical, otherwife no uncertainty concerning it could have place. It cannot therefore in itfelf be the caufe either of *grief* or *joy*, but, as we ufually exprefs the particular ftate of mind, of *hope* or *fear*. In the obfervation made by Mr. Hume, that " an " object, whofe exiftence we defire gives fatisfaction, " *whenever we think of thofe caufes which produce it*," his own ideas are manifeftly entangled in the inaccuracy of the ftatement. It cannot poffibly be the *object* we defire that gives the fatisfaction he mentions, for then the defire would be accomplifhed; but it is *thinking of thofe caufes*, which produce, or are calculated to produce it. Thus has he inadvertently afcribed an influence to the object, primarily and folely, which ought to be afcribed fimply to the ftate of our minds concerning it. The object itfelf, inftead of giving this fatisfaction, will remain the fubject of our hopes and fears, as long as we remain in a ftate of uncertainty concerning it. When we advert to the *probabilities* of its exiftence, the mind may derive both *hope* and *joy* from the predominant influence of thefe probabilities upon us, and when *improbabilities* gain an afcendant influence, our *fear* will prevail, and this will be accompanied with a certain degree of *grief* at the *difappointment* of the hopes we had indulged. Thus by being agitated by the "*pro* and *con*" of probabilities and improbabilities, we feel a pleafing expectation at one moment, and a painful reverfe at another. Here are of

confequence

consequence two temporary sensations, alternately excited respecting this desired object; but they are immediately excited by the detached evidences on the side of an happy or unhappy issue. Without hope we should sink into the extreme of fear; without fear, our joy would be complete: and when the grand result shall be known, these temporary sensations will cease, and the mind will be under the influence of unmixed joy or grief according to the event. The joy and grief accompanying hope and fear therefore, retain their own characteristic natures without any transmutation having taken place. After we have indulged hopes, by contemplating the promising side of the question, we are grieved and chagrined at the disappointment of these hopes, as often as improbabilities alarm our fears. On the contrary, when probabilities appear strongly in favour of what we ardently desire, we *rejoice* that our hopes are encouraged.

Thus the passions of fear and hope are not mixtures of grief and joy, in the same manner as a coloured ray of the sun passing through a prism is a composition of two others; but they are all distinct passions, and have their own distinct causes of excitement. Hope and fear respect the grand issue; grief and joy, the encouragements or discouragements which may alternately present themselves respecting it.

Note R.

After " our understandings cannot fully reach and comprehend." Page 149.

From Mr. Grove it was natural to expect precision; and although this is manifest in most parts of his Treatise on the Passions, yet in his description of admiration, he has not only deviated from the best authorities, but also from himself.

That admiration is not excited by *novelty* alone is plain, because there are many novelties which no one can admire; such as are indifferent, insipid, or displeasing. That it cannot be synonymous with *surprise*, is plain, because were we to tell any one that we were surprised at his excellencies, he would probably be surprised at our ill manners. Nor is it the same with *wonder;* for when a lover admires the charms of his mistress, we cannot suppose this to be *wondering* that she possesses them.

But that the term Admiration cannot be confined to the impressions which simple novelty is able to make, is obvious from the subsequent remarks of Mr. Grove, and the more pertinent phraseology employed in other parts of his works. He acknowledges that *greatness* or *excellency* is the most general and most proper object of admiration. But neither of these are necessarily novel. He further observes that " *admiration* according to the different character of " its object is called *esteem* or *contempt*." But his definition confines our ideas to the simple character of novelty;

nor

nor can admiration be applied to opposite characters, without a destruction of the simplicity he ascribes to it, and I may add without exciting a degree of surprise at the versatility of its nature. He has also remarked, that even *littleness* may excite admiration; but he allows that the works of nature or art, which are of an unusual *smallness*, are admired, not so much for their smallness, as for the *greatness of the wisdom and skill* conspicuous in them. For " we can behold a particle of mere undiversified mat-
" ter," says he, " though incomparably smaller, without
" such wonder." In another passage, speaking of the advantages of sleep, he says " we shall discern one reason
" more to *admire the wisdom* of the Creator, in appoint-
" ing so great a portion of our time for sleep."

Thus it appears that Mr. Grove feels the necessity of opposing his own definition, and also the peculiar propriety of applying the term to indubitable marks of excellency.

The extreme confusion and contrarieties which run through the chapter from whence the above extracts are made, proceed from his considering admiration as synonymous with surprise; and they fully indicate the great importance of affixing distinct ideas to each expression. Every author admits that the terms to *admire, admiration, admirable*, may always be applied to some kind of excellency without the shadow of an impropriety; and the above observations manifest that they cannot at all times be used synonymously with either *surprise* or *wonder*. This circumstance fully indicates their proper place in the accurate arrangement of our ideas.

NOTE

Note S.

After " or which has a preponderancy of excellence." Page 226.

To enter deeply into this delicate subject, would not be consistent with my plan, but the following queries are proposed to those who are more disposed. Since the Female Sex complain, with apparent anguish of heart, that men have taken the lead in directing the wheels of government, in the establishment of the arts, and prosecution of the sciences, by *usurpation*, how came they to be such general and extensive usurpers, without possessing a superiority of correspondent qualifications?—Can any other example be produced of predilections being rendered so universal and so permanent, by circumstances merely incidental?—Again, excepting we have recourse to the constitution of nature, who can explain the reason why each sex should regard the qualities in the opposite sex most similar to its own, with such marks of disgust or contempt; and delight in qualities directly opposite? This is contrary to all the laws of the social affections in every other instance; for similarity of dispositions and manners is considered, in every other case, as the foundation of love, and the cement of affection and friendship.

May we not safely assert that there is, generally speaking, an original diversity in *tastes* and *dispositions*, liable however to some exceptions? If this be admitted, a correspondent

respondent diversity of *pursuits* will naturally follow. We may also subjoin that these tastes and dispositions are in most instances, remarkably correspondent with the corporeal powers of obtaining or accomplishing their objects.

NOTE T.

After " by a cautious manner of communicating the tidings." Page 285.

HISTORIANS present us with many instances of fatal effects from the excess of joy; but it plainly appears from their narratives, that the subjects were, at the instant preceding, under the pressure of extreme anguish of mind.

Pliny informs us that Chilo, the Lacedemonian, died upon hearing that his son had gained a prize in the Olympic Games. " Cum victore filio Olympiæ expirasset " gaudio." We may consider the excess of joy in this case, as an indication of his previous solicitude concerning the issue. (Plin. Maj. LIB. VII. SECT. 7.) But the following instances are more express.

Valerius Maximus tells us that Sophocles the tragic Writer, in a contest of honour, died in consequence of a decision being pronounced in his favour. " Sophocles " ultimæ jam senectutis, cum in certamine tragædiam " dixisset, ancipiti sententiarum eventu diu solicitus, ali" quando tamen una sententia victor, causam mortis gau" dium habuit." (Val. Max. LIB. IX. CAP. 12.)

Aulus Gellius mentions a remarkable instance of what

may

may be termed, accumulated joy, in Diagoras, whose three sons were crowned in the same day as victors; the one as a pugilist, the other as a wrestler, and the third in both capacities. " Diagoras, tres filios habuit, unum pu-
" gilem, alterum lutorem, tertium Pancrastiasten; eosque
" omnes videt vincere coronarique eodem Olympiæ die;
" et cum coronis suis in caput patris positis suaviarentur;
" cumque populus gratulabundus flores undique in eum
" jaceret, ibi in stadio, inspectante populo, in osculis,
" atque in manibus filiorum animam efflavit." (Aul. Gell. noct. Attic. LIB. III. CAP. 15.)

Livy also mentions the instance of an aged Matron, who while she was in the depth of distress, from the tidings of her son's having been slain in battle, died in his arms in the excess of joy upon his safe return. (Liv. Lib. XXII. Cap. 7.)

Not to enumerate more instances; we are told by the Italian historian *Guicciardini*, that Leo the Tenth died of a fever, occasioned by the agitation of his spirits, on his receiving the joyful news of the capture of Milan, concerning which he had entertained much anxiety. (Istoria de Guicciardini, Lib. XIV.)

In all these instances the previous state of mind, with its pathological effects upon the body, made the impulse of joy the stronger, and contributed to render it fatal.

Note *U*.

After " will contribute to explain the rest."
Page 297.

Dr. Haygarth, in his late Publication on *the Imagination as a Cause, and as a Cure of the Disorders of the Body*, has presented us with many curious and interesting facts relative to its influence; to which I beg leave to refer the Reader. Such incontestible proofs of the power of the imagination in medical cases, may vindicate some of the strenuous advocates for *Animal Magnetism*, from the charge of intentional fraud, brought against them by the totally incredulous; while they demonstrate the absurdity of all their theories.

I have in the text attributed the power of the imagination to produce certain changes in the corporeal system, to the Passions or strong Affections, which in such cases always accompany it; and the experiments made by the Doctor and his medical friends, abundantly corroborate the sentiment. In some of the patients, the salutary influence of *hope*, and afterwards of *joy*, was evidently very great:—in others, the mind was obviously in a state of *surprise* and *astonishment* at the mysterious powers supposed to be seated in the instruments;—in others, it was agitated by alternate *hopes* and *fears*;—and in others, it was under the strong impressions of *terror*. The directions given to the *Tractors* served to point out, as it were, the influence of this pre-disposition of mind to the parts particularly affected, by a law not more inexplicable,

though

though more uncommon than the operation of the will in producing voluntary motion. Nor is the process dissimilar to that of conveying the electric fluid to various parts of the body, as practised in medical electricity. Since every passion is frequently excited by the imagination alone, without any real or just cause, and since these passions are in their appearances and effects perfectly the same as those produced by realities, the medical influence of the imagination is obviously reduced to the same principle. The remaining difficulties therefore attending the subject are not greater than those which belong to the influence of the passions in general. When it shall be explained in what manner each passion instantaneously produces its own specific change, whether it be of an exhilarating, irritating, depressive, or languid nature, we shall be able to explain the medical Power of the imagination, which is able to excite passions and affections, from *ideal* causes.

Note W.

After " where the sole object is to establish indisputable facts." Page 298.

THE Section to which this Note refers is an abridged translation of some parts of the Author's Inaugural Dissertation, *De Animi pathamatum vi, et modo agendi in inducendis et curandis Morbis;* published at Leyden in the year 1767. In which his professed object was *to theorize;* and by adducing numerous proofs of the influence of the passions both in inducing and removing disorders, to demonstrate the fallacy of the Boerhaavian system,

which

which attributes the proximate causes of diseases to certain changes in the fluids. He attempted in that Dissertation to explain the *modus operandi* of the passions and affections, upon principles equally adapted to the influence of every other cause of morbid or salutary change. It was his intention to have considered the subject more amply; and to have presented it to the world in another form: but in the earlier part of life he was deprived of the requisite leisure; and in subsequent years the gradual rejection of the Boerhaavian doctrine, and the very learned dissertation of Dr. Falconer on the same subject, to which the *Fothergillian* Medal was adjudged, conspired to render the execution of his design the less necessary. The Reader will find in the Doctor's Treatise, numerous instances given illustrative of the doctrine and principles now advanced, and such authorities quoted as will remove every doubt.

See also Sir George Baker's Observations, in the Medical Transactions. T. III. XI.

Note X.

After " The other compounds partake of mixed effects." Page 307.

These Observations on the influence of the passions and affections upon thought and language, united with those repeatedly advanced on the power of sympathy, point out to us the reason of an axiom universally admitted, that the orator must *feel* his subject to insure his power

over

over the feelings of others. As the warm feelings of a mind duly cultivated, will always suggest a train of ideas and expressions correspondent with its peculiar state, thus is some degree of feeling highly necessary for a successful imitation. If the rhetorician or orator be totally destitute of sensibility, there will be such an artifice in his style and manner as can alone deceive those who are ignorant that artifice exists. It is however acknowledged, that by constant practice, or in other words, by being *hackneyed* in their profession, both language and manner may become the result of habit, and may be employed with effect, when the feelings which gave them their original energy are obtunded. Veteran actors have been known to imitate various emotions in a just and forcible manner, long after they had lost their sensibility. The retained Counsellor has been known to imitate that pathos in a bad cause, which a good cause alone could have at first inspired: and the corrupt Senator may in his degenerate state, counterfeit all that zeal and energy, which was genuine at the commencement of his political career. But so true is nature to itself, that it absolutely demands the passions and emotions to be perfectly represented. Defect diffuses a langour, excess produces disgust. The eloquence dictated by an unfeeling heart, mistakes bombast for sublimity, rant for strong feelings, the cant and whine of a mendicant for the pathetic. It confounds or misapplies every trope and figure which it has collected from systems of rhetoric. It is loquacious where it ought to be concise; amuses itself with drawing of pictures and gathering of flowers, when it should have been borne down with a torrent of rapid thought and diction. In a word,

it

it presents us with every indication that the author has been merely employing his head, and playing with his imagination; without making any attempts to warm his own heart. It is therefore impossible that he should succeed in warming the hearts of others. He may excite the admiration of some, the contempt of many, but the genuine feelings of none.

> False eloquence, like the prismatic glass,
> Its gaudy colours spreads on every place:
> The face of Nature we no more survey;
> All glares alike without distinction gay.
>
> POPE.

THE END.

ERRATA.

P. 49. l. 14. For exifting, r. exciting.
P. 97. l. 4. For affection, r. affectation.

www.ingramcontent.com/pod-product-compliance
Lightning Source LLC
Chambersburg PA
CBHW080051190426
43201CB00035B/2161